WALTER STEPHEN was born  :ed at
schools and universities in Glasg egrees
in Geography, Economic History ncipal
Teacher of Geography in disting burgh
he became Adviser in Social Studies in Edinburgh and Senior Adviser in
Lothian Region. In Edinburgh he set up and ran Castlehill Urban Studies
Centre, the first successful Urban Studies Centre in Britain, and the History
of Education Centre.

As an independent scholar he has been active in investigating Interesting
Victorians and has been responsible for books on Patrick Geddes (planner
and polymath), Willie Park Junior ('The Man who took Golf to the
World') and Frank Fraser Darling (a Victorian in spirit if not by birth, who
lived among the red deer and founded the environmental movement). His
contribution to 2009, the Darwin year, was 'The Evolution of Evolution:
Darwin, Enlightenment and Scotland'. His 'Walter's Wiggles: The Random
Thoughts of a Random Fellow' is a place-related travel book set in Europe
and North America.

His infatuation with Empresses began in the 1950s with Carlota of
Mexico and Elisabeth of Austria. In the 1960s he delivered rolls and bread
to Balmoral and Birkhall, his father being By Appointment Baker to Her
Majesty the Queen and Her Majesty the Queen Mother, the last Empress of
India. Since then he has tried to unravel the complexities of the European
Imperial families and clarify what was duty and what was pleasure in their
lives.

The Gypsy Empresses
A Study in Escapism

WALTER STEPHEN

Hills of Home
Edinburgh

First published 2012

ISBN: 978-0-9555190-3-1

Typeset & Printed by
Printpoint (Edinburgh) Ltd, Dalkeith

The author's right to be identified as author of this book under
the Copyright, Designs and Patents Act 1988 has been asserted.

Contents

Illustrations	Colour Plates	7
Illustrations	Figures	9
Acknowledgements		11
INTRODUCTION	A Study in Escapism	13
CHAPTER 1	*Belles Demeures en Riviera, 1835-1930*	21
CHAPTER 2	*'Kennst du das Land?'*	40
CHAPTER 3	The Gypsy Empresses	52
CHAPTER 4	Elisabeth, Empress of Austria (1837-1898) *Manège* not *Ménage*	58
CHAPTER 5	Eugénie, Empress of France (1826-1920) The Survivor	79
CHAPTER 6	Carlota, Empress of Mexico (1840-1927) The ghostly Empress	92
CHAPTER 7	The Empresses of Germany Augusta of Saxony-Weimar (1811-1890) A superior being Victoria of Great Britain (1840-1901) Ninety-nine days Augusta of Schleswig-Holstein (1858-1921) *Kinder, Küche und Kirche*	107
CHAPTER 8	The Russians Alexandra Feodorovna, Empress of Russia (1798-1860) Diplomacy in the sunshine Marie Alexandrovna, Tsarina of Russia (1824-1880) An inconsolable *mater dolorosa* Maria Feodorovna, Dowager Empress of Russia (1847-1929) Sad *Fiancée* and Dowager Empress and Katia Dolgourika/Catherine Yourievski The shadow Empress	123
CHAPTER 9	Victoria, Empress of India (1819-1901) Our own dear Queen	167
Epilogue		181
Bibliography		186

Illustrations – Colour Plates

COVER   In Geneva, this fine statue by Philip Jackson stands on the spot where the Empress Sisi was murdered in 1898

PLATE 1A   Menton/Roquebrune – plaque commemorating Sisi's connection

PLATE 1B   Villa Thompson, Nice. Built 1878. Now *Musée des Beaux-Arts Jules-Chéret*

PLATE 2A   Dr James Henry Bennet in the Menton he helped to create

PLATE 2B   'Where the lemon trees bloom'

PLATE 2C   The gypsy stereotype – Aachen style

PLATE 3A   Elisabeth, '98 – the Empress and her City

PLATE 3B   Madame Tussaud's, Berlin – Romy Schneider as Sisi

PLATE 3C   Villa Cyrnos, Roquebrune, 1892

PLATE 4A   *The Empress Eugenie and her Ladies on the Beach at Trouville,* by Boudin (1824-98)
(By kind permission of Culture and Sport Glasgow (Museums))

PLATE 4B   Praca Dom Pedro IV, Lisbon. Recycled statue of Maximilian

PLATE 5A   Russian Cathedral, Nice

PLATE 5B   Her Imperial Majesty in Birmingham

PLATE 6A   Outside the Loch Maree Hotel – *Bhan righ Bhictoria* slept here

PLATE 6B   Ardgour – the Queen's profile

PLATE 7A   The Queen's View – looking up the Avon to Ben Avon

PLATE 7B   The Queen's Well in Glen Mark

PLATE 8A   Menton – Queen's well on frontier with Italy

PLATE 8B   *L'hôtel Excelsior Regina à Cimiez c1900*

PLATE 8C   Cimiez, Nice – The gracious *Impératrice des Indes*

Illustrations – Figures

FIGURE 1   The Scots Kirk at Menton

FIGURE 2   Henry Dryerre's gravestone in Menton

FIGURE 3   Rumpelmayers - *'le roi des pâtissiers'*

FIGURE 4   The caves at *Balzi Rossi/Rochers Rouges*
             - with lift, museum and restaurant

FIGURE 5   Liszt thumping the keyboard in 1886
             (Olrig Stephen, after *La Vie Parisienne*)

FIGURE 6   Weather vane in the garden of Villa Cyrnos

FIGURE 7   Here lay the body of the Grand Duke Nicholas

FIGURE 8   The Zugswang Trail
             (Olrig Stephen)

FIGURE 9   Victoria and John Brown at Tomintoul
             (Noted and adapted by Olrig Stephen)

FIGURE 10   Crossing the Poll Tarff
             (From *Leaves from the Journal of Our Life in the Highlands.*
             1868 edition, by kind permission of the National Library of
             Scotland)

Acknowledgements

THE ORIGINS OF THIS PROJECT were remote in time and the gestation period has been lengthy. Reading Montgomery Hyde's *Mexican Empire* in 1950 introduced me to the complexities of the Hapsburgs. Later in the 'fifties I lived in Switzerland, where I saw the delicious Romy Schneider playing the equally delicious Empress Elisabeth and visited the various battlefields, like Morgarten ('the Swiss Bannockburn'), where the gallant Switzers had defeated the overbearing Hapsburgs and Burgundians.

In Vienna Gordana Semmelrock happily took me to the famous Hotel Sacher for *Sachertorte* but was puzzled that I should also wish to be taken to where the Hapsburgs are buried in the *Kapuzinerkirche*. In Menton, a paper by Anne-Michelle Slater of the University of Aberdeen caused me to look twice at a little bridge, to read the plaque more closely and begin to make the connections between the bridge, she who caused it to be built, and the other Empresses who escaped to the Côte d'Azur. The indefatigable Rhoda Fothergill of the Perthshire Society of Natural Science set me off on a course which eventually brought together more humble escapees from northern Europe, through the expertise of Almudena Arellano of the Musée Municipal de la Préhistoire Régionale, Menton.

As ever, the staff in our great national institutions have been supportive beyond the call of duty. Figure 10 (*Crossing the Poll Tarff*) is reproduced by kind permission of the National Library of Scotland. The breezily atmospheric PLATE 4A (*The Empress Eugenie and her Ladies on the Beach at Trouville*, by Boudin (1824-98) is reproduced here by kind permission of Culture and Sport Glasgow (Museums).

The equally atmospheric – but in a threatening, lowering way – *La Rade de Villefranche*, also by Boudin, hangs in the Musée des Beaux-Arts Jules-Chéret in Nice. I have to report that permission to reproduce it here was twice refused by the Musée d'Orsay in Paris. A request for clarification, so that there might be negotiation, was ignored.

The incisive drawings and Zugswang Trail (Figs 5, 8 and 9) are by Olrig Stephen.

INTRODUCTION
A Study in Escapism

THE BOUNDARY BETWEEN Menton and Roquebrune-Cap Martin on the French Riviera is a little river – the *Torrent de Saint-Roman* - which dries out in summer. From 1848 till 1860 the neighbouring towns of Roquebrune and Menton, till then part of the Principality of Monaco, were granted the status of *villes libres* (free towns). After a plebiscite, in 1861 a treaty between Sardinia, Monaco and France tidied up the Riviera coast and Roquebrune, Menton (and Nice) were handed over to France. As a result, the little bridge over the torrent – so small that few people realise that they are crossing a bridge – is called *Le Pont de l'Union*, later retitled *Le Pont de la Paix*. On the parapet is a plaque (PLATE 1A)which reads as follows:

> *Pour perpetuer le souvenir de ses sejours*
> *de Sa Majesté Elisabeth*
> *Imperatrice d'Autriche et Reine de Hongrie*
> *1894 – 1895 – 1896 – 1897*
> *Les habitants de Menton ont fait placer en 1899*
> *cette inscription commemorative*

What lies behind this text? Why should the citizens of a French town want to remember foreign royalty, however distinguished? And why should she have wanted to spend so much of her life here? And why here? And what happened in 1898 to change the pattern of Imperial residences?

When we add to the plaque the knowledge that, when the Empress Sisi (as I shall usually call her) was resident here, Eugénie, former Empress of the French, had a villa built for herself on Cap Martin and our own Queen Victoria, Empress of India from 1877, visited adjacent Menton, a definite pattern begins to emerge. Here we have some of the great ones of their world choosing to spend substantial periods of time in a place which had little to do with their national interests. On the French Riviera they carried out no public functions. They often pretended that they were incognita and were pleased to think that they were visiting in a private capacity.

The Gypsy Empresses

Ten ladies with the title of Empress, or similar, form the subject of this book; plus another who thought she should have had the title. Victoria became Queen through inheritance and married years later. Sixteen years after she was widowed she was created Empress of India in a deliberate political attempt to reconcile the recent differences between India and Great Britain. The others on our list were empresses as a result of their marriages and did not necessarily share the nationalities of their husbands, who usually went beyond their national boundaries in search of suitable mates. Again with the exception of Victoria, it could be said that these women were adjuncts to their husbands, who were men of power. Power resided with the husbands, although, as in any marriage, some of the women were able to contrive some influence for themselves. To know these women it is essential to know their husbands, whose word was law.

To understand these women and their lives it is also necessary to understand the society they grew up in, which was that of the court, of the absolute monarchy – on paper at least. The late nineteenth century could be said to be The Age of the Double Standard, summed up by the following statistics relating to the Metropolitan Museum of Modern Art in New York:

3% of the artists whose works are on display are women,
83% of the nudes on display are female.

On the perceived importance of women in society, it is worth quoting from Roy Soweto's *The New Dawn* at some length.

When Jacob Bronowski, in the early 1970s, presented his celebrated and seminal television programme on the rise of mankind from primitive origins to its contemporary elevated status, he called it *The Ascent of Man*, although The Ascent of Men would have been a more appropriate title. Seven women were given a mention in the series and in the resulting book: Queen Anne because she knighted Sir Isaac Newton; Queen Isabella I, because she, with her husband Ferdinand, backed Columbus; Marie Antoinette, because she was, well, Marie Antoinette; Queen Victoria, because in her time she ruled the world's greatest power, and Madame Curie for obvious reasons.

One of the other two women who got a mention, Ellen Sharpless, was included for the not so obvious reason that she made a pastel portrait of Joseph Priestley (an inclusion made even less worthy since Priestley discovered oxygen two years after the Swedish apothecary, Carl Wilhelm Scheele). One woman did get in on merit. Dame Kathleen Kenyon was from 1961 to 1966 director of the School of Archaeology in Jerusalem and was responsible for the excavation of Jericho to its Stone Age beginnings and for revealing it to be the oldest known site that has seen continuous occupation.

Bronowski could include such a mixed bag of token women in his account because it was so blindingly obvious to him that mankind had ascended almost entirely due to the efforts of men. If this was true of the twentieth century, how much worse could it have been in the nineteenth, before women were allowed to vote, or have their own property?

On marriage, the Empresses took on several responsibilities. They were expected to embody a satisfactory alliance with another power. By being beautiful and gracious, simply by being seen, they would enhance the Emperor's power and prestige, and they would ensure the continuance of the line – 'an heir and a spare'. They might even be able to advise their spouse on matters of import. In return they had a splendid – if very restricted - lifestyle and were under constant surveillance, which could be tiresome.

To understand the women and their times it is essential to consider their husbands and their relations with the countries they ruled. Without getting bogged down in detail we must understand why some were contented while others were uncomfortable in their roles.

Besides their husbands, there were other men in their lives, often gathered around like bluebottles around a piece of bad meat, vying for a piece of the action. One thinks of our own Mary, Queen of Scots, who irritated the Scottish nobles with her train of handsome young Frenchmen, *les cadets,* hence 'caddies', adept at carrying the Queen's golf clubs or scarf. Her jealous husband and some of these nobles murdered her secretary, David Rizzio, because they thought he and the Queen were too friendly. (1)

The Empress Sisi would march around Cap Martin, followed by her Greek teacher, Christomanos, reading from Homer. When she became too hot she would disappear behind a bush, remove her outer layers and throw them to her companion to carry. And there were those winters hunting in the English shires while Franz Josef toiled at his desk in Vienna.

Courtiers and politicians hated John Brown for his officious gatekeeping of Victoria and, later in her life, in her Indian phase, resented the special favours shown to the Munshi (Abdul Karim). But whom can a poor lonely Empress trust? Remember The Emperor's New Clothes? Where can one find a little boy who tells the truth?

Names are a stylistic problem for the writer. The great ones have so many. Think of the present heir to the British throne. On his notepaper he is HRH The Prince of Wales. In general usage he is Charles, or Prince Charles. In Scotland he becomes the Duke of Rothesay. His latest wife has something to do with Cornwall.

In the Hotel Elisabethpark in Bad Gastein (which has a Café Sisi on its Franz Josef Strasse front) is the framed original licence signed by Franz Josef. There follow row upon row of titles beginning: Emperor of Austria, King of Hungary, Duke of Styria, right down to Knight of some parcel of land one has never heard of.

The Russians were even more untidy, partly because of the practice of the empresses changing their names on marriage. Alexandra Feodorovna was Charlotte of Prussia. Marie Alexandrovna was Maria of Hesse. Maria Feodorovna, as we shall see, was Marie Dagmar of Denmark, daughter of Christian IX. Out of three Empresses there were two Marias and two (but not the same two) Feodorovnas. French was the language of the Russian ruling class, so that the same person may be Natasha or Natalie. Thus Katia (Catiche) Dolgorouki, whom I am calling 'the shadow Empress', was the morganatic wife of Alexander II, and was the only Russian-born of the four ladies more fully dealt with below. Later called Catherine Yourievski, she devoted the latter part of her life to a vain struggle for recognition against the Dowager Empress Maria Feodorovna. (2)

Marie Dagmar, daughter of Christian IX of Denmark, was generally known as Dagmar. She was engaged to Tsarevich Nicholas. When he died she became 'The Sad Fiancée'. When she married his brother Alexander and he became Tsar she changed her name to Maria Feodorovna and her title to Tsarina or Empress. His death made her the Dowager Empress. Ideally each character should have one name, but imagine how boring it would be – and tiring for the author – to have the name 'Maria Feodorovna' perhaps six times on every page of a chapter. There is also a principle of good writing called elegant variation, which means, quite simply, that one does not keep on using the same word over and over again. Her family must have been aware of this, since within the family she was known as 'Minnie'. So here we have the answer. When young she is Dagmar. When we want to give her full pomp or presence she is the Empress or the Dowager Empress. Day by day she is Maria Feodorovna. If discussing her relationship with Tsar Nicholas, her son, she could be the Dowager Empress or Minnie, depending on the subject.

Two of the three German empresses were called Augusta. To muddy the waters further, their husbands were both called Wilhelm. The Empress Frederick, as Princess Victoria, was the daughter of the Queen Victoria who was made Empress of India in 1877. Further complication came with Vicky's fifth child ('Moretta'), baptised Victoria, who married Adolf of Schaumberg-Lippe. For two years 'Dona', Wilhelm II's spouse, had two Dowager Empresses metaphorically looking over her shoulder and sorting her out. (3)

The pedigrees of the Empresses did not always appeal to their husbands' subjects. Elisabeth of Austria was a Wittelsbach, daughter of Maximilian I, King of Bavaria. Although Franz Josef was her cousin, her treatment by the Austrian court was unfortunate, to put it mildly. Eugénie – Maria Eugenia Ignacia Augustina de Guzman y Palafox – was the daughter of a Spanish count and a Scottish mother. Like 'Sisi' a great beauty and a superb horsewoman, jealousy must have been a strong component of the dislike demonstrated towards her by the hangers-on of Napoleon III. Carlota (a cousin of Queen Victoria) was a daughter of Leopold, King of the Belgians, a meddler who had a higher opinion of himself than historians have had of him. She was hardly likely to appeal to the mixture of decayed hidalgos and barefoot Indians which was Mexico in the mid-nineteenth century. Vicky, Queen Victoria's eldest daughter, was subjected to lifelong attack and conspiracy by Bismarck and even her son, Wilhelm II.

Imperial travel was of three kinds, which could overlap on occasion, and which might compete with each other. At home they travelled about their territories, opening parliaments, launching battleships, inspecting the troops, visiting hospitals, inaugurating universities. In the political world there is a concept known as 'effective sovereignty'. In effect it is: 'use it or lose it'. It is not enough to claim territory or just 'to show the flag'. The monarch or government must be able to demonstrate that they are using it effectively. Thus the Falkland Islands and their Dependencies had splendid stamps bearing the Queen's head. When the British government withdrew a fisheries cruiser from South Georgia the Argentinians could validly claim that we had ceased to display effective sovereignty – and moved in.

Abroad there were diplomatic and other State visits.

Given the importance of the hereditary principle in the nineteenth century and the interlocking of the European dynasties, there was a continuous programme of family visits, royal weddings, funerals and the like, where pleasure was often subordinated to duty. For example, most of the royals and imperials of Europe visited Sydenham, to see the Crystal Palace, and what could be more natural than to take in Windsor or Balmoral at the appropriate season? There is a wonderful old photograph of HRH Prince Heinrich von Preussen (the Kaiser's brother and grandson of Queen Victoria) driving off at the Balmoral golf course, with his kilt swirling around him, woollen stockings and sporran.

State visits were part of royal duties abroad. In 1855 the Emperor and Empress of the French paid a State visit to England, which lasted from 16 to 21 April. Prince Albert welcomed them at Dover and escorted the Imperial couple to Windsor Castle, where a splendid suite was set aside for them. There were morning walks and long conversations about the Crimea. The Household Troops were reviewed in the Great Park and a ball held in the Waterloo Room - for once, French susceptibilities were ignored. The Emperor and Empress went to London and attended a banquet in the Guildhall. They attended a gala performance of *Fidelio*. (Not, perhaps, a good choice of opera, since it is a celebration of married devotion and Napoleon III was a notorious philanderer). On the Emperor's 47th birthday Victoria gave him a pencil-case, which she would meticulously record, as she did with all her gifts. Napoleon and Albert attended two war councils and the Queen herself attended the second, which she found 'one of the most interesting scenes I ever was present at'.

Almost at once the visit was returned. Victoria, Albert, the Princess Royal (who will re-emerge as Empress of Germany) and the Prince of Wales landed at Boulogne on 18 August and left Paris on the 27th, having taken in an International Exhibition (three times), the *Comédie Francaise*, the *Louvre*, and a gala performance at the *Opéra*.

Another, even higher-level Imperial occasion, took place in 1867. The Great Exposition was Napoleon's 'last and greatest party'. It was to prove 'the grand finale of his "bread and circuses" regime'. The Prince of Wales (the future Emperor of India) 'delighted in the gay city he so relished'. Tsar Alexander II was the real guest of honour, since Napoleon wished to draw him into an alliance against the growing threat of Prussia. There was a lot of ground to be made up. The French Emperor's uncle had burned the Moscow of Alexander's uncle, while the scars of the Crimea were still raw.

The person everyone wanted to see was the giant Chancellor of Prussia, Count Otto von Bismarck. His master, King Wilhelm, set the edgy French at ease and seemed utterly relaxed himself. It was said he spent his time exploring Paris as if intending to come back there some day - as indeed he did, when he was declared the first Emperor of Germany by

Bismarck.

At first the visit went well. At a great military review at Longchamp Alexander was in excellent humour. The climax was a massed cavalry charge of 10,000 cuirassiers who halted in perfect order within five metres of the royal party and saluted with drawn sabres. Gravely the Tsar and the King saluted their host, and bowed to the Empress Eugénie.

On 12 April was the premiere of Offenbach's *La Grande Duchesse de Gérolstein*. Offenbach reflects better than anyone else the temper of French society under Napoleon III. His music vibrates with frenetic gaiety, sparkling wit and catchy tunes which resonate for hours after first being heard. Like the Second Empire, it is brilliant, showy, and with a satirical edge - the portrayal of Zeus in *Orpheus in the Underworld* pulled no punches and bore a marked resemblance to the amorous Emperor.

Like every Offenbach score, the *Grande Duchesse* bubbles with joyous melodies, patter songs and luscious waltzes. Gérolstein is a tinpot little German state and its ruler a sixteen year old girl fixated on soldiers – '*Ah, que j'aime les militaires!*' She loves their moustaches and the plumes in their hats. She has her own regiment and praises them with choruses full of '*Ta ra, ta ra*' and '*rataplan, rataplan*', 'Sound the trumpets and beat the drums', 'In honour of war, In honour of love'. Gérolstein is taken into an unnecessary war because the Chancellor, Baron Puck, needs to divert attention from difficulties at home. The army is led by a stupid German general called Boum.

The Tsar and his party roared with unimperial laughter. A little apprehensively, the French court half feared they had gone too far and kept a close eye on Bismarck, who seemed to be enjoying himself more than anybody. Alistair Horne suggests that his enjoyment really lay in some very secret joke of his own. Perhaps he was already planning the victory parade of the German armies down the Champs Elysées a mere four years later.

Then it all went terribly wrong. At one of the parades a certain Berezowski, a young Polish patriot, rushed from the crowd and fired a pistol at the Tsar. He missed, but the white gloves of the Tsarevich were spattered with blood from a wounded horse. No doubt Alexandra Feodorovna, Empress of Russia, whom we will meet later, was nearby to witness this disturbing incident. The Tsar – whose fate was to be killed by an anarchist bomb in St Petersburg 14 years later – was much shaken by this incident, became suddenly unfriendly and Napoleon's hopes for an agreement with Russia proved vain.

Many of the great ones were content with the social and political round but some more than others felt the need to escape from the formality and sycophancy of the imperial or royal court. What concerns us here is how these great ladies spent their lives when they were not on duty. As we shall see, the gypsy strain led them to many interesting places and encounters. This could easily turn into a catalogue or a railway timetable, but, fortunately, most of these great ladies were attracted at some time to the Riviera or the Côte d'Azur and this provides a useful common denominator to apply to their wanderings.

End Notes

1 James VI and I was nicknamed 'The Scottish Solomon'. He thought highly of himself as an intellectual – which he was – but many would slyly remember that, in the Old Testament, Solomon was the son of David.

2 Another hazard is the Russian calendar. Russia used the Julian calendar until the Revolution of 1917, being one of the last countries to 'go Gregorian'. The October Revolution took place on 25 October 1917 (Old Style). In our calendar this was 7 November. As a result there are many anomalies in books about Russia and it makes sense to check if the author is using Julian or Gregorian dates.

3 A very fine 'team photo' of Vicky and her family was taken in 1900, less than a year before her death. The women are standing and the men are seated, Victorian style. Vicky was only five foot two when she was young and is stuck between Dona – who is a good half-head taller, and Moretta, the tallest of her children, who is a full head taller.

CHAPTER 1

Belles Demeures en Riviera 1835-1930

BELLES DEMEURES EN RIVIERA, 1835-1930, by Didier Gayraud, is as imposing as its subject. It is what the Germans call a *Handbuch* in that it requires two hands to pick it up – just. A kind of superior paperback, it has thick card covers folded over for extra strength and 280 pages of heavy, glossy paper.

After a brief introduction, the plan of the book could not be simpler. Starting at the west at Théoule-sur Mer 167 villas (68 of them in Cannes) are described on the stretch of coast to the mouth of the Var. From Nice to just over the Italian border is the length of coastline of greater relevance to this study and 177 villas are described for this section, 80 of them in Nice alone. This makes finding them quite easy but is not very useful if we are looking for trends. In many cases, the eruption of villas on to the scene was not systematic, but piecemeal. (There were exceptions, like the development of the Cap Martin peninsula by the English tramway financier Calvin White from 1889 and the Garavan area of Menton a few years later).

Gayraud sets the scene with the discovery of Cannes in 1834 by the British parliamentarian Lord Brougham and Vaux, and his building of a big villa there in the following year. A stream of English followed, attracted by the fine scenery and mild winters. (Summers were too hot and could even be injurious to health). The PLM (*Paris, Lyon, Mediterranée*) railway reached Cannes in 1863, Nice in 1864 and was pushed on to Villefranche and Menton. A lack of precise planning regulations encouraged the mushroom growth of great mansions along a coastal strip 100 kilometres long and only a few kilometres deep, in a diversity of styles found nowhere else.

There were pastiches of Gothic castles, Indian and Persian palaces, at least two villas in the Scottish Baronial style, Venetian palaces, baroque follies from Aquitaine and Swiss chalets surrounded by palm trees. There were Moorish villas and villas in the Italian style. Théodore Reinach, a retired advocate and Deputy for Savoy, director of the *Gazette des Beaux-Arts* and author of a History of the Israelites, acquired a property at

Beaulieu-sur-Mer in 1902, rased it to the ground and replaced it with the Villa Kérylos, An ardent Hellenophile (Kérylos = swallow, harbinger of summer), he caused to be constructed an exact replica of an ancient Greek palace, with courtyards, statuary, replica furniture, musical instruments and the rest. Ancient Greek music was transposed for the piano, there were concerts and recitals and Gabriel Fauré performed for a selected audience in the grand amphitheatre of the Sorbonne in Paris. Reinach wintered every year at Kérylos till his death in 1928, benefiting from the cunningly concealed underfloor central heating, the electric lighting disguised as oil lamps and the baths and showers offering about a dozen healthy sensations. The villa was bequeathed to the Institute of France who have turned it into a museum where the little people can, for a few hours, immerse themselves in the marvellous, if slightly demented, world of the lover of the ancient Greeks, frequently used by the film-makers.

For each villa the standard treatment is to give at least one fine contemporary photograph of the exterior, with the address and location. The origins – the first owner, the architect, the architectural details, the gardens - follow. Seldom did ownership last long, tenancies were common, and we are taken through the vicissitudes of these splendid buildings, which often reflected major dislocations of society. Thus many of them were turned into hospitals and rehabilitation centres during the First World War. The American love affair with the Riviera started in the 1920s when ex-GIs came back to the France they had loved as convalescents and jazz and cocktails became the bread and butter of the Riviera. The Riviera began to be democratised when one hotel kept open in the summer of 1922, the beginning of a new kind of sun and sea tourism.

The Wall Street crash almost finished the Côte d'Azur. For example, Osborne O'Hagan was: 'a member of the London Chamber of Commerce of Irish origin' and had Casa del Mare (1903) at Roquebrune, one of at least 25 villas individually designed by Georges Tersling. In its own park and with a beach of over 300 metres, O'Hagan made Casa del Mare a cultural centre for the Riviera, with regular concerts for invited audiences of 200. O'Hagan disappeared in 1930 and his sister auctioned off the marble statues in the park, the rare plants in the gardens and the magnificent marble staircase.

In World War II most of these fine buildings – now under Italian occupation - were requisitioned again. Somerset Maugham, the hugely successful English writer, had bought the Villa Mauresque in 1926. After the war, he returned to find that it had been occupied, successively, by

Italians, Germans and French. The façade was pock-marked with shell and bullet holes, the two cars he had left in the garage had disappeared, the cellar had been emptied and the dogs he had kept in the garden had been eaten. But his carefully hidden pictures had survived and, 'with a new "secretary", he repaired the house, halved the size of the garden and his staff, and started writing again' until his death in 1965.

Some villas re-emerged in public ownership, or were turned into hotels. Many have had their grounds packed with modern infill. Others have been sub-divided for the mass market while others were demolished for comprehensive redevelopment. Hard-pressed villa owners have been very successful in making their homes and gardens available to film-makers. Thus, Casa del Mare was bought in 1970 by the film producer Dino de Laurentis and the Italian film star Silvana Mangano.

That some stretches of the Côte - notably Cap Martin and Cap Ferrat -have retained their exclusivity was demonstrated by a recent headline in *The Scotsman*: 'Oligarch picks up Hunter's villa for £50 million'. Sir Tom Hunter, retail and property entrepreneur, began his career by selling training shoes from the back of a van. His villa was 'one of the most impressive in the south of France' and was 'reputed to have the largest private infinity pool in Europe'. Having received an offer 'he couldn't refuse' Sir Tom sold his villa to an unknown Russian oligarch, thus turning the clock back a hundred years, to the golden years before the Revolution of 1917.

The *belles demeures* of the Empresses will be considered at the appropriate places but it is important to remember that they set the general tone of the Mediterranean coast and gave society standards for aspiring social climbers from a variety of origins. The Empresses need not feel lonely, there were plenty of royals, aristocrats and hangers-on with whom they could mix, if so inclined. To avoid tedium I have given an example of each class – royals, aristocrats, the big money people, artists, industrialists and some interesting people difficult to pigeon-hole.

A mixed blessing – but an astute businessman – was Leopold II, King of the Belgians, resident of Villefranche and Cap Ferrat for many years. Born in 1835, he was five years older than Carlota, whom we will meet later, and had a doubtful track record. He became immensely rich from heading up the company that exploited the Congo, but his methods – forced labour, mutilation, production quotas - so scandalised the world that in 1885 the Congo was, in effect, taken from him and control handed over to the Belgian government.

From Villa Léopolda (address – 1600 Avenue Léopold II) he expanded to Les Cèdres on Cap Ferrat, on the way picking up eighteen building plots in the coastal mountains and also the west side of Cap Ferrat - 50 hectares of the world's prime real estate. His financial methods were often doubtful and involved his personal doctor and nebulous enterprises. Villas were built for his mistress, for one of his illegitimate sons, and for French or Belgian officers returning from the Congo. (These were named Boma, Matadi and Banana, no doubt provoking reminiscences about the good old days by the Congo when the blacks knew their place).

The Villa Léopolda - much later - was used for the filming of *The Red Shoes* (1950) in which the lovely flame-haired Moira Shearer provided a role model for a generation of young girls. The Villa Léopolda was in the news again in 2009, when it was considered the world's most expensive property. Owned by Lily Safra, the widow of a Lebanese-Jewish banking billionaire who had been murdered by his male nurse in Monaco in 1999, it was sold for £347 million to Mikhail Prokhorov, a Russian metals magnate and investor. 'The price tag was seen as the latest sign of property one-upmanship between Russian oligarchs on the Riviera'. Prokhorov failed to follow through on the deal and Mrs Safra therefore took the house off the market and retained the deposit of £35 million. Prokhorov then sued Mrs Safra. One of the lawyers commented that neither party was strapped for cash. 'Both are hugely rich. The house price is the same amount France hopes to retrieve from tax fraudsters in Switzerland'.

By contrast, in Monaco, in 1910, was built Danichgah (house of the poet) for Arfa Mirza Riza Khan, Prince of Persia, composer of the Persian national anthem and his country's first representative at the League of Nations. He did all the right things during World War I and in the 1920s attracted to the Riviera the Shah of Persia and other Middle Eastern notables.

Aristocrats – particularly Russian aristocrats – were ten a penny on the Riviera. Mathilde Kschessinska will enter this narrative later as the young mistress of the Tsarevitch who became Nicholas II. She was the prima ballerina *assoluta* of the Imperial Theatre in St Petersburg and the mistress, in succession, of three Grand Dukes. When Nicholas became engaged to Princess Alix of Hesse-Darmstadt, she moved on to Grand Duke Serge Mikhailovich, who kept her for eight years, when she moved on again to the younger Grand Duke Andrei Vladimirovich. After renting villas on the Riviera for several years the couple acquired a villa in Cap-d'Ail with large balconies and balustrades and a vast west wing with a round tower. They called it Villa Alam, and it became a lively social centre for Russians on the Côte. (The diminutive of Mathilde is Mala which, reversed, gives Alam. Very bourgeois!).

Space being limited, Kschessinska purchased a parcel of land across the road and built there a replica in the same style as Alam, which became the garages and domestic quarters. Alam was used for several seasons, while Kschessinska performed around Europe for the rest of the year. Caught in St Petersburg by the Revolution the couple returned to Alam after six years to find it much decayed. The 'club' on the Riviera - Eugénie at Cap Martin, Queen Marie of Rumania, Princess Radziwill and Princess Yourievsky (of whom much more later) at Nice – lent a hand and Kschessinska re-emerged as Princess Krassinsky-Romanovsky, hostess to Diaghilev and the Ballets Russes, founder of a ballet school in Paris and patroness of a school for the Russian refugees on the Riviera.

Very few of the great villas are accessible to today's public, but one of the finest is. (PLATE 1B) Villa Thompson is set in splendid gardens, where its superb front of six Corinthian columns overawes the visitor. From the south the villa looks symmetrical, but internally the third of the building on the right (east) is grandiloquent public space, while the other two-thirds is made up of more conventional – though still spacious – living space. The main entrance is from the east where the entrance hall and patio was a winter garden, full of statuary and rising to the full height of the house. A monumental staircase rises gently to a great hall, on the way passing a mezzanine glazed apse in which is set a marble Hebe. It takes little imagination to people these spaces with a crowd glittering with jewels and military decorations, entertained by the musicians in their gallery.

This 'sumptuous palace' was begun in 1878 by Prince Leon Kotschoubey, privy councillor to Tsar Alexander II, and was built as a replica of the Palace Razumovsky de Batourine in the Ukraine. Work went slowly, the prince died and his widow, Princess Elisabeth Vassilievna Kotchoubey, already bored with her palace and the slow progress, sold the unfinished building.

In its place she bought the Villa Haussmann, on Mont-Boron, high above Nice. Here Haussmann (1) had already entertained Napoleon III in 1869. Princess Kotchoubey entertained lavishly and received in 1896 Queen Victoria and her ladies.

The American industrialist James Thompson bought the villa in 1882, engaged a leading Nice architect and had the house completed in sumptuous style. From the entrance hall the marble staircase to the first floor was completed at a cost of 130,000 francs – the price of a small villa. The reception hall - fifteen metres high - became the setting for great dinners and receptions, with the music emanating from an orchestra of twenty-five musicians. Lenin, who was in Nice in 1911, would have found here ample fuel - if any were needed - for his revolutionary ideas as he contrasted this gross display with the plight of the peasants in his winter homeland.

The 'sumptuous balls' went on till the Twenties, till the crash came. The city of Nice bought the building and gardens. It is now the Musée des Beaux-Arts, with a decent collection of known painters and half a dozen 'lollipops'. In addition, three local painters are featured. In three totally different styles they are, at the least, interesting and sometimes disturbing.

Around the coast of Cap Martin, from Menton to the railway station at Roquebrune-Cap Martin, runs an ancient right of way – the Path of the Customs-men. This was a great nuisance to the great ones high on the cape, who wanted exclusive access to their picnic places, boathouses and landing-places down by the sea and found themselves the subjects of scrutiny by the little people. Even these powerful manipulators could not change the law, but two found a way round – or, rather, over it.

Cyprienne Dubernet was a shopgirl who married the boss, owner of *Les Grands Magasins du Louvre,* in Paris. After his disappearance she married again and, in 1909, she decided to build the Villa Cypris (or Cyprus, home of the goddess of love but also a reference to her own name. 'The fair Cyprian' was a Victorian euphemism for a prostitute).

. Her daughter. Virginie Hériot, was obsessed by the sea and had her own villa – Tatiana – built by Tersling at Cap Martin in 1902 – before her mother came to the Côte. She owned a succession of vessels, including *Ailée,* a yacht bought from Kaiser Wilhelm II, sailed the coasts from north Africa to Scandinavia, was the first woman to devote herself to sailing, wrote several books, won the gold medal at the 1928 Olympics and was awarded the Legion of Honour.

Mother's villa is absolutely extravagant. Cypris itself is big and Byzantine, with a lavish supply of columns and arches. Below, running down towards the Mediterranean, is a great processional double staircase, flanked by columns, and leaping over the public path to a long gallery of arcades. This is where Madame used to repair in order to look out to sea and admire her daughter's exploits in the bay. Seen from the path, this pavilion overhangs the sea and is a kind of Byzantine cloister on piles, with its own chapel, stained glass and decorated brickwork.

The path is a delightful walk round the headland, with the grey rocks and blue sea, the wind-blasted pines and the occasional peep into the villa gardens. One stretch is, however, grey, damp and sordid; when one must creep through a low and depressing concrete tunnel. To the north is the Hotel du Cap, built by the Danish Georges Tersling and with fine gardens in a number of different styles. South of the tunnel is a big spread of rocky shore, most of which has been concreted over to give a firm footing for rows of deck chairs, sun beds, a café-bar and the other paraphernalia of a sunshine holiday. Hotel patrons can thus move to and fro in security.

The Hotel du Cap began as the Villa Kahn in 1902. Kahn (born Abraham, renamed Albert in anti-Semitic France) began as a bank clerk and amassed an enormous fortune in banking, then in diamond mines in South Africa, then in copper in the Congo. Unlike many of his kind, he retained some ideals and tried to work towards universal peace. He set up a number of foundations. He was interested in colour photography and employed teams of top photographers to roam the world recording societies in danger of extinction. A series of his films has appeared on British television, including a truly revolutionary World War I film - in colour - of how the French rescued, treated and rehabilitated casualties at Verdun.

The Villa Kahn proved to be too small for Kahn and his entourage. In the twenties he renamed Kahn Zamir ('birdsong' in Yiddish) and acquired two other - neighbouring - villas in Cap Martin - Miramar and Dunure, both built in 1892 - and some other properties. Sir George White was one of the few Scots who appeared on the Riviera as villa owners. From Ayrshire - as the name Dunure implies - White pioneered the introduction of tramways, notably in Bristol, and was nicknamed the 'Tramway King'.

The Wall Street crash of 1929 put an end to all this speculation and investment. Kahn had colossal obligations and could not satisfy his creditors. One ray of light emerged from the wreckage of his properties. In Paris his residence near the Bois de Boulogne was bought by the department of Seine and has been turned into the Albert Kahn Museum, behind which is the most beautifully-manicured garden, surely one of the finest urban gardens in the world. Kahn was permitted to live in a part of the Paris property till his death in 1940.

One has a healthy respect for those who have been successful in making things that are helpful to society. Among the social butterflies who had inherited wealth, or married money, or had acquired it by gambling with the money of others, or robbing the poor widows, were some I would consider had earned their place on the Riviera, who had invented useful things or enriched the lives of ordinary people. At Beaulieu James Livesey installed himself in the Villa Livesey of 1890, anchoring his two steam yachts in the bay. A British railway engineer, he was a world advisor on railway construction and inventor of an alloy of iron and steel for the manufacture of rails. Nearby, the Chateau Marinoni (1881) was built for the inventor of machines for removing seeds from cotton and for folding newspapers. Trained as a printer, he improved mechanical type and invented a rotary press which enabled his *Petit Journal* to exceed a daily circulation of over a million.

Nearby, above Cap Ferrat, the industrialist Emile Crozet-Fourneyron, owner of steelworks in the Lyon area, had La Vigie built in 1898. Almost next door, Arthur Wilson, a British shipowner, acquired 4 hectares and built Villa Maryland. Also above Cap Ferrat was the villa of Edouard Vial (1875) a Nice shipowner with interests also in gas heating and lighting. A frequent absentee, the Villa Vial was let to a stream of Americans, the most notable being the Vanderbilts.

Cap-d'Ail lies between Beaulieu and Monaco. Here were built in 1902 not one, but three Villas Lumière – Villa Antoine-Lumière, Villa Auguste-Lumière and Villa Louis-Lumière. The Lumière brothers, Auguste and Louis, invented cinematography in 1895 and colour photography in 1905, while father (Antoine) was the manager and entrepreneur. Antoine suffered from ' the malady of the stones' and, before settling on the Riviera, had had grandiose schemes near the Lake of Geneva, with vineyards, housing and a rack railway to transport the grapes, and at Lyon. Antoine kept a tight rein on his family while entertaining lavishly, the result being estrangement and the division of the property.

At Roquebrune-Cap Martin Sir Walter Becker, a shipowner based in Italy who was also 'Consul General in Piedmont for the King of Siam,' had Tersling build Delphine - *'une vaste villa'* - in 1910. Also in 1910, in 12 hectares at Roquebrune-Cap Martin Tersling built Zoraïde for Kenneth Clark, the American thread manufacturer whose son was to become head of the British Museum.

The Rev JE Somerville conveyed very well the feverish rate of development on Cap Martin.

The fine Cap Martin Hotel has been erected on the promontory, the chosen abode of the royalties and aristocrats of Europe. A Mauresque Pavilion decorates the extremity of the point close to the rocks and the sea, where of an afternoon hundreds congregate, who are quite as intent on tea and cakes as on the splendid views to be had all around. Several lots of the Cap have been sold off and villas been built, among others, Villa Cyrnos, the residence of the ex-Empress Eugénie. Roads have been made through the pines, and the electric tramway from Mentone to Nice passes through the northern part of the property, surmounting the ridge of the Cap by a steep gradient zig-zag and a cleverly constructed tunnel.

Cap Martin offered in abundance:

...a short but quiet and delightful drive, with grand views...ruined chapels and convents, myrtle in abundance...time-worn rocks, a lighthouse, permitting through its telescope a peep at distant Corsica, a restaurant near the shore, and a Roman arch erected after 1848!

Charles Henfrey had made his pile by the construction of railways in India. He had a chalet on the shores of Lake Maggiore and in 1879 Queen Victoria passed a month there. Having learned that Henfrey had a Chalet des Rosiers at Menton the Queen made her first visit to the Riviera in March 1882 – the first of many. Unobtrusively, she travelled as 'Countess of Balmoral' in a special train driven by the head of the Great Western Railway!

Head and shoulders above these technocrats was Gustave Eiffel (1832-1923), creator of France's greatest icon and a myriad of great bridges and other works, grandiose and with the beauty of function. By 1896, when he came to Beaulieu under a cloud, his best work was behind him, but his CV was formidable. An expert in 'beautiful transparent structures' in wrought iron and steel, his bridges, stations, markets, even churches, post offices and similar public buildings were to be found all over Europe and South America, in Africa, Asia and the Philippines (still Spanish in the nineteenth century). The Eiffel Tower was built for the 1889 *Exposition Universelle* and was visited by two million people in that year alone. Critics hated it. Ordinary people - and posterity - loved it and it now seems incredible that the original intention was to dismantle it after the exhibition. Paris without the Eiffel Tower? *Incroyable!* On an island in the Seine near the Tower is a miniature version of the Statue of Liberty, which reminds us that it was Eiffel who built the metal framework around which the exterior of the statue was fitted. All done in Paris, dismantled and re-assembled in the New World.

Ferdinand de Lesseps is well known as the builder of the Suez Canal

(1869) and the unsuccessful promoter of a canal across the isthmus of Panama. In fact, de Lesseps was a retired diplomat and financier, not an engineer. In 1879, as President of the Panama Canal Company, he started the work on a Panama Canal without locks, like Suez. Unlike Suez, Panama was mountainous and covered in tropical forest. Eiffel was brought in to design ten locks but management was incompetent and the company went bankrupt in 1888. Of the 21,000 Frenchmen who went to Panama to dig the canal, 10,000 died of yellow fever. Hundreds of thousands of small investors were ruined. (The United States bought out the assets in 1904, a new line was chosen and the Panama Canal was opened in 1914).

The Panama Canal Scandal was the *cause célèbre* of 1893. De Lesseps – and others, including Eiffel – were accused of bribing politicians and journalists and embezzlement, were found guilty, fined and sent to prison. Eiffel's apologists say that he was merely a contractor working for the company and not responsible for its affairs. But money intended for the locks had ended up in Eiffel's pocket. Eiffel accepted that he had been, perhaps, a little careless – and found himself sentenced to two years in prison. After serving a long week, the verdict was reversed by the Court of Cassation, on the grounds that he had been found guilty more than three years after the crime was committed.

Next to the Villa Kérylos in Beaulieu was a little villa ('bourgeois in plan') which had been built in 1880 for Joseph Durandy, engineer in Nice and president of the General Council of the department. Eiffel had two sons who felt stifled by their father. One entered the wine trade in Bordeaux, while the other stayed at home but devoted himself to painting. On the other hand, Eiffel's son-in-law, Adolphe Salles, managed the Eiffel factories and was Eiffel's business partner. (Salles married Claire, Eiffel's oldest and favourite daughter, on the condition that she must always live in her father's house). When Eiffel purchased the little villa he found it prudent to buy it through his son-in-law, so that it became known as the Villa Salles. (It is now the Hotel Eiffel, in the Rue Gustave-Eiffel).

At Beaulieu, Eiffel was in semi-retirement, taking long walks, riding along the tracks of Cap Ferrat and the beaches and cruising along the coast in his steam-yacht Aïda. He immersed himself in meteorology, with several weather stations in the gardens, linked up with his others at Bordeaux and Sevres, near Paris. This led on to making practical use of the Eiffel Tower for aerodynamics, meteorology and radio-broadcasting. 'Home improvements' transformed the original villa. An extra storey was added, as were a loggia and arcades. In 1912 an additional hectare was turned into a park. Then came a long gallery overlooking the sea, garnished with statues and marble columns. Carefully aged Roman ruins were placed in the grounds. All very satisfying, but perhaps a little trivial to one whose lifetime was founded on massively useful public works.

In the late nineteenth century the proper place for a poet or an artist was in a garret, starving. Such folks were common enough in the houses of the great ones, but as guests to be shown off, or singing for their suppers. Yet there was a sprinkling of cultural and aesthetic villa owners, a couple of operatic singers, for example. The claim of Paris Singer to fame is based on his long association with Isadora Duncan, the dancer. She died before his villa, Mes Rochers, was finished. No doubt their extravagant lifestyle was sustained by Paris's father, Isaac Merrit Singer, inventor and manufacturer of sewing machines.

Most of Monaco is a miracle of engineering but a catastrophe of taste. Hidden from the Mediterranean by the Grimaldi Forum and flanked on either side by gross multi-story blocks is the Villa Sauber, a gem reminiscent of Garnier, set in a delightful garden. Robert Sauber (1868-1936) was well-placed in the English artistic scene, specialising in portraits and illustrations, like a series of 'Familiar Figures of London'. His name was unknown to me; much of his work that I have now seen is clean, pleasant and attractive – but scarcely memorable. 'Sub-Sargent' might be a layman's impression. Yet it must have sold well because Sauber, disgusted by the English winter when he could only work for two hours in the day, was able to decamp to Monaco where a splendid four-storey villa was built for him in 1904, with all the twiddly bits and a fine garden. Villa Sauber is now part of the national museum of Monaco and in 2009 held a very fine centenary exhibition of the Ballets Russes on the Côte d'Azur.

The last two villas I wish to mention are just over the border in Italy. Charles Garnier (1825-1898) in many ways personified the style of France in the late nineteenth century. The Paris Opera House (1875) made his reputation, which was enhanced by the Monte Carlo Opera House and the Casino which he transformed. Having taken his sickly son to Menton in 1871, he visited Bordighera, over the border in Italy, fell in love with the place and bought 30 parcels of land totalling 20 hectares. Four years later the Villa Charles Garnier 'of vast dimensions' was complete and became his winter home 'capable of receiving my friends'. Raphaël Bischoffsheim followed Garnier to Bordighera and commissioned him (in 1878) to build an extravagant villa (Etelinda).

Bischoffsheim was born in Amsterdam (in Gayraud's words – 'of a rich family of Israelite bankers'). He worked as a railway engineer in Italy before succeeding his father as a financier. Raphaël had two loves, women and astronomy. He bought 45 hectares on Mont Gros, between Nice and Villefranche, and commissioned Garnier to build him an observatory of the very highest class for the period.

Garnier was an artist, not an engineer, and was soon in trouble. He called in Eiffel, who designed a giant cupola of 95 tons to cover the workings of the building and which could move round as the telescopes followed the movements of the heavenly bodies. The cupola was made from 620 sheets of iron held together by 55,000 rivets, the whole resting on a float in a tank of water and antifreeze. According to an eye-witness:

>...it floats so lightly that the hand of a Parisian girl can make it
> turn with the aid of a little winch.

James Henry Bennet (PLATE 2A) was a consumptive London doctor who came to Menton in 1859, to the Hôtel des Anglais, searching for health but probably, like so many others, to die. But he did not die and became the principal propagandist for the benefits of the Mediterranean climate. His *Winter and Spring on the Shores of the Mediterranean* was translated into several languages and started the flood of the sick from northern Europe to the azure coast. In 1870 he was ready to move over the Italian border, to an old castle of the Grimaldi family of Monaco. Immediately adjacent he built a grandiose pile of stone with marble terraces and other trimmings, set in a garden of 26 hectares. However Bennet acquired his money it was socially acceptable and Queen Victoria drove round to call on him on her first visit to Menton.

The Château Grimaldi had some interesting owners after Bennet's long-postponed death in 1895. (The photograph in *Belles Demeures* was probably taken in 1904 and shows a motor car with four passengers and a chauffeur outside the gates, which carry a 'Castle for Sale' sign). It was bought by Ella Waterman, a rich American from Philadelphia whose father had made a fortune from mining. At that time it had two grand salons, a magnificent dining room, a billiard room, a library, thirteen master bedrooms and five servants' rooms. The old tower had been restored to give another six rooms and a caretaker's flat. In 1904 Kaiser Wilhelm II - anxious to benefit from the charms of the Riviera but unwilling to risk settling in France, where he was unpopular - was unsuccessful in a bid for Château Grimaldi.

In 1925 the property passed into the hands of Doctor Serge Voronoff, Russian by birth but a naturalised Frenchman, from Cimiez, the outrageously classy suburb of Nice.

As Shakespeare says:

Golden lads and girls all must,
As chimney-sweepers, come to dust.

but Voronoff spent a lifetime helping the rich who wanted to live for ever. In 1920 he successfully grafted monkeys' testicles on to men desirous of regaining their youth and virility and went on to repeat this operation many times. This was followed by delaying the menopause in women by transplanting the ovaries of female monkeys. The good doctor published widely and inspired novels and a film, none of them of any distinction. The chateau was transformed into a clinic with operating theatres and the like and the grounds were filled with animal enclosures, so that Voronoff's supply of top quality organs was assured.

Despite the almost comic quality of his venture and the pathetic hopes of his clientele, Voronoff was a serious pioneer of organ transplantation and bone grafting, which he had carried out with great success on World War I casualties. In 1935 he was made an Officer of the Legion of Honour. Château Grimaldi was badly damaged during World War II and rebuilt by Voronoff, only to be subdivided into forty apartments.

In 2011 I was doing some work on the Perthshire Society of Natural Science. In Edinburgh, on a certain September Monday I received from Rhoda Fothergill, the indefatigable secretary, the list of PSNS members in 1899, so that I could make a socio-economic analysis of the membership. Of the 399 members eighteen were ministers and one jumped off the page at me. James Ewing Somerville attracted my attention because he was a Life Member and was the only member to take up two lines on the list. He had two addresses. In summer he lived at Castellar, Crieff - and Castellar is a picturesque hill-village, just north of Menton, on the Riviera. His winters he passed at the Villa Isaune in Menton.

The next day I was in the National Library of Scotland pursuing *The Scottish Geographical Magazine* for 1904 for an article on the PSNS. Scanning the contents I found that one Ralph Richardson, FRSE, FSAScot, had a paper of 11 pages published on *Primitive Man, as Revealed by Recent Researches in the Caves near Menton*. Richardson:

The Gypsy Empresses

...had the privilege of visiting the Caves during March 1902 in company with that experienced cave explorer and archaeologist, the Rev JE Somerville, the well-known Scottish clergyman of Mentone, who gave me the history of the researches and discoveries which have made the Mentone Caves famous.

There are nine caves, known as the Balzi Rossi, of which Richardson visited three. The second was:

A Cave, as yet unnamed and unexplored, into which the sixty-year old Mr Somerville and I let ourselves down with difficulty, and inspected with the aid of candles. We found it encrusted with stalactites and stalagmites, some of considerable size. No human relics have been discovered yet.

However, the museum afforded Mr Somerville, who had:

...studied the Caves and their contents with great care and with perfect impartiality for the past fourteen years,

ample opportunity to interpret the evidence.

That was Tuesday and on Thursday afternoon I was in Menton. There is still an English Church in Menton, so I took a shot of it, just in case. I went browsing in the main bookshop, picking up a big, glossy, illustrated *Impératrices sur la Riviera*. There, tucked in near the bottom of page 38, was the following sentence:

The Low Church or Scottish chapel (Salle Saint-Exupéry) was opened in 1890 by the Rev James Ewing Sommerville (sic) who exercised his ministry from 1886 to 1920.

On Friday the search was on for the church, which was not on any map or list. But it was there, on one of the principal streets. A fine stone building with, above the entrance door, a clear sculpted panel of the Burning Bush – the symbol of the Church of Scotland.

On Saturday I covered the Balzi Rossi caves, just over the border in Italy, the two museums on the site and the fine archaeological museum in Menton. The cave Richardson and Somerville explored has been blocked off for safety reasons.

I now had a good picture of the good minister as a pillar of the Menton community. He was editor of the *Continental Presbyterian* and in *The Expository Times* of 1910 wrote an article on *An Invitation to the Thirsty*. The Rev Dr Murray Mitchell was minister of the Scotch Church in Nice, and died there. He had written two papers on the district. Somerville added a third chapter to bring the subject up to date. The result was – *Les Îles de Lérins: The Iona of the South*.

FIG 1 *The Scots Kirk at Menton*

Dr. George Müller was one of several writers who helped to publicise the attractions of Menton and its surroundings, living in the area for thirty years till his death in 1891. In 1910, Somerville salvaged and edited Müller's *Mentone and Its Neighbourhood: the Past and the Present*, bringing it into the public domain. His editing task was not easy.

> He is perpetually breaking into rhapsodies over the scenery and moralising as he goes along, while his sesquipedalian sentences are fraught with terror to an English reader.

Somerville added chapters on the Menton caves, the Balzi Rossi, his main interest, Ligurian forts and the Via Aurelia, the Roman road that runs along the coast.

When I got back from Menton I immediately looked out James Geikie's *Prehistoric Europe: A Geological Sketch* published in 1891, in which Geikie makes four specific references to the Mentone caves. (2) 'Paleolithic man was…unquestionably a true troglodyte', he says, and goes on to give an admiring description of Cro-Magnon man – 'tall', 'remarkable strength and muscularity', '… the Mentone man was as much as 6 feet 0.8 inches'. Reindeer, mammoth and deer remains abound but Geikie notes the Common Marmot (*Automys marmotta*) as evidence of an earlier cold climate. He mentions the glutton twice. (We now call it the wolverine.)

> The occurrence of the glutton at Mentone…is in perfect harmony

with the appearance of a northern fauna in southern France.

I cannot resist pointing out that I have seen the wolverine at 14,000 feet in the Sierra Nevada of California.

Without doubt a recurring duty for Somerville would have been the burial of the stream of Scots sent to Menton to throw off their illness, and the tidying up of their affairs. One of the most touching stones in the cemetery at Menton states quite baldly:

FIG 2 *Henry Dryerre's gravestone in Menton*

HENRY DRYERRE, BLAIRGOWRIE
POET MUSICIAN JOURNALIST
DIED AT MENTONE
31 MARCH 1905
THE GOODNESS OF GOD ENDURETH

The very baldness of the inscription is interesting, with the minimum of verbiage. Was there no-one at his death to give the stone mason more information? Blairgowrie is a small town fifteen miles from Perth.   How could such a small town support a Poet, Musician and Journalist? Was Dryerre not rather an exotic name for a place well-known today for travelling berry-pickers and folk music? How could Dryerre afford to die in Menton? He could be an interesting case-study of one of the more modest who came to the Riviera and did not return.

In *A Social History of Blairgowrie and Rattray* Dryerre (1848-1905) is recorded as a Bookseller, Stationer, Newsagent and Music Teacher at 10 High Street, Blairgowrie. (Not quite so grand as the gravestone would have us believe. His shop in Blairgowrie, with flat above, is now a pet shop). He published *Love Idylls, Ballads and Other Poems* in 1884, in 1901 *Dryerre's Guide to Blairgowrie, Rattray and district* and, in 1903, *Blairgowrie, Stormont, and Strathmore Worthies* (446 pages, with fifty-one biographical sketches, forty-eight portraits etc.).

EM Theobald, author of *Shakespeare Studies in Baconian Light*, in his *Passages from the Autobiography of a Shakespeare Student* (London, 1910), clearly held Dryerre in high esteem.

Another very able advocate of our thesis is Mr. Henry Dryerre, who lived at Blairgowrie, and was a constant writer for the *Glasgow Argus*, to which he contributed a valuable series of papers on Baconianism. (3) I have visited both Stronach and Dryerre, going to Blairgowrie, especially in order to visit professionally Mrs. Dryerre, who soon after died of cancer. Dryerre was a delicate man, and when 1 first saw him 1 was struck by the milk-white pallor of his complexion. He was then suffering from the elementary stage of pernicious anaemia. He spent a few days with me at Blackheath, on his way to the Riviera, where he hoped to find recovery in the warmer atmosphere of the Mediterranean coast. My eldest daughter was at Monte Carlo at the same time, and they often met. When poor Dryerre's condition was hopeless, Emma went to see him, and directed the landlady to provide, at her expense, everything necessary for his comfort. He died soon after, and his daughter remained in the south, having been affianced to a young Italian who resided there. Dryerre was one of the most tender-hearted men I ever knew, and when we parted he kissed me most fervently. He went with me to Knockholt and helped me on my return home, when I had met with a serious accident, tearing the capsule of my knee-joint, and causing injuries which necessitated the use of splints and bandages for some months. I was a bed-ridden invalid when Dryerre took his loving and, as it proved, lasting farewell. A volume of Wordsworth, elegantly bound in morocco, which he gave me, is among my most valued literary treasures. It is the edition admirably edited by Henry Morley.

Like so many of the bright young persons of his time he went to Menton in search of health, only to die there and be buried by the Rev J.E. Somerville. Did he die alone? Or was the good minister able to share with him memories of distant Perthshire?

Enough has been said to give a picture of the richness, indeed opulence, of the landscape created on the Côte d'Azur over the nineteenth century. At the beginning of the century the foothills of the Alps plunged straight into the Mediterranean, a beautiful but hard environment with poor harbours used by a few fishermen, backed by rocky slopes with thin soils, burnt by the summer drought, with twisted pines and *garrigue* vegetation of lavender, rosemary and lentisk, overgrazed by goats. By the end of the century the landscape had been transformed by human hands. Roads and railways drew the area into contact with developed societies in north Italy, northern France, Germany, Britain, even Russia. Splendid villas, set in gardens with exotic plants from other continents, set the pace for the growth of towns and villages to provide for the construction workers and those who served the great ones – and the lesser ones who followed in their wake. Bored sophisticates required entertainment, so that was provided through the casino, the opera house, the ballet, golf and the racetrack.

Of course, the Côte d'Azur was not unique, the same processes were operating all over Europe and North America as countries industrialised and growing numbers acquired great wealth, or even just enough wealth for an annual holiday. The Prince of Wales (later Edward VII) regularly visited Biarritz and the German spas as well as the Riviera. The Empress Eugénie led the fashionable world to enjoy the bracing breezes of Deauville, Trouville and Dieppe. Odessa and the Crimea were boltholes for the Russians.

In Britain existing spas and watering places expanded and the railway (and railway hotels) helped obscure collections of fishermens' huts to become sizeable towns. Thus Blackpool grew from virtually nothing to a population of 100,000 in the century to 1931. Even in Scotland there could develop somewhere like Strathpeffer with a spa (for health), with a branch line from the Highland Railway (for access), a handful of villas (for those retired from service abroad), two or three big hotels and a handful of boarding houses (to suit the length of one's purse). And Queen Victoria set the fashion for escaping to one's Highland estate in pursuit of sport.

What marks out the Côte d'Azur is the scale, the sheer size of the enterprise. Even today, Nice airport is the second busiest in France, although Nice is only the sixth largest city. To this stage there has been an assumption that there were good reasons for its being such a powerful magnet. It is now appropriate to turn to a close examination of the reasons why so many rich and important people – and particularly the Gypsy Empresses – found it important to see and be seen on the Côte.

End Notes

1 Baron Haussmann (1809-1891) was Napoleon III's right-hand man in the re-creation of Paris in the 1860s, when 60% of its buildings were transformed. Insanitary quarters were swept away, a network of Grands Boulevards was created, a new water supply was brought in, parks laid out etc.

2 There were two Geikies, both distinguished geologists, Sir Archibald (1835-1924) and James (1839-1915), both experts on the Ice Age. Sir Archibald was Director of the Geological Survey in Scotland, the first Murchison Professor of Geology and

Mineralogy at Edinburgh and Director-General of the Geological Survey of the United Kingdom.

James followed his brother through the Geological Survey to become the second Murchison Professor at Edinburgh. As Regional Surveyor he was based in Perth and was an active President of the PSNS. His greatest book was *The Great Ice Age and its Relation to the Antiquity of Man* (1874). Its central issues, continental and highland glaciation, cyclic climate change and multiple glaciations and consequent sea level changes, form the theoretical basis into which the caves of Menton and their early inhabitants fit.

3 Baconianism in this context refers to the theory that Sir Francis Bacon (1561-1626), lawyer, philosopher, essayist and scientist, wrote the plays usually attributed to Shakespeare and that the historical Shakespeare was merely a front to shield the identity of Bacon, whose political ambitions would be negated if it were known that he wrote plays!

CHAPTER 2
'Kennst du das Land?'

THE GERMANS HAVE a word for it. We know *Heimweh* (homesickness) and how they wax tearful at the thought of the *Heimat,* its forests and its snowy peaks. But they also have *Fernweh*, which we could call farsicknesss, the longing for faraway places. The people of northern Europe have always had this longing for the south, for its warmth and colour. Goethe wrote *'Kennst du das Land wo die Zitronen blühn?'* expressing the melancholy ache for a faraway golden land - *'Dahin! Dahin! Möcht ich mit dir, o mein Geliebter, ziehn!'* (There, there, I would go, O my beloved, with thee!). Aschenbach longs for the exotic south at the beginning of Thomas Mann's *Death in Venice.*

Where the lemon trees bloom is along the Mediterranean coast, what we now call the French and Italian Rivieras, where Menton has the mildest winters of mainland France and every town has its Festival of Lemons in the spring. (PLATE 2B)

Ambroise Thomas's *Mignon* is a nineteenth century opera version of Goethe's *Wilhelm Meister* and from it *'Connais-tu le pays?'* became a great favourite for the soprano in the opera house and the salon, prostrating audiences with its affecting nostalgic simplicity. Mignon sings of dim memories of her childhood – the land from which she was abducted – and in Act III all is satisfactorily resolved. (*Mignon* is not experimental or fringe theatre. At the time of writing it had been performed 1833 times at the *Opéra Comique* in Paris alone).

Our own Lord Byron had his own ironic parody:

> Know ye the land where the cypress and myrtle
> Are emblems of deeds that are done in their clime?
> Where the rage of the vulture, the love of the turtle,
> Now melt into sorrow, now madden to crime?

while Elgar celebrated a more generalised feeling with his overture: *In the South – Alassio.*

The ultimate 'flight to the South' is described by the Crawfords in *Michael and Natasha: The Life and Love of the Last Tsar of Russia:*

During the long six months of winter some of the very rich would exchange the bitter cold and swirling snow of St Petersburg for the warmth and sunshine of southern France. From 1898 onwards the luxurious St Petersburg-Cannes express – dubbed 'the train of Grand Dukes' – left the Warsaw station in St Petersburg twice a week, packed with aristocratic Russians.

To the general 'feel-good' character of the Mediterranean came to be added the incentive of a supposedly healthy environment. James Henry Bennet, latterly of the Chateau Grimaldi, was an influential figure who convinced the consumptives of northern Europe that Menton was the place to regain their health. Himself a consumptive, he arrived in Menton in 1859 in a search for health – or a quiet place to die. Unusually, as it turned out, he found health there and the unhappy event of his death was delayed till 1895. In the interim he devoted his energies to passing on the good news. He was enthused and became the chief advocate for Menton as a centre for recuperation and the leading figure in the British colony on the Côte. His book: *Winter and Spring on the Shores of the Mediterranean* was a Victorian favourite and helped to sell Menton as the place to spend the winter, or even to end their days. New words became fashionable: *'les hivernants'* - those who were there to spend the winter - and the 'valetudinarians', paying a protracted farewell. A stream of valetudinarians and health-seekers poured in to make the best of the mild winters.

In Menton a Russian Grand Duchess set up a residence for young consumptives of noble birth. The cemeteries of Menton and Nice have large sections devoted to 'les Anglais' and the Russians, but there is a fair sprinkling of others from northern Europe - Germans, Dutch, the occasional Dane and Swede. There are even a few Swiss, although by that time places like Davos were attracting the likes of Robert Louis Stevenson in search of a cure.

Bennet was highly regarded in his time and prospered to such an extent that, on her first visit to Menton, Queen Victoria drove round to call on him. In Menton he is not forgotten. His bust, on a sturdy pillar, stands in the busy Rue Partouneaux, among the municipal buildings and hotels he helped to generate. (PLATE 2A)

Robert Louis Stevenson was an only child and a sickly one, spending long spells in bed when young and, in adolescence and adulthood, always on the move in the quest for health. He had some of the symptoms of consumption, but some of these disappeared in time and it may be that two winters at Davos, high in the Swiss Alps, brought about a cure. Although he was only forty-four when he died suddenly in Samoa, the cause of death was not consumption but a cerebral haemorrhage.

RLS had several spells on the Riviera (to say nothing of inland visits to Paris, St Germain, Montpellier and the Cevennes). He visited Menton twice and fortunately lived to tell the tale. In early 1863 there was a family tour of five months from Marseille to Menton and on to Rome, Venice and Munich. In the winter of 1863-64 he joined his mother in Menton. In 1873-74 he was alone in Menton, first in the Hotel du Pavillon, then, after a Christmas visit from his friend Sidney Colvin, in the Hotel Mirabeau.

Stevenson was now 24 and pining for Mrs Sitwell, a dark beauty twelve years his senior, to whom he was writing every week. He was brought back to life by the company he met at the Mirabeau. Princess Zassetzky and her sister Madame Garschine had taken a villa but ate and socialised at the hotel. There were two little girls also, but Stevenson could never sort out which belonged to which. There followed a 'sunlit winter of laughter and high spirits' as RLS won over the little girls and became the epicentre of the small and cosmopolitan society of the Mirabeau. His mental therapy complete, he began to write again and tore himself away from Menton to creep back to Paris and Edinburgh.

Raoul Mille, in his *Riviera III,* has a chapter on Stevenson and his role in 'the discovery of the South'. He gives some detail on life at the Mirabeau and how time was spent pleasurably. He does his best to turn up the temperature, but is unable to reveal anything more than joyful companionship.

In 1882, after receiving a clean bill of health from Dr Ruedi in Davos and spells in Kingussie, Strathpeffer, Braemar and Pitlochry, and having acquired a wife and stepson, RLS leased a kind of chalet at Hyères for nine years. Although he said he had had there the only unalloyed happiness of his life, after nine months he was driven out by continuing ill-health and 'Fanny's medical fads'. So it was back to Britain, to Bournemouth, to the United States, to the Adirondacks and California, and to the South Seas.

Edvard Munch (1863-1944), the Norwegian painter famous for 'The Scream' (1895) was one of five children of an army doctor. Two of his brothers died young, of tuberculosis. He was very close to his sister, who died of tuberculosis at fifteen. After the death of Munch's mother at thirty, also of tuberculosis, Munch's father found himself in a precarious financial situation, to which his reaction was to descend into depression and excessive Puritanism.

Munch, the artist, shuttled between Norway, Copenhagen, Paris, Berlin, Florence and Rome. All his life Munch was more than concerned about his health. He was obsessed with sexuality, death - and nature. Melancholy and depression about his tuberculosis and death haunted him. He was reluctant to father children because of what he might transmit to them. In 1902 he tried to shoot himself, damaging a finger in the process. In 1908, after severe depression, hallucinations and attacks of paranoia he underwent a six-month treatment for alcoholism in a Copenhagen clinic. In 1937 the Nazis confiscated ninety of his paintings in Germany, considering them 'degenerate art'. On his death in 1944 he bequeathed to the city of Oslo over 1000 paintings, 18,000 engravings and almost 5,000 watercolours and drawings.

Munch was remarkable for the way he switched styles and frequently in later life would return to an earlier style. At 29 he had a spell in Nice - for pulmonary reasons. His palette lightened to match the brilliant Mediterranean light (*'la lumière éblouissante'*), although one dark picture ('The Vampire' – Munch was fond of vampires and such) seems to have set off a local Nice painter on a career of very strange paintings. In the former Villa Thompson, now the Musée des Beaux Arts, he has a whole room of black-haired women, eyes streaming with blood or tears, or with bleeding hearts.

Despite his pedigree and irregular life style, and whether or not his sojourn on the Riviera was beneficial, Munch managed to survive miserably for 81 years, working furiously all the time.

One of the most sobering walks in Menton today is to leave the busy, cheerful streets of the old part of town and trudge uphill to the Cemetery of the Vieux Chateau. For some years access to the cemetery was limited as winter gales had uprooted the sad cypresses, which, in turn, had pulled down walls and uprooted gravestones. All was put right for 2007 and the Rugby World Cup and now we have access to the whole cemetery.

A series of terraces is packed with ranks of tombs and graves in different styles and several languages. A Sunday walk up to the Vieux Chateau cemetery could hardly have been cheerful for the ailing as they inspected last year's crop of new graves and wondered – who next? Some were old and had achieved some importance in life, but too many were young consumptives who had died far from home and family, with no-one to ensure that their last resting places had more than the minimum of recorded information. A brother (12) and sister (15) had died within a week of each other. It is a sad feature of the graves of the young that many only have names and dates – there are no personal touches. It is as if they had been abandoned by their families and the hotels had been left to carry out the chore of burial and commissioning a stone.

As we browse along we notice and give a nod of recognition to one of the most touching stones, that of:

HENRY DRYERRE, BLAIRGOWRIE
POET MUSICIAN JOURNALIST
DIED AT MENTONE
31 MARCH 1905
THE GOODNESS OF GOD ENDURETH

Poor Dryerre! Surely an exotic name for douce Blairgowrie! Now we know something of the sensitive soul sent off to die alone where the lemon trees bloom, with the least possible fuss or attention.

William Webb Ellis (1806-72) and his brother were the sons of an Army officer who was killed in the Peninsular War. They were awarded free places at Rugby where, he – as his gravestone records –

...with a fine disregard of the rules of football first took the ball in his arms and ran with it thus originating the distinctive feature of the rugby game.

Ellis rose to be Rector of St Clemence Dane's in London, contracted tuberculosis and travelled frequently to Menton for remedial visits, staying in the Hotels d'Italie and de Grande Bretagne. A few days before his death he bought a grave in the Vieux Chateau cemetery, among the other British, German and Russian valetudinarians. Then he made his will and died.

His grave was rediscovered in 1958, but a few years ago the major storm uprooted trees, threw down walls and smashed gravestones in his part of the cemetery. Only in 2007 was that part of the cemetery splendidly restored in time for the Rugby World Cup, which Menton also marked with an exhibition in the Palais d'Europe and a Webb Ellis Trail ending at the grave. (There was already a Rue Webb Ellis in the smart district of Garavan.)

WB Yeats died in Menton in 1939, requesting: ' If I die here, bury me up there on the mountain, and then after a year or so, dig me up and bring me privately to Sligo'. In 1948 his body was interred at Drumcliff and on the stone were engraved these lines from his *Under Ben Bulben*:

> Cast a cold eye
> On life, on Death.
> Horseman, pass by!

with his dates. His youthful bride, Georgie Hyde-Lee, whom he married at 52, lies beside him - but does not get a mention.

In the nineteenth century it was the mildness and gentle sunlight of the winters that appealed. The consumptives notoriously loved frantically for their short lives but the healthy had a great deal of time on their hands and many perceptive people put themselves to a great deal of bother to help to entertain their guests – and to relieve them of their wealth! One could have breakfast at Rumpelmayers or take afternoon tea at London House, where one might see the Empress Sisi enjoying a cup of chocolate.

Visiting, promenading, taking tea, and driving in the country, visiting the antiquities and picturesque hill villages, satisfied the quieter members of a family but the upper crust were accustomed to something more exciting at home. Public gambling was illegal in France but the opening of the casino at Monte Carlo (Monaco) was the springboard for sophisticated entertainment along the coast. (The

FIG 3 *Rumpelmayers – 'le roi des pâtissiers'*

Prince of Wales, later Edward VII, was such a frequent visitor to Baden Baden because, being in Germany, it had a casino as well as a spa). Monte Carlo acquired a splendid new opera house which outrivaled the existing one at Nice. Theatres sprang up and the Riviera became second only to Paris as a centre for ballet – partly because of the large number of Russians on the coast and the links with the Imperial ballet companies 'back home'. Diaghileff's *Ballets Russes* were the ultimate flowering of ballet as an art form, combining Diaghileff's vision and entrepreneurship with the music of Stravinsky, the colour and costumes of Bakst and Cocteau and a stream of brilliant dancers, notably Nijinski and Pavlova. And there was a constant stream of twinkies and handsome sailors from the fleet at Villefranche.

To work up an appetite there was the sea, with boats of every size and shape - for those with long purses, at least. Sea bathing was refreshing and, after the First World War, the sun became a force to be worshipped rather than, as before, avoided. In Nice a 300 square metre 'Skating Ring' was established, where the sexes could mingle in public. Young men could show off their skill and confidently support tremulous partners, while there were countless opportunities for eager social climbers.

The more intellectual might visit the *Rochers Rouges*, inspect the caves and the finds, perhaps even converse with the good minister. From the 1920s photograph it will be noted that the museum was dwarfed by the lift to a hotel on the clifftop and the restaurant. Priorities!

FIG 4 *The caves at Balzi Rossi/Rochers Rouges –with lift, museum and restaurant*

Tennis, of course, was a fashionable import practised in all the hotels. (Note the two courts below the Excelsior Hôtel Regina - PLATE 8c). It was considered to be suitable for a wide range of players. It was capable of developing the body as well as character. It encouraged elegance, physical and moral beauty. The game brought out *le fair-play* – and it was free!

In the 1890s golf ceased to be an esoteric set of skills practised by uncouth and unintelligible fishermen and miners along certain favoured coastal locations, like St Andrews, Musselburgh and Prestwick. These Scottish artisans took the game to the world and within a few years millionaires in the United States and the aristocracy of Europe – under the tutelage of such as Willie Park Junior, twice Open Champion – made it 'the' game for top people. Thus Cannes Mandelieu was founded in 1891 (there are now three golf courses at Cannes) and Monte Carlo in 1910. The *Royal and Ancient Golfers' Handbook* for 2001 lists 34 courses in Provence and Côte d'Azur.

Horse racing is, of course, the ideal occupation for the idle rich. It gets them into the open air. It offers them the opportunity to meet others like themselves and to show off. Many of them own horses, can ride well and are interested in the sport as well as in winning. And it is exciting – the sweating animals at full stretch, the emotions coming to a peak six times in one afternoon. Ideal for bored sophisticates and carers seeking respite from their dying charges. So the Riviera acquired its race-tracks where the punters could follow the classic road to ruin – fast women and slow horses.

High summer heat and drought and inefficient drains made the Côte d'Azur intolerable to the leisured classes. The First World War changed all that. In May 1919 local hotel owners held a *Fête France-Amerique* when the wartime Riviera Leave Zone - where so many Americans had learned to love France - closed down. 1922 was the first year when a hotel was kept open for a summer season and in 1923 the Negresco, the Ruhl and other big players joined in. Thus, just before the Wall Street Crash and the Great Depression, a new pattern of mass summer tourism began to take off.

Where do the gypsies fit in to this landscape? Gypsies? They were an alternative society. Mysterious (in popular imagination originating in Egypt), with their own language and customs, passionate, exotically dressed, unwilling to conform. About the gypsy there is always a whiff of danger – no wonder that rigid regimes felt obliged to persecute them.

Gypsies were everywhere in literature and music – George Borrow started it off for the English with his travel books. Matthew Arnold's *The Scholar Gypsy* retells an old legend about a poor Oxford scholar who joins the gypsies, immersing himself in their culture and mastering their secrets. Intending to learn everything that the gypsies could teach him, he would leave them and reveal the secrets to the world. The scholar gipsy, having given up 'This strange disease of modern life, With its sick hurry, its divided aims', is 'Free from the sick fatigue, the languid doubt', which rules society. He will never master all the secrets and is therefore not subject to ageing and death.

Prosper Merimée's *Carmen* does what she pleases, whatever the cost to herself or to others. It was in the brothels of Paris that Bizet found the gypsy music he so brilliantly transformed to turn Merimée's short story into everyone's favourite opera. Hungarian gypsy music, actually Hungarian music played by gypsies, turned up in all sorts of places. Liszt – himself Hungarian, although not a gypsy – could not have been more romantic or passionate. His *Hungarian Rhapsodies* are still popular, even as advertising jingles, especially since Disney started a fashion for using them as background for wildlife films. Johannes Brahms, a stolid Hamburger whose idea of a good night out was a game of cards as one of

'The Three Johnnies' (Hans Richter, Johann Strauss and himself), came up with sets of Hungarian dances.

Other serious composers wrote Gypsy Dances, Gypsy Rondos or *Rondos a la Ongarese*. In Imperial Vienna one could take in one evening Johann Strauss's *Gypsy Baron* and the next Emmerich Kalmann's *Gypsy Princess*. The Hungarian *czardas* turns up in *Die Fledermaus* as a brilliant show-stopper. (André Previn has said that, if he had a choice, he would like to die conducting Kiri Te Kanawa singing the *czardas* from Act II of *Die Fledermaus*). The second act of a classical ballet is often some sort of entertainment based on a suite of dances, and one of these is usually a Gypsy Dance, or a Spanish (Gypsy) Dance. It was the blind (or blindfolded) gypsy fiddler who provided the romantic music for a romantic dinner in a *chambre séparée*. Piercy's suite, *Gypsy Idyll*, is marked 'with expression' and 'with sadness' while *Gipsy Blood* is to be played *con fuoco* – with fire.

The Empress Elisabeth became passionately involved in matters Hungarian. Stunning in Hungarian national dress she sometimes embarrassed Franz Josef as he sought to deny the subject peoples of his empire their individuality. At other times she was able to use the personal loyalty the Hungarians showed to her to defuse situations which might have split the empire. She took piano lessons from the Abbé Liszt, but showed no great aptitude. No musical highbrow, she loved the gypsy music of Primas Horsty Timor and promoted him in society circles. Her instrument was the zither, which she and her father, Duke Max, played on the escapades of her youth.

Verdi managed to interweave damaged childhoods and the antisocial behaviour of the gypsies in *Il Trovatore*. A very complex plot is centred around Azucena, whose gypsy mother was burned alive at the stake. To avenge her she steals the Count de Luna's son but, half-crazed, throws her own child into the flames by mistake ('thus preserving' as Kobbé says 'with an almost supernatural instinct for opera, the baby that was destined to grow up into a tenor with a voice high enough to sing *"Di quella pira"'*). Strong stuff, ornamented by the gypsy chorus and the Anvil Chorus – the ironworker being another of the traditional gypsy roles in society.

When Violetta - *La Traviata* - returns to Paris to give the party which turns out to be her last, the gypsies (Spanish this time) are dragged in to liven up the proceedings. The gypsy's curse is a crucial element in the plot of Gilbert and Sullivan's *The Gondoliers or the King of Barataria*, a tale of confusion between brothers - or are they? The *Raggle-Taggle Gypsies* exist in some form or other in every folk-song collection in western Europe. *The*

Gypsy's Revenge (PLATE 2C)) was advertised in Aachen early in 2012 by fetchingly dishevelled hair and artfully revealing clothing.

Our own Adam Smith was stolen by gypsies when a child – the only exciting incident in a valuable but quiet life. There is no evidence to suggest that this potentially traumatic event had any effect on *An Inquiry into the Nature and Causes of the Wealth of Nations*.

Even that tough old cynic, Noel Coward, wrote a sentimental gypsy song. Sargent, the American painter of flash portraits of the cream of society, built a very successful career on *La Jalia*, a huge evocation of gypsy low life. How many children have been stirred by William Brighty Rands' *The Pedlar's Caravan*? Probably even more than by his other main contribution to the imaginative life of children, *The Boy's Own Paper*.

I wish I lived in a caravan,
With a horse to drive, like the pedlar man!
Where he comes from nobody knows,
Or where he goes to, but on he goes!

The roads are brown and the sea is green,
But his house is just like a bathing machine;
The world is round and he can ride,
Rumble and splash to the other side!

With the pedlar man I should like to roam,
And write a book when I come home;
All the people would read my book,
Just like the Travels of Captain Cook!

They wandered across Europe, seemingly randomly, but often in complex seasonal patterns – think of the berrypickers of Blairgowrie, the tattie howkers in the Lothians, the horse traders and grooms at Aintree, The Curragh and Cheltenham. They had specific skills, like the working of iron or a way with horses, but like the untouchables in India they had to do jobs no one else was willing to do.

Folk music is redolent with gypsies – like 'The Raggle-Taggle Gypsies, Oh!' or "The lady of the manor was dressing for the ball'. Charles Murray ('Hamewith') in *The Gypsy* describes how, when her 'Lord is awa' at the Corbie's linn', my Lady comes down the stair to 'the antlered ha'":

The Gypsy Empresses

Whaur, bonnet in hand, stood the gypsy there
As raggit as she was braw.

'O I hinna kettles to clout,' she said,
'An' my spoons an' stoups are hale,
But gin ye gang roon' to the kitchen maid
She'll gie ye a waucht o' ale.'

'It's never the way o' the gentry, na,
When visitin' 'mang their frien's,
To drink wi' the maids in the servants' ha'
Or speak about stoups an' speens.

'An' we are mair sib than ye think,' quo' he,
For his Lordship's father's mine;
Tho' the second wife was o' high degree,
His first was a gypsy queyn.

'An' the younger son got the lands an' a',
But the gypsies bettered me;
He is only laird o' a fairm or twa,
I'm king o' the covin-tree.

'Sae I am guid-brither to you, my lass,
An' head o' the auncient name;
An' it wouldna be richt for me to pass
Withoot cryin' in by hame.' (1)

Nobel prizewinner Ivo Andric in *The Bridge on the Drina* paints a much darker picture of the gypsy from his Serbo-Croat background. In Visegrad neither Christian nor Turk is given the responsibility of extracting the truth from a suspect; instead Merdjan the Gipsy has to heat and apply red-hot chains to the suspect. Then, in meticulous detail, Andric describes how Merdjan and two other gipsies have to impale the suspect on an eight-foot stake – while still keeping him alive.

At a later stage, the parish priest is beheaded and his head is stuck on the bridge. It is the gipsy children who mockingly stick a cigar in his dead mouth.

Do we really believe that Queen Victoria yearned to impale Mr

Kennst du das Land?

Gladstone on a stake, no matter how much the clicking of his false teeth irritated her? Can we imagine the Empress Eugénie roughing it round the camp fire, toasting some disgusting piece of carrion on a stick? When the Empress Sisi headed off to the Riviera did she live in a caravan, like a pedlar man? If she was a gypsy, she was a gypsy with a circus in her wake – a court chamberlain, a master of horse, a doctor, a chaplain, a secretary, a treasurer and a troupe of domestics, hairdressers, housekeepers, chambermaids, coachmen, plus two goats to ensure the correct balance of her diet, the procession being followed by Commissioner Xavier Paoli and the French police.

The German Empresses lived by *Kinder, Küche, Kirche* - the family, the household, the Church – and seem never to have wanted to stray. But some of the others, in varying degrees, had the occasional itch to throw off the shackles of court convention. In the eighteenth century Marie Antoinette and her circle played at being shepherdesses in the gardens of Versailles. In the nineteenth century the Riviera was the place where the great ones could leave behind their duties and relax. They could get up to all kinds of nonsense, and still be insulated from the less attractive sides of society.

End Note

1 From Charles Murray, *Hamewith and other Poems* (Constable & Co Ltd, London, New Edition, 1944).
Sib = related, queyn = young woman, covin-tree = the large tree in front of the mansion where visitors were received.

The poem concludes when the Lord returns:

> But the bluid ran thin in the gard'ner Sim,
>   He'd heard o' the cairds afore,
> An' the auld romance had nae charms for him,
>   He lockit the hen-hoose door.

Note the contempt for the settled laird – the gardener. A caird was a travelling tinker and therefore to be regarded with suspicion. The union which brought about the gypsy was unlikely to have been blessed by the church. So the fox had to be kept from the chickens.

CHAPTER 3
The Gypsy Empresses

VICTORIA GLENDINNING, HERSELF a prize-winning biographer, has said that all biographers fall in love with their subject. There is much truth in this, although there must be exceptions, like Alan Bullock and Hitler. It should therefore be made quite clear that this book is A Study in Escapism and not a series of biographies, that the author is trying to tell the truth simply and is not in love with any of his subjects – although some are more attractive than others. All one is trying to do is to examine the lives of a number of great ladies for signs of unconventional behaviour in an era when they were supposed to be the embodiment of conventional behaviour.

Yet it does not require sophisticated computer analysis to realise that these *grandes dames* are not treated equally. For some of these ladies there is, quite simply, little unconventional behaviour to observe and record. They were born into a high position in society. They married, had children, were supplanted by younger models and/or died. They had an easy life, lived in palaces and had the best of clothes and jewels. Their routines were safe and predictable and they were surrounded by loyal servants and deferential courtiers. The empresses had varying degrees of power in their own countries, but this was often limited to the influence that any wife might have on her husband in an age of autocracy.

The hereditary principle became firmly established in Europe after the collapse of the Roman Empire and invasions from the East. In a society in turmoil the little people found it useful, even essential, to band together under a strong leader who would defend them against their enemies. In a kind of contract the overlord would supply a strong right arm, keeping the peace and encouraging trade while his subjects paid taxes to maintain him and turned out to defend the state when required. The succession of the eldest son was a clear-cut mechanism for transfer of power once the strong right arm began to fail, the assumption being that, just as property should pass from father to eldest son, the desirable qualities of the father would be passed on to the son. (1)

Most kings and emperors had a coronation, performed before God and the people, which was a kind of marriage ceremony in which the monarch promised to perform God's will and support His church and to protect and care for his subjects. Very often this developed into a belief that the king had a special relationship with God, was almost divine himself. Indeed, our own James VI (and I) wrote defending the 'Divine Right of Kings', although his behaviour suggested he was only too human. (2)

Great ones with the special qualities that made them great would have to ensure that these qualities were passed on and therefore must marry others like themselves, offspring of the great. So there grew up a class of European rulers, marrying and intermarrying among theirselves, despite all the evidence that this was an unwise and even dangerous practice. 'Marrying out' might have refreshed the gene pool but such morganatic marriages resulted in the loss of the rights of succession.

In this respect family pride often overruled common sense. Franz Josef of Austria, Tsar Nicholas of Russia, even Kaiser Wilhelm of Germany had - more or less - absolute power. They could each sign a decree, which was enthusiastically followed up, sending a million of their subjects to their deaths. Yet they felt unable to overturn a practice established for some prejudicial reason two centuries before.

By the nineteenth century there had developed a barbed wire entanglement of relationships. From this evolved a loose network of private and family relationships, which formed much of the basis for the lives of the Empresses. Dynastic links were made for political reasons or merely to keep things within the family – the Hapsburgs were notorious for this. Religion could be a problem, with the limited availability of suitable Protestant candidates, a similar problem to that faced by our own Royal Family. There was resentment at minor Germans being promoted and would-be Tsarinas had to change their language and name before being accepted.

Our own Queen Victoria (later Empress of India) had nine children, all of whom married well. She was the mother of one of the Empresses of Germany ('Vicky') who was, in turn, mother of eight children, all of whom also married well. Carlota became Empress of Mexico when the Empress of Austria's brother-in-law was forced upon the Mexicans by the husband of the French Empress.

Eugénie in exile settled in Farnborough, in Hampshire, where she and Victoria could visit each other. On the Cote d'Azur, Eugénie, Sisi and Victoria regularly visited each other, Sisi even helping Eugénie to design her villa on Cap Martin.

In this welter of high politics and family squabbles how dispassionate is the author? I think I make clear the distinction between factual reporting and comment. Since this is a study in escapism it must be true that I am more interested in and sympathetic towards the escapists than the strait-laced stay-at-homes.

Before proceeding to examine each Empress in some detail a thumbnail sketch of each might help to sort them out.

Victoria's reign is usually divided into three parts. Her life with Albert was happy and fruitful. They travelled a great deal and, especially when based at Balmoral, made expeditions and had adventures of a sweet and simple kind. After Albert's death in 1861 there was a period of black retreat from public life as 'The Widow of Windsor'. This was succeeded by a kind of Indian summer when she was persuaded to come back into the world. She was created Empress of India in 1876 and, although she never went there, she resumed the travelling life.

Eugénie and Carlota might be called the synthetic Empresses. Eugénie and Napoleon III might be considered well-matched. He might be called a chancer and she was certainly called a gold-digger. The frenetic Second Empire lasted only twenty years – yet this was nine years more than the imperial rule of his more respected uncle, the warmongering Napoleon Bonaparte. Then Eugénie's travels began in earnest.

The Mexican debacle was one of Napoleon III's half-baked schemes - remembered mainly as a subject for Manet, the French Impressionist. Maximilian's Mexican Empire lasted only 3 years, ending in the death of the puppet by firing-squad and the madness of his unfortunate widow.

There could be no doubt but that the Empress Sisi was the most-travelled of the Empresses. Too sensitive for her own good, her life alternated between spells of trying to fit the expected stereotype of Empress of Austria and Queen of Hungary and flight to another, gentler, world. Her death was characteristically unsatisfactory - murdered by an anarchist who had come to Geneva to kill one of the French royal family (who had just left the city) and instead killed the next aristocrat he could find. The irony was that this free spirit was an easy victim because she was about to board a lake steamer, accompanied only by a lady-in-waiting.

The Riviera was a second home for the three so-called Russian Empresses considered. (Two were German-born, the other Danish.) Alexandra Feodorovna had a part to play in obtaining the use of Villefranche-sur-mer as a naval base for the Russian fleet after the Crimean War. Marie Alexandrovna's tale is of the beautiful young girl loved madly by the Tsar till, worn out by bearing his children, she was superseded by another beautiful teenage blonde. Maria Feodorovna ('The Sad Fiancée') fought her mother-in-law's cause and founded the Russian cathedral in

Nice. As Dowager Empress she shuttled around Europe before and after the Russian Revolution.

For good measure I have thrown in Katia Dolgourika aka Catherine Yourievski (Alexander II's schoolgirl love). After Marie Alexandrovna's death they were married – but only morganatically and very conveniently for Alexander, who was able to have his cake and eat it.

As for the Germans, Augusta of Saxony-Weimar (1811-1890) was already sixty-one years old when the German Empire was declared but was Empress for sixteen years. Victoria of Great Britain (1840-1901) married Crown Prince Frederick of Prussia in 1858 and had a long wait of sixteen years as Crown Princess of the German Empire until her husband succeeded as Frederick III in 1888. Unfortunately Fritz's reign lasted only ninety-nine days, leaving Vicky to live out thirteen years as Dowager Empress. (There was a spell of about two years when Germany had two Dowager Empresses.) Augusta Victoria of Schleswig-Holstein (1858-1921) was Kaiserin for thirty years, until her husband's flight to Holland and abdication. After Augusta's death Wilhelm married Hermina of Reuss, who died in unexplained circumstances in 1949, in Frankfurt an der Oder, at that time in East Germany. As she was not an Empress she does not qualify for consideration here.

The German Empire lasted only 46 years. Two of the Empresses lived unremarkable lives while Vicki's life is more interesting for us because of the family tensions rather than for her wanderings.

The late nineteenth century was the high point of empire in at least an organisational sense. Napoleon III's Second Empire was one of many constitutional experiments carried out by the French over more than two centuries and collapsed when it foolishly challenged the Germans. Maximilian's Mexican Empire was projected in the wrong century. Both Eugénie and Carlota had many years to reflect on their experiences. The other Empires - the Austro-Hungarian Empire, the Russian Tsars, the short-lived German Empire and the Ottoman Empire - were all casualties of the revolutionary changes resulting from the First World War.

One of the first gramophone records I owned was Johann Strauss's *Emperor Waltz* of 1889 (on three sides). This is a big concert-hall piece rather than a ballroom item. 'Imperial in inspiration, it is also imperial in stature', says the programme. It has a lively opening march, which gives way to a tentative waltz ('the most dignified of its kind'), which is followed by a succession of brilliantly tuneful waltzes - 'stately', 'dignified', 'imposing', 'almost symphonic proportions' – 'and a brilliantly ceremonial ending'.

'A thoughtful solo cello' gives a clue to my interpretation of the *Emperor Waltz*. It is achingly sentimental, suffused with gentle melancholy, picturing perfectly the decay of the Austrian Empire and forecasting accurately a future nostalgia for a lost world.

Alas for childhood's imagination. Strauss's great waltz was written to celebrate the historic state visit of Kaiser Franz Josef I of Austria to Kaiser Wilhelm II of Germany in Berlin in 1889. It should not be the Emperor Waltz, but the Emperors' Waltz, designed to flatter them both and offend neither by parading national tunes. Clever Strauss, that he could turn out a work that pleased his clients and yet forecast their fate!

'The Last...' is a favourite title for books dealing with this period. Franz Josef died, toiling away to the last, in 1916. His grandnephew Charles was shown the door in 1918 and the Hapsburg domain split into the republics of Austria, Hungary and Czechoslovakia and the kingdom of Yugoslavia. Germany was also dismembered and made to pay for the cost of the war. The result was financial chaos and a sense of grievance which made it easy for Hitler to lead his people into ventures which were supposed to set things right. In Russia the tyranny of the Tsars was ousted by the Russian Revolution and civil war, to be replaced by the tyranny of the Party and the eventual dismemberment of the Union of Soviet Socialist Republics. The Ottoman Empire was complex and corrupt, with only a toehold in Europe in the nineteenth century, but, like its allies Germany and Austria, it paid the price of defeat - internal collapse and dismemberment. Almost a century after the World War I 'peace settlement' parts of the former Ottoman Empire - Lebanon, Israel, Palestine, Iran, Iraq, Saudi Arabia - make up a litany of grief and distress.

Curiously enough, the British is the only one of the Empires to survive, albeit in modified form. Despite our near-collapse financially in two world wars and the growth of independence movements, there is still a Queen heading up a constitutional monarchy. Colonies have evolved into separate states, but most of these have chosen to be part of the Commonwealth. Some have seceded and been re-admitted. There is even a former Portuguese colony - Mozambique - which has chosen to enter the Commonwealth and has been welcomed.

Is it too simplistic to observe that those who had total authority, the autocrats, the Kaisers, the Tsars, failed to use that authority wisely and fairly, and were swept away? While our own muddled constitutional monarchy - with no written constitution - has contrived to keep its family of nations bumbling along in more or less the same way?

End Notes

1   At the same time as the development of the hereditary states of Western Europe, the kingdoms and caliphates of the Muslim Near East were bedevilled by murder, jealousy and conspiracy as brothers and uncles were manipulated by the women in the harem in their desire for control.

2   One of the refreshing things about the Church of Scotland is that Andrew Melville, one of the early Reformers, addressed James as: 'God's sillie vassal on earth'. The meaning of 'silly' may have morphed a little since the 16th century, but Melville's courageous character assessment of James strips away pretension and puts him on the same plane as the rest of us.

CHAPTER 4

Elisabeth, Empress of Austria (1837-1898)
Manège not *Ménage*

IN 1618, AS THE EMPEROR MATHIAS lay dying, the Hapsburg dynasty was the greatest power in Europe. They owned Austria, Hungary, and all the surrounding territories that were not in the hands of the Turks. Burgundy, the Low Countries and parts of Alsace were theirs. Lombardy, Naples, Sardinia and Sicily were Hapsburg territory. Hapsburgs were Kings in Spain and Portugal, and with them came Chile, Peru, Brazil, Mexico in the New World, with many important islands from India to the Philippines. Marriage, rather than conquest, was the secret of their success in acquiring and securing territory. One prince could be brother-in-law, son-in-law and cousin to another, as CV Wedgwood says: 'Thrice-bound to him in love and duty'. This happened twice, with Philip IV of Spain and the Emperor Ferdinand III and the Elector Maximilian of Bavaria and the Emperor Ferdinand II.

The *Kaisersgruft* (Imperial Burial Vault) is not one of the most cheerful tourist sites in Vienna. Right in the middle of the old city it is seldom visited, not least because it is not advertised and gaining admittance is like an episode from an old mystery in black and white. The *Kapuzinerkirche* is unobtrusive, but it is what lies underneath that is important. Here are the Hapsburgs, 145 of them, starting with Matthias, in rows of black coffins with simple deathsheads, each with the imperial crown.

In an extension the style changes, with an enormous elaborate sarcophagus covering the remains of Maria Theresia, Empress in her own right and an eighteenth century mother-figure similar to our own Queen Victoria. Her son, the reforming Josef whom we always associate with Mozart, chose simplicity. In something like an old tin trunk he lies at his mother's feet.

A further extension is well-lit and spacious. In the middle is a marble plinth with quite a plain sarcophagus. Here Franz Josef is at rest. On either side are the Empress Elisabeth and their son Crown Prince Rudolf, both of whom suffered violent deaths.

And here, all during the hot summer of 1857, came the Empress Elisabeth in a closed carriage with the blinds drawn down, descending into the crypt to weep and pray, wallowing in self-reproach, by the tomb of her two year old Sophie, who had died of measles while her younger sister survived.

Many years later, on 9 February 1889, the Empress retired to bed early in the Hofburg, the Imperial Palace. She got up, dressed, veiled herself so closely as to be unrecognisable and left the palace by a side door. A passing cab took her to the Capuchin monastery, where she summoned the Prior. Lifting the veil she said. 'I am the Empress. Please take me to my son'. Despite the Prior's remonstrances she descended into the gloomy, icy vault, ill-lit by a few hastily-gathered torches. All was silent for many minutes – only interrupted twice by the loud and anguished cry of 'Rudolf! Rudolf!' emerging from the crypt, causing the young monk acting as night-watchman to cross himself in fear. Then, quite calm and collected, she left the monastery, having achieved some degree of consolation. She would not be able, however, to leave behind thoughts of the sordid end of the Crown Prince Rudolf, heir to the Hapsburg Empire, who, having made a suicide pact with Maria Vetsera and shot her, sat in the locked room for six or eight hours beside her naked body before he could summon up the courage to fulfil his part of the bargain. Nor was the rottenness of the Hapsburg monarchy better demonstrated than in the disgusting treatment of the body of the comparatively innocent Vetsera - and her mother - in a pathetic attempt to keep the Imperial name unsullied, so that Rudolf could lie beside his ancestors.

Probably the key to understanding the early relationships around the Emperor Franz Josef of Austria and his bride Princess Elisabeth of Bavaria is the Archduchess Sophie of Bavaria. Sophie was the cleverest, the most handsome, and the most determined of 'the Bavarian sisters of misfortune', the daughters of Maximilian I, King of Bavaria. Her oldest sister married Francis I, Emperor of Austria and the last Holy Roman Emperor. Sophie was forced into marrying Francis Charles ('That imbecile! Never!'), younger son of Francis, so that her half-sister became her mother-in-law. When Francis died, his successor Ferdinand I proved to be weak and incompetent. In 1848, the Year of Revolutions, he was forced to grant a popular constitution and fled to Innsbruck. He was persuaded to abdicate in favour of Franz Josef (and lived happily for another 27 years). Sophie's husband, Francis Charles, was persuaded to give up his right to the succession (and bumbled on happily for another 28 years), leaving

Sophie's eighteen year old son, Franz Josef, Emperor.

His first actions were to overturn the new constitution, to crush the popular discontent and to restore to the Catholic church the privileges withdrawn by Maria Theresia's son, Josef. A young Emperor needed a young wife and Sophie lined up for him her niece Helen. Helen was, however, morose, awkward and shy, and, when Franz Josef snatched a summer holiday at Bad-Ischl, it was the younger sister, the fifteen year old Elisabeth, he fell for, in probably the only romantic and spontaneous action in his life.

What was so special about the young princess? Her father was Duke Max:

> ...in whom the Wittelsbach strain of eccentricity manifested itself in an irresponsibility bordering on the pathological.

He kept the company of artists, writers, and frequented low taverns. His greatest skills were playing the zither and trick circus riding, both talents which were passed on to Sisi, who was to become one of the finest horsewomen in Europe. He would disappear for long periods when he went about having romantic ventures and exercising his *droit de seigneur*. Worse, he even wrote articles for the liberal, gutter press! But he was charming and would return to be welcomed by all his family and another child would be conceived. Sisi grew up wild and undisciplined in an untidy, but happy home. All her life she was surrounded by the biggest of dogs, the bane of tidy-minded courtiers. In her teens she and her father 'went walkabout' in the countryside, playing the zither and singing for their suppers. As her father said to her:

> If you and I, Sisi, had not been born princes, we would have been performers in a circus.

All her life, she was to give offence to the court by her rejection of suffocating protocol and her obvious preference for lively, if humble, company. In 1861, after her sojourn in Madeira, she spent a week in Spain incognita, 'to avoid the tedium of a royal visit'.

> Too delicate for the strain and fatigue of a royal visit, she was nevertheless well enough to visit all the churches and gardens of Seville and even to attend a bull-fight which, given her love of horses, she found 'both horrible and cruel'.

Her accomplishments – out of the saddle – were limited. Despite the zither, we hear little of her music. She had lessons from Franz Liszt, but this was more of an expression of her love of all things Hungarian than a serious undertaking. Nevertheless, Liszt may have had a deeper influence than mere keyboard brilliance. To quote *The Oxford Companion to Music:*

> Two opposing forces were continually at war within him. He revelled in the glamour he created, but when satiated with all this he would shut himself away from the world, full of disgust, the desire to write great works strong upon him. Then his delight in the world's applause would prove too strong, he longed again to see fashionable society at his feet and he would emerge again from his isolation.

> In his last years his raking discontent made him more than ever restless. He travelled incessantly, urged on, it would seem, by a burning desire to make amends, for he gave his services wherever they could be applied to a useful purpose, as he had for long given all his lessons, free of charge.

Sisi was shy and spent much of her youth in the fantasy land of romance – knights and maidens and forests. All her life she wrote poetry which was - in English translation at least – rather banal and insipid. But she was undoubtedly beautiful - tall for the time, unbelievably slender in an age when feminine beauty was an accumulation of curves. Her hair was auburn and, again against the fashion, was never cut. Her hands were

FIG 5 *Liszt thumping the keyboard in 1886 (Olrig Stephen, after La Vie Parisienne)*

supposed to be too large and rough - but who but a spiteful lady-in-waiting would notice that, especially when they were always covered by the finest of gloves? Her teeth were discoloured - a consequence of inbreeding. With her shyness this meant that she hid behind a fan and spoke in little above a whisper – which added to her attraction. (PLATE 3A)

The Gypsy Empresses

Franz Winterhalter (1805-73) was the Victorian master of the swagger portrait. He could even make Victoria look glamorous. His full-length portrait of Sisi reveals her:

> In a vaporous white ball dress, studded with stars, with diamond stars in her hair, she appears ethereally beautiful, elusive and intangible.

> One understands why Franz Josef could refuse her nothing, why wounded soldiers in hospital begged for her picture to hang above their beds, and peasants in Hungary burnt candles to her image.

Portraits of Sisi on horseback, sketches and caricatures, convey a vision of grace, erect with a miraculously slender waist. Eugénie, subject of another Winterhalter portrait, twelve years Sisi's senior and who could have been jealous, said she was 'the loveliest crowned head in Europe'.(1)

Empresses, queens and princesses are always beautiful and gracious – at least until someone younger comes along to tickle the husband's fancy. Fashion photographers and portrait painters can transform quite plain girls into raving beauties. Henry VIII had Anne of Cleves ('the Flanders mare') brought over on the strength of a miniature only to dump her when the reality fell short of the image. Is there such a thing as an objective view of beauty?

Sisi attracted dozens of admiring descriptions – but how can we gauge their accuracy? Fortunately we have her vital statistics for her later years. When she was wintering at Roquebrune she weighed 45 Kg (99.2 lbs). Since she was quite tall - 1 metre 75, or 5ft 9 ins - this gave her a Body Mass Index of 14.1. Since anything below 18.5 is now considered underweight, she was clearly seriously underweight. A modern fitness trainer would advocate a muscle-building regime but fitness was not a problem for Sisi and she would have required to have been force-fed a rich diet to bring her back to something approaching normality – and that would have been totally abhorrent to her.

The possible marriage between Franz Josef and Elisabeth raised doubts at the time. The Habsburgs were notorious for their inbreeding, most obvious with the Habsburg lip and heavy jaw, brought out so well in the portraits of Velasquez. (2) The Wittelsbachs had a taint of madness and their creativity could wobble between hyperactivity and depression. Franz Josef and Elisabeth were first cousins and their union was to be the 22nd marriage between Habsburg and Wittelsbach. A special dispensation had to be obtained from the Pope.

The marriage of Franz Josef and Elisabeth lasted for 44 years. A ball-by-ball account of its ups and downs would be impossibly long, repetitive and unnecessarily tedious. Rather I propose, as briefly as is reasonable, to examine the how and why of Sisi's becoming a Gypsy Empress and to describe what that meant for her. There follow a number of incidents, spread over many years, which provide food for thought about Sisi and her reactions.

The conventional description of the early days of the marriage, based partly on Sisi's own accounts, is that a young girl, 'shy and wild, cultured, full of enthusiasm and with a tendency to dreaminess and melancholy', was brought into a rigid and protocol-ridden community, to be bullied and condemned for her free-and-easy ways. Thus, having been told that she was the highest in the land, she was not allowed to order a glass of beer if she was thirsty. Empresses did not drink beer – except when on holiday in Bad-Ischl.

Archduchess Sophie led the bullying campaign and succeeded in blunting young Franz Josef's passion for his bride and directing his energies into the massive task of running the Empire as an absolute ruler. Court etiquette and military pageantry were to become to him as sacred s religion.

Sisi's reaction was to withdraw or flee from the court.

> I had no choice but to live like a hermit. In the larger world I was persecuted and judged badly. They hurt and slandered me so much… And yet God, who can see into my soul, knows that I never harmed anybody.

> It was for these reasons that I decided to seek company that would not only not disturb my tranquillity but would be pleasant to me. I turned inwards and I clung to Nature. The woods, the forests do not betray. It's true that it is difficult to live in solitude, but one grows accustomed in the end. Nature is much more grateful than human beings.

A month after her wedding she said: 'Oh! Why did I abandon the path that was leading me to freedom!' and to a friend wrote:

> Matrimony is an absurd institution. They sell you at 15, when you're still a little girl, and they make you swear an oath you do not understand

and which you will regret for the next 30 years or more, yet have no way
of breaking.

Recent research, however, has shown from Sophie's diaries that, at a
personal level, she was more than well-disposed towards Sisi. Certainly, the
hidebound court gave her a hard time - as we shall see - but was this any
worse than has happened in many aristocratic families? Sophie certainly
pushed hard at her son in political and diplomatic matters but did not set
out to wreck the marriage. Franz Josef was dull, unimaginative and a slave
to duty. Sisi was overimaginative and unpredictable and became hysterical
when her husband felt compelled to prefer the company of ministers and
generals to her own.

Sisi's first child was christened, without her being consulted, Sophia,
after her grandmother, who immediately took the child to the Imperial
nursery on the same floor as her quarters, and hand-picked the nurses and
maids. Sisi was not allowed in charge of her child, but was this so terrible
in the Viennese capital in 1855? The child care of the upper classes has
always been a hit or miss affair compared with 'middle-class morality'.
Was Sisi a bad mother? Or was she merely typical of her time? When
her second daughter was born there was a blazing row with Sophia, and
the Emperor ordered that the nurseries be moved to be adjacent to the
Empress.

There is no evidence to suggest that Sisi was any better at bringing up
her children than Sophia had been. The latter considered Sisi unfit to be a
mother, more interested in her horses than her children. A *bon mot* current
at this time was '*Manége* not *ménage*' – horsemanship not housekeeping.

Yet she was not totally selfish and irresponsible. She could turn up
trumps in an emergency and arouse admiration for the support of her
husband at stressful times - as in Hungary, as we shall see, and several
times in the troubled north Italian territories. At the battle of Solferino the
French and Austrians slugged it out with more violence than intelligence.
Casualties were horrific, almost the only provision for the wounded being
a field hospital set up by the Empress.

Franz Josef's empire was a hotch-potch of different faiths and
peoples. Joseph Roth (1894-1939) was, by general agreement,

The great elegist of the cosmopolitan, tolerant and doomed Central
European culture that flourished in the dying days of the Austro-
Hungarian Empire.

In *The Radetzky March* of 1932 he has the 'illusionless, mocking, fearless and self-assured' Chocknijki telling:

> ...all and sundry that the Emperor was a senile idiot, the government a bunch of morons...the state authorities corrupt villainous and lazy. Austrians of German stock crooned waltzes in their cups. Hungarians stank, Czechs were born to clean shoes. Ruthenians treacherously disguised Russians. Croats and Slovenes, whom he called 'stoats and ravens', were broom-makers and chestnut-roasters, and Poles, of whom he himself was one, fornicators, barbers and fashion-photographers

In 1857 the Emperor and Empress made a tour of Hungary as part of a campaign to heal the wounds of the savage repression of 1849. In Budapest Gisela, the second child, fell ill with measles and further touring was suspended. Gisela soon recovered but her elder sister Sophie contracted the disease. The Empress was filled with remorse, but the imperial couple were persuaded to continue their tour. A telegram summoned them to return from Debreczin, but there was nothing to be done. A distraught Sisi had to sit for twelve hours while her child died in agony. As we have seen, Sisi was in despair at having allowed her sense of duty to contribute to her daughter's death.

As her children grew up and the first wrinkles began to appear Sisi's absorption in her own beauty and the physical regime necessary to maintain it became obsessive. Wherever she went, her gymnastic apparatus accompanied her, and every day she had a session on it. She became intolerant of the stuffy conversations at court. For many public functions she just did not turn up. If the Emperor insisted, she would wear some clinging garment that emphasised her height and slenderness, outshining the grand ladies loaded with glittering schmuck. Or she would have a plain dress and a simple bonnet 'like a retired maid in a Sunday dress'.

In her life there was a string of young men with whom she would discuss philosophy and poetry. Some of them were lame dogs, like Christomanos, her Greek teacher, who was a hunchback. She had what was seen as a perverse sympathy for 'freaks' and for visiting other unfortunates. She solved the problem of what to give the girl who has everything for Christmas by wheedling out of Franz Josef a fully-equipped lunatic asylum - which helped to make Vienna the most advanced city in the world for the treatment of mental illness.

She explored Vienna after dark in disguise and attended a masked ball at the *Musikverein*. As 'Gabrielle' (3) she met and had a long correspondence with a young diplomat. Mr Collett was a crippled young Englishman who was in love with the Empress and contrived to be in Bad Kissingen when she made her annual visit there. They discussed poetry and religion and she had two of his poems set to music, so that they could be sung to her in the evenings.

These adventures were harmless, but indiscreet. The young men must always have known that this was a very special lady as her behaviour, by the usual standards, was awkward and her questions came out as commands. But if any of them tried to go too far he was summarily frozen out.

Two of her young men deserve special mention. Hungary was a major component of the Empire and a great source of trouble to the Emperor. Sisi fell under the spell of one Count Julius Andrassy, a leading Hungarian nationalist and politician, who had contrived to plant a Hungarian patriot (Ida Ferenczy) among Sisi's maids of honour. Andrassy was handsome, dashing and slightly dangerous, having been exiled after 1849. Sisi swallowed everything Hungarian. She learned the language, loved the music and dressed in national costume. At Franz Josef's side she pushed for Hungary's nationalist aspirations, causing him great embarrassment.

1866 'brought out all that was best and noblest in Elisabeth'. Prussia invaded Austria, crushed the army at Sadowa and advanced on Vienna. Sisi worked in the hospitals and 'stood by her man'. On his behalf she went to Budapest to secure the loyalty of the Hungarians, who were in danger of seceding.

The visit was a personal triumph for Elisabeth. The Hungarians fell in love with her. Franz Josef had her stay on in Budapest, hoping that she would temper the Hungarians' ambitions. However, under Andrassy's influence she made a nuisance of herself by being over-zealous on the Hungarians' behalf.

Reluctantly, however, it became recognised that a contented Hungary was Austria's only salvation for the future. A Dual Monarchy was created, the 1848 constitution was restored, and a Hungarian Chamber of Deputies revived. Count Andrassy was appointed as Minister for Hungarian Affairs. On 8 June 1867 Franz Josef and Elisabeth were crowned King and Queen of Hungary in Budapest. Liszt wrote the music for the Coronation Mass and wrote to his daughter: 'Erszebet' (Elisabeth in Hungarian) 'was a celestial vision' in an adaptation of Hungarian national dress by Worth, the top couturier in Europe.

An empress or queen is supposed to serve her country by establishing a rapport with other rulers. Sisi and Eugénie got on quite well, despite their very different characters and the contrasting qualities of their husbands' characters and ambitions. In a private capacity, Sisi visited Britain on many occasions. Victoria admired her and may even have felt a little jealous of her attraction and freedom, but there was little rapport between them. Indeed, Sisi twice refused invitations to dine at Osborne, the Queen's residence on the Isle of Wight. By contrast, there was a mutual sympathy between Sisi and Vicky, Victoria's eldest child who became – for a short time - Empress Frederick Victoria of Germany.

Captain 'Bay' Middleton of the 12th Hussars was one of the finest riders to hounds in Britain. ('Bay's a phenomenon, but one day he'll break his neck' was an accurate prediction, as he was to die in a point to point some years after his association with Sisi). Sisi spent several hunting seasons in the English shires and Ireland, bringing her own stud with her from Hungary and a substantial entourage, not forgetting her own gym. Middleton was singled out to pilot her through her first season – an arrangement so successful that it was repeated for the next six years.

Wary at first, Middleton found a horsewoman as professional as a huntsman, tireless and ready to spend all day, and every day, in the saddle. They formed a mutual admiration society, outdoing each other in daring, wearing out the courtiers and other house guests. Sisi loved the free and easy social life of the hunt, the roughness and plain speaking, the merry recounting of the day's sport after a good dinner.

Joan Haslip says that 'Elisabeth was certainly infatuated, even if she was never in love'. Certainly there was concern at the close relationship, although Sisi did not disguise her pleasure from Franz Josef, who seems to have liked the amiable young soldier. Others, however, resented his being included as a guest at hunts and shooting parties in Hungary and Bohemia. He may have been an officer and a gentleman in England but in the eyes of the Hungarian nobility was little more than a groom or other servant.

'Mad King Ludwig' of Bavaria, builder of crazy castles and patron of Wagner, was another of Sisi's lame dogs - and a cousin. Deposed and locked up as insane, he died in extremely odd circumstances. Sisi was the only woman he could relate to and his death was another blow, not least because of the suggestion of tainted blood.

A major turning point in the imperial couple's relationship came in 1861, when it became apparent that Elisabeth was seriously ill. She had been infected with a sexually-transmitted disease by her loving husband, although this was represented as tuberculosis, which was, of course, more respectable.

Most of us learn our history from film and story, which makes this a suitable point at which to cue in Romy Schneider. The Austrian film actress Romy Schneider, was born in Vienna in 1938 and died in 1982 in very messy circumstances - less than a year after her son had bled to death in an accident.

In 1956 I was working in the German-speaking part of Switzerland and noted three interesting things about the film scene. Richard Dimbleby had done an April Fool spoof on 'Panorama' about the spaghetti harvest, in the style of an anthropological investigation. This was shown on the Swiss newsreels as an example of how stupid the English were – the gallant Switzers did not realise it was meant to be a joke!

That was the year of *War and Peace,* starring Mel Ferrer and Audrey Hepburn, both resident in Switzerland at that time. Like many another, I had tried to read the book but had given up after thirty pages, defeated by those awful Russian names. But after the film I was able to get through the book in as near one sitting as could be contrived for such a major work.

The real hit that summer in Austria, Germany and Switzerland was, however, *Sissi, die junge Kaiserin* (Sisi, the young Empress). There were queues outside every cinema, and it ran for weeks in every town and city. Romy Schneider, then virtually the same age as the part she was playing, was Empress of Austria. The plot was simple enough. Sisi, the young Empress, was portrayed as slowly adapting to life in the Hofburg and at Schönbrunn. Hedged in by sterile protocol, she found it especially hard to live with her mother-in-law, the Archduchess Sophie – seen through the camera lens as a genuine busybody, constantly interfering with how the Emperor performed his duties and how Sissi was bringing up her first-born daughter.

What I didn't realise at the time was that *Sissi, die junge Kaiserin* was the middle film in a trilogy in which the empress was played by the delightful Romy. *Sissi* (1955) was even more sweetly sentimental, with the 16-year old Princess Elisabeth of Bavaria following her mother and sister Helene to the Austrian court in Bad Ischl, where the engagement of Helene to the young Emperor Franz Josef was to be announced. When Sissi is out fishing Franz Josef meets her and falls in love. She loves him in return but with the marriage comes the bonus of his arrogant and headstrong mother.

1957 saw the release of *Sissi – Schicksalsjahre einer Kaiserin* (Fateful Years of an Empress). In it the Austrian empress enjoys travelling through

Hungary, where she eventually finds the politically priceless affection of the local Count Andrassy too intimate. This is only temporary relief from the frustrations of court life in Vienna, where dutiful Franz Josef remains chained to his desk, trying to run the empire single-handed. His chillingly strict mother continues to interfere, even in the upbringing of the daughter.

When Sissi was diagnosed with potentially fatal tuberculosis, Franz Josef had to allow Sophie to remove the daughter (also called Sophie, who died at the age of two – fact) on the doctor's recommendation. Sissi was in danger of losing the will to live while exiled to recovery-inducing climates in Madeira and Corfu. Desperately needed psychosomatic therapy appeared in the shape of her indestructibly positive mother Princess Ludovika of Bavaria, who lovingly nursed both Sissi's sickness and her taste for life on idyllic walks.

Comic relief is provided by Colonel Böckl, the clumsy bodyguard whose doting on the Empress borders on the improper. Each move that Sissi makes finds him struggling with the local language and falling in love with his private language teacher.

Finally she is well enough to rejoin her husband on an official visit to Venice, part of Austria's remaining possessions in northern Italy. Nationalists prepare for the Hapsburg sovereigns a hostile welcome, which may even develop into a violent uprising. However, the emotional Italians melt as they witness the ostentatiously loving reunion of mother and daughter on St Mark's Square and all ends happily. If only!

Schneider left behind the saccharine image of these early films and moved on to more serious roles and an international stage, only to appear again as Elisabeth of Austria in *Ludwig* (1972), Visconti's film about King Ludwig II of Bavaria (Elisabeth's cousin). *Ludwig* was a dark film, full of homoerotic undertones, and Schneider's Elisabeth was a much more complex, mature and even bitter character than the young Sissi. Reportedly, the only one of Schneider's roles she had displayed in her home was a portrait of her taken from the Visconti film.

'Sissi sticks to me just like oatmeal' Schneider once said, and one wonders whether her own private life was just disastrous, or whether it had been subtly moulded by the parts she had played so well, Her private life was turbulent in the extreme but nose-dived completely after her 14-year old son punctured his femoral artery attempting to climb the spiked railings at the home of his stepfather's parents. He got off the fence and into the house, only to die on the way to hospital. When Romy Schneider died she was declared to have died of cardiac arrest, although no postmortem was carried out. It was suggested that she committed suicide by taking a lethal cocktail of alcohol and sleeping pills.

Curiously enough, Romy Schneider's first film, at the age of sixteen, was *Mädchenjahre einer Königin* (*The Story of Vicky* – a biopic about the young Victoria – a part also played by some great British actresses from Anna Neagle to Judi Dench). Another part she played was Katia Dolgourika aka Catherine Yourievski, whom I have called 'the shadow Empress' and who comes in at a later stage in this book. She was also played by Danielle Darrieux, the great French film star. How complex!

The ultimate recognition of Schneider's celebrity came with the opening of the Berlin Madame Tussauds, where she is on view as the Empress Sissi, complete with the diamond starbursts in her hair. (PLATE 3B)

The birth of Crown Prince Rudolf in 1858 was a matter for great rejoicing. The Empire now had a clear line of succession and there was every sign that the young prince would grow up to be a charming and delightful young man. In fact, he grew up to be an unpleasant, spoiled brat, with a train of badly selected tutors, some merely incompetent, others nurturing his viciousness. It could not have helped that his early years coincided with the beginnings of the really serious wanderings of Sisi, disgusted by her husband's behaviour.

Superficially popular with the populace, Rudolf reacted against his conventional father, flirted with Liberal politicians and became an unofficial opposition leader – more to spite him than out of any real conviction. Writing in the *Neues Wiener Tagblatt* did not enhance relations with the Emperor.

His dynastic marriage to Stephanie of Belgium (niece of Carlota, whom we will meet later) was a disaster. (4) He got bored 'and turned to other women for diversion'. In contracting a 'serious illness' he was said to 'have fallen a victim to his own excesses' and his instability and capriciousness increased. One of these 'other women' was the young Maria Vetsera, who was understandably swept off her feet by her noble lover. Suicide was very much the fashion in late nineteenth century Vienna – the preferred method of dealing with potential scandal in the army was to leave the miscreant in a locked room with a loaded revolver and wait for the sound of the shot. Rudolf did not even have the courage to pull the trigger; after disposing of the unfortunate Maria he sat all night dithering, no doubt wondering whether he might still be able to live after disposing of his lover. (5)

The death of Rudolf drove Sisi deeper into an even greater depression than her infection with venereal disease. Then she had disappeared from the Viennese court for two years, spending several months in Madeira, where she was cured, cruising in the British royal yacht *Victoria and Albert* and discovering the Adriatic, where she fell in love with all things Greek. In Corfu she had a villa built – the Achilleon – complete with appropriate statuary and a temple dedicated to Heine, her favourite poet. But by the time it was complete, she had lost interest and moved on. Kaiser Wilhelm II later bought the Achilleon, cleared the place out and replaced Heine with a statue of Elisabeth. He joined in the archaeological digs on the island, with his own little spade – and his entourage had to follow suit and suffer the 6 to 8 hours of the working day.

In 1884 it was noticed that the Emperor had developed quite an interest in the theatre, and particularly a youngish actress, Katherina Schratt. Alexander III of Russia played Cupid by setting up a special performance at Kremsier, after which the relationship took off. (It lasted 44 years). Katherina was a good enough actress, pretty and possessed of all the ordinary virtues that Sisi lacked. Elisabeth did not react with hostility or hysteria to the affair. Instead she showed kindness and generosity towards the younger woman, who became recognised as 'the friend' rather than the mistress.

At Schönbrunn, the summer palace, Franz Josef would rise from his simple soldier's bed at four or five and work solidly till about nine, when he would toddle round to Madame Schratt's rather nice house in the grounds for breakfast, with the fine china and banal court tittle-tattle that drove Sisi off to solitude in the Vienna Woods. She continued to work in the theatre and was provided with a fine three-decker house in the Kärntnerstrasse hard by the Opera House. After Franz-Josef's death she 'got religion', living to 97 as a shining example to us all!

And so to the 1890s and Roquebrune/Cap Martin. By now Sisi was in her late fifties but still slim, lithe and attractive. True to her preference for the anonymity of grand hotels Sisi came to the *Grand Hôtel du Cap Martin*. Cap Martin was a high-class hunting ground until 1890 when it was bought and sub-divided for villas of the highest class. An English company - The Cap Martin Hôtel Ltd - bought 13 hectares and began the construction of a vast hotel of 250-300 rooms of the highest class, in 1890. An extra floor and two big wings were added later, first used by Sisi and Eugénie. One was called the Pavillon Sisi.

There is no sitting on the fence with Sisi. One either finds her a spoiled brat who took the benefits of being married to the Emperor without paying the price for it, or a lovable little girl who walked into a trap and punished herself for her social inadequacies for the rest of her life. For me, Sisi's sojourns at Roquebrune were totally admirable, the perfect model for any attractive woman approaching the age of sixty.

She was, of course, incognita, although how she thought her train of chamberlain, head groom, doctor, chaplain, secretary, treasurer, plus hairdressers, chambermaids, housekeepers and coachmen, backed up by the security presence of Superintendent Xavier Paoli and his police, to say nothing of the portable gymnasium, could slip in unnoticed is beyond belief.

Sisi's day began at five, when she dressed - always in black now - and went out to a favourite place to observe the dawn, returning about seven. (There was a similar sunset ritual, round the other side of the Cap).

The morning might be taken up with exercise in the gymnasium, followed by a bath in tepid distilled water. Then came an electric massage. Her hair, which was never cut, could take up two hours. Or she might slip out, avoiding her security men, and go for long walks along the coast or over the mountain paths to the hill villages. On one of these walks she decided that the people of Borrigo needed a bridge over their occasionally violent stream. So she paid for a bridge to be built – which she did not live to see completed. On a wet morning she would explore the empty streets in nearby Menton. Often she would walk by the Mediterranean accompanied by her Greek secretary Christomanos, reading Homer aloud to her as she stormed along. On a hot day she would disappear behind a bush and strip off surplus garments which were thrown over the bush for poor Christomanos to carry back to the hotel, under the discreet surveillance of Paoli's men.

Her diet was radically different from that of the other hotel guests. Breakfast was a cup of tea and a biscuit. At eleven she might have a cup of soup and an egg. One or two glasses of blood might be taken. The Masai killed their animals for their blood but Sisi searched out two of the best local cattle which were bled on alternate days and were returned to her special herd in Vienna after the season.

Socially she paid duty visits to Victoria in Nice. In 1895 and 1896 she was joined by her sister Trani, five years her junior. They looked and dressed the same and caused confusion to the locals. Trani was a good walker, but could not keep up with Sisi for six or seven hours. She hated the sea while Sisi revelled in its wildness.

Eugénie lived in the Grand Hotel while her Villa Cyrnos was being built. (PLATE 3C) The two Empresses got on well and Sisi was consulted about matters of design. They often walked together (Eugénie at seventy was still said 'to have the legs of a young girl'). It must have been hilarious watching these two great ladies in black. Eugénie discoursed on Europe, the Spanish-American war, the anarchists and their assassination attempts, the troubles of Alsace-Lorraine under German rule, her schemes for restoring the monarchy in France and, of course, the death of her beloved son. Sisi rambled on about Hungary (whose language she had learnt), Heine, her favourite poet, the sky, the birds and the wonders of Nature, trouble in the Balkans and the end of her son Rudolph. Neither listened to the other!

Sisi took great pleasure in wandering about and making casual acquaintances, or sitting at the back of a café people-watching. She would chat with the girl on the cash desk at Rumpelmayers. She took great pleasure in not being recognised – although we cannot believe that the locals were unaware of the identity of the beautiful stranger in black.

She had one delightful adventure. She took the train to Monaco with her lady of courtesy Countess Sztaray and Superintendent Paoli. In the first-class compartment were two English ladies who amused Sisi by looking down their noses at the intruders. The little party went straight to the casino, to the roulette room, where Sisi observed what was going on, took 5 francs out of her little purse and put it on number 33. 'Let's see if I have any luck on 33', she said. At the third attempt, 33 came up, the croupier pushed 175 francs towards the Empress. She picked up the tokens in her two hands, turned to her companions and said: 'Let's go quickly, I have never acquired so much money'. And off they went. Such self-discipline!

In the 1894 season Sisi was joined for two weeks by her husband. – 'incognito', which meant that, for once in his life uniform was discarded in favour of a suit and a *melon* (bowler hat). Incognito the imperial couple may have been, but only a fool could have missed the extra telegraph lines being put into the hotel and the two suites of courtiers taking residence in the two pavilions of the Grand Hotel – his and hers!

As usual, Franz-Josef rose at five to deal with the affairs of the state, sending off eighty telegrams before ten. But mid-morning he and Sisi - like any other long-married couple - would amble along the *Promenade du Soleil* to Rumpelmayers for coffee and a *Viennoiserie*, 'Count Hohenembs' doffing his hat to all the ladies and exchanging a few gracious words with the gentlemen. Visits were paid to Albert I of Monaco and Victoria in

Nice. Franz-Josef and Sisi took the train to Nice, strolled along to the Nice Rumpelmayers in the Boulevard Victor-Hugo. Having consumed the choux pastry of *le roi des pâtissiers*, the imperial couple took a cab up to Cimiez - just like any other visitors. Franz-Josef was very impressed by Eugénie's garden at the Villa Cyrnos and noted the gardener's name. But after two weeks it was back to Vienna, with Sisi seeing him on to his special train at Menton station. A special train, but not an armoured train, as was thought necessary for the Tsarina in 1879. The emperor embraced Sisi twice and pleaded with her not to live off oranges and vanilla ice cream. Sisi returned to her more vigorous lifestyle for another month before following her husband back to Vienna.

For whatever reason, Sisi did not return to Roquebrune in 1898, preferring instead to winter in San Remo on the Italian Riviera. And so to Geneva and to 10 September 1898. Sisi was staying at the *Hôtel Beau-Rivage* when it was decided, in the afternoon, to go to Prezny a couple of miles along the lakeside. It would have been in character for her to have walked there, trailing her lady of courtesy, Countess Irma Sztaray, behind her, yet on this occasion Elisabeth decided to take the steamer which left at 1335. On the promenade she encountered young Luigi Lucheni, who stabbed her in the heart with a sharpened file. As she was helped back on her feet after having been stabbed, she said 'It is nothing. Come, we must hurry to catch the boat'.

She boarded the ship, but as it set off she felt unwell. Her corset had kept back the flow of blood but its removal revealed the serious nature of the wound. The *Genève* put back to the shore, the ailing Empress was carried back to the *Hôtel Beau-Rivage,* where she died, her last words being: 'What happened to me?'

There is a savage irony in the fact that Sisi, who had said 'But who would want to hurt me?' should die in Geneva, the cradle of the Reformation, in a country that had been committed to perpetual neutrality since the end of the Thirty Years War in 1648; the city which was home to the Red Cross, founded by Henri Dunant after the horror of Solferino, where the incompetence of the Emperor Napoleon had been more than outmatched by the stupidity of Franz Josef. And at the hands of Lucheni, who had come to Geneva to assassinate a French royal and, frustrated at finding him gone, had decided that any aristocrat would do, even an empress in thinly-disguised incognito.

Lucheni did not attempt to flee the scene of his crime. There is a photograph of him being escorted to his trial by two gendarmes. He has a mocking smile and wears his hat at a dashing angle. There being no capital punishment in Geneva he was sentenced to life imprisonment. Ten years later he hanged himself in his cell.

Sisi's life was full of secrets and Jacques Foëx, in a centenary essay called *L'épaule de Sisi* (Sisi's shoulder), came up with an intriguing assertion, that Sisi had, on one of her beautiful shoulders, the tattoo of a ship's anchor. If this is true it is quite startling. Even the shy and reclusive Sisi must have attended great occasions *décolleté*, with her 'Imperial shoulders which forced the admiration and jealousy of the court' in full view. Where did she acquire the tattoo? In Madeira or Corfu, 'where she went secretly into the port to have her flesh marked?' Or perhaps in 'one of her escapades in Algiers, or Cairo, or in the sleazy quarters of Paris?'

And what did the anchor mean for her? The low life of the sailors' dockside dens? Or the loneliness and ceaseless movement of the sea, the seaspray and the cry of the gulls? After all she did write:

> I am like a bird of the tempest...
> And every time a wave breaks on the bridge,
> I want to break into cries of jubilation.

Whatever its provenance, it is clear that Sisi's tattoo was an expression of defiance.

To Countess Irma Szataray, her *dame de compagnie*, she made a statement of faith:

> I believe in God, but not as much as you do. I may become religious again one day. I often yearn for death. I know you do not fear it, but I tremble at the idea. What frightens me really is the step between life and death.

That step was taken for her sooner than she had supposed.

Given their troubled marriage it may seem difficult to reconcile some statements by the Imperial couple. Thus Sisi said: *'Ich hab' den Kaiser so lieb! Wenn er nur kein Kaiser wär.'* (The Emperor is so dear to me. If only he weren't the Emperor!) After her death Franz Josef said: *'Sie wissen nicht wie Ich diese Frau geliebt habe'.* (You have no idea how much I loved this woman). His letters to her were signed *'Dein armer Kleiner'*, sometimes translated as 'In humble love'. I would prefer the less formal and more familiar 'Thy poor little thing'.

The Gypsy Empresses

Much talk of *Liebe*, of Love; but what is this thing called Love? Both German and English are lacking in subtlety. If we look at the New Testament the word 'love' is scattered about freely and seems to mean different things in different contexts. In the original Greek *eros* is hot, sweaty, and passionate, while *agapé* is brotherly love, the love of the Last Supper, of:

> greater love hath no man than this, that he shall lay down his life for another.

Franz Josef was a simple man of his time, accepting and enjoying the double standard. Elisabeth was more naïve, expecting a marriage which was scarcely possible in her time and situation. She had been through four pregnancies in a diseased marriage and was, quite simply, disgusted by the dirty ways of men, taking refuge in the comparative simplicity of an active life in the open air and an idealised view of the past.

A good fiction writer can often catch the spirit of the times better than the more pedestrian historian. George MacDonnell Fraser has Flashman say in *Flashman and the Tiger*:

> What could it matter what the Emperor and Empress of Austria thought of a mere British soldier? She had an eye for men, and it was common talk that Franz-Josef had warned her off various gallants with whom her relations had probably been innocent enough, but I hadn't been among 'em. I dare say I could have added her scalp to my belt, but I'd never tried, for good reason: everyone knew that Franz-Josef, whose ambition seemed to be to bag every chamois and woman in Austria, had given her cupid's measles, and while the poultice-wallopers had doubtless put her in order again, you can't be too careful. And while she looked like Pallas Athene, I suspected she was half-cracked – flung herself about in gymnasiums and went on starvation diets and wrote poetry and asked for a lunatic asylum as a birthday present, so I'd been told. She and Franz-Josef hadn't dealt too well since he'd poxed her, and she'd taken to wandering Europe while he pleaded with her to forgive and forget. Royal marriages are the very devil.

End Notes

1 Winterhalter specialised in the crowned heads of Europe.

The Gypsy Empresses are prominent in our Royal Collection: Victoria (several times), Eugénie (twice), Carlota, the Empresses of Germany - Vicky (several times) and Augusta, Wilhelm I's spouse, 'a superior being'. He also painted Alexandra, Edward VII's spouse, who was a later Empress of India but is a marginal figure in this book.

2 It always seems strange that such a macho lot as Spanish manhood should speak with a lisp. It was not always so, but the Emperor Charles V's jaw was so deformed that he could not speak properly and the court - in order not to show him up - had to mirror his speech, which became politically correct.

3 'Gabrielle' was only one of the pseudonyms adopted by Sisi, who loved secrecy and deception. 'Countess of Hohenembs' was a favourite role. In 1890, distraught after the death of Andrassy and her daughter's wedding, she embarked on a long sea voyage in a chartered English cutter, the *Angelie,* in the guise of 'Mrs Nicholson'.

4 Princess Stephanie of Belgium exhausted her supply of good fortune at the age of six, when she contracted typhus, received extreme unction – yet survived. At seventeen she was bullied into marriage with Rudolph in a wedding so magnificent that the printed list of wedding presents ran to 79 printed pages. She and her sister Louise, also unhappily married, were referred to as 'the two Belgian peasants' by the sophisticated court in Vienna. After Rudolph's death it was proposed that she marry his cousin, Franz Ferdinand, who was to die a violent death at Sarajevo in 1914.
   When she did remarry, it was for love, in 1900, to her father's chamberlain, Count Elemer Lonyay de Nagy-Longya. The happy couple visited Menton in 1900 and 1902 and in 1903, as countess, she was made an honorary member of the *Menton-Lawn-Tennis et Croquet Club de Menton.*

5 Mayerling has spawned a large crop of interpretations. One of the strangest is Dr Enrique Lardé's *The Crown Prince Rudolf: His Mysterious Life after Mayerling;* so outrageous that one almost expects Flashman to come bounding off the next page. We are now inured to revisionist history, but Lardé out-revises all. Let me use his own words:

I will therefore discuss:
   1. What really happened at Mayerling.
   2. The simulated burials of Baroness Maria Vetsera and the Archduke.
   3. The slanders directed against the Crown Prince.
   4. Why the Archduke ended up in El Salvador.

5. Why he adopted the pseudonym 'Justo Armas'.
6. How the Archduke was shipwrecked in the Straits of Magellan.
7. Why Empress Elizabeth, his mother, was assassinated.
8. The social environment found by the Archduke in El Salvador.

When we add in the Archduke's hiding in Europe for a year while his cousin, Archduke Johann Salvator of Tuscany trained to become a ship's captain and bought a ship which he then sailed to South America where the ship was wrecked and he was drowned. And why Justo Armas spent the rest of his life walking barefoot and 'with his heels totally raised'. And why the Austrian secret police should have been active in two continents. To say nothing of the Jesuits.

CHAPTER 5

Eugénie, Empress of France (1826-1920) The Survivor

ALTHOUGH EUGENIE WAS a woman in her own right with a long. interesting and complex life I feel it best to set the stage for her with a brief and simple - if that is possible - description of her husband Charles Louis Napoleon Bonaparte, later known as Louis Napoleon, later still as Napoleon III, Emperor of the French, born in Paris on 20 April 1808, died in exile at Chislehurst in Kent on 9 January 1873.

French historians make no pretence of objectivity and there are many pejorative assessments of Napoleon III, such as: 'the Bourgeois Emperor', 'a sphinx without a secret', 'a great unfathomed incapacity', 'a melancholy parrot', 'a hat without a man'. The historians tend to project on to him all the weaknesses of French society of the time that he was responding to. For me, Napoleon never seemed to take himself completely seriously and had a soft streak unlike our usual perception of an elected dictator. For example, he was execrated because he did not screw out of the Austrians all that he might have after the victory of Solferino – but his critics had not been there and had not seen the fearful sufferings resulting from the stand-to between Napoleon and Franz-Josef.

The difficulties begin with his birth. Josephine de Beauharnais, a widow with two daughters, was the first wife of the great Napoleon. The Empress Josephine was beautiful and charming but spendthrift and of shaky morals. Her daughter Hortense clearly inherited similar qualities and married Louis Bonaparte, her stepfather's brother, puppet King of Holland till he abdicated in 1810 and fled to Bohemia. It was not a happy marriage and 'doubts have lingered regarding Louis's paternity'. Hortense was bright and extrovert, her husband 'morose and neurotic, possibly a repressed homosexual'.

There were two children, confusingly called Napoleon-Charles and Napoleon-Louis. The consensus admits that 'Hortense certainly had lovers and in 1811 was to give birth to an illegitimate son', but concludes:

Nevertheless, even if accusations that Louis Napoleon was not really a Bonaparte cannot be refuted definitively, most biographers are agreed that he was in all probability the son of Louis, conceived during a brief reconciliation with Hortense, following the sudden death of their first-born child in May 1807.

So far, so good. Now let us take a stroll around one of the great cemeteries of Paris. Pere Lachaise is famous as the last resting place of the great and the good of France – and Oscar Wilde. On the Left Bank the Montparnasse Cemetery is less formidable, more attractive and the last home of a slightly lower stratum of greatness and goodness, such as Alekhine, the great Russian chess master, and Serge Gainsbourg, *'chanteur-compositeur'*, best known for his wife, Jane Birkin's, singing of *'Je t'aime'*. In the *Avenue Transversale*, near Samuel Beckett, is a fairly modest column, topped by a moustached bust. The inscription reads:

J Ottavi, Orator
Parent de Napoleon
born at Ajaccio 24/7/1809
died at Paris 9/12/1841
En descendant de la tribune
Erected by his friends and admirers.

This is all very odd. Poor Ottavi, cut off in his prime as he stepped down from his public platform in 1841. But important enough to have an expensive memorial in an expensive cemetery and not be bundled away in some obscure plot. Who was born at Ajaccio, home-town of the Bonapartes and birthplace of the great Napoleon? Ottavi? Or *Napoleon*? It looks as though Ottavi was a fellow-Corsican who became entangled with Hortense, the result being the future Emperor Napoleon III. No other person could have been the 'Napoleon' referred to as having been born in 1809. Napoleon III's official birthday is always given as 20 April 1808 but he was not baptised until 1810 - at Fontainebleau. The godparents were the Emperor Napoleon and his new Empress, Marie-Louise of Austria.

Whatever the circumstances of his conception and birth, the young Louis Napoleon was definitely Hortense's son and, as such, fitted into the highest levels of society. He had a special place in Napoleon's affections and was spoiled by Josephine, pensioned off as 'Dowager Empress'. With the collapse of the Empire, Hortense and her son went into exile, shuttling between Bavaria and Switzerland. In 1830 Louis Napoleon enrolled in the Swiss army as a volunteer and in 1831 he and his brother joined in with Italian revolutionaries. Napoleon Charles died and Louis Napoleon was sentenced to death by the Austrians. He was romantically rescued by Hortense, taken to Paris. Exiled again, they became celebrities for three months in London before returning to Switzerland.

From 1832 Louis Napoleon saw himself as the heir to Napoleon and a potential Emperor of the French. His older brothers were dead, as was the Duke of Reichstadt ('Napoleon II'), Napoleon's legitimate son by Marie-Louise of Austria. In 1836, as a captain in the Berne militia he published a *Manuel d'Artillerie*. An attempted *coup d'état* in Strasbourg lasted three hours before he was off on his travels again, expelled to the United States, then London and Switzerland. From London was launched his second *putsch* – another semi-comic fiasco. A landing at Boulogne was briskly dismissed. The Prince, as he now was, was wounded and had to be rescued from the waves. He was taken to Paris, tried, found guilty and sentenced to 'imprisonment in perpetuity'.

Perpetuity lasted six years, during which he busied himself with literary production (*The Extinction of Poverty*, 1844), study and regular sex. In 1846 he escaped from prison, coolly walking out in the guise of a workman, carrying a plank, and reaching London in twelve hours via Belgium. In 1848, 'the year of revolutions', while in Vienna Prince Windischgrätz drowned an insurrection in blood and Franz Josef agreed to shoulder the imperial burden of his incompetent father, Louis Napoleon enlisted as a special constable at Marlborough Street police station in anticipation of unrest in the streets. By September the time was ripe for a return to France – he was elected to the Constituent Assembly to represent the department of Yonne. On 20 December 1848, at the age of forty, Louis Napoleon was formally invested as the President of the Second French Republic. In 1851 he had himself made President for a further ten years. In November 1852 a plebiscite seeking approval for a change of regime was held, which he won by 8 million votes to 0.25 million. On 2 December 1852 Louis Napoleon Bonaparte was proclaimed Emperor Napoleon III and installed at the Tuileries.

> It is a truth universally acknowledged, that a single man in possession of a good fortune, must be in want of a wife,

said Miss Austen. Even truer for an emerging emperor. Who would be attracted to this bizarre adventurer with the squeaky voice and the heavy Swiss-German accent? He was small, had short legs and only looked good when on horseback. Ugly, his long nose, moustaches and beard were a gift to cartoonists. Bored by the petty nobodies around him he seemed half-asleep – an appearance explained by his devotion to the pleasures of the flesh. His contemporaries and most historians found him easy to underestimate, starting with his collapse and the collapse of France in 1870 and working back from there. Anyone with an open mind will recognise that this reputation for incapacity was ill-founded.

From fashionable society and the *demi-monde* there were plenty of candidates to choose from. A succession of mistresses included the French actress Rachel and the English courtesan Miss Howard, who followed him to France and helped to fund his ambitious activities. She was, however, deemed an unsuitable consort for an emperor and was pensioned off with a title and a generous allowance. His cousin, Princesse Mathilde Bonaparte had been engaged to him in 1836 but, despite an unhappy marriage, was disinclined to give him a second chance. A judicious alliance with one of Europe's ruling houses would have pleased his advisors but a number of foreign princesses also turned him down.

Finally, the choice was Maria Eugenia Ignacia Augustina de Guzman y Palafox y Portocarrero. Born in Granada on 5 May 1826, Eugénie, as she became known, first met her future husband in 1849. Cleverly she avoided many attempts to seduce her, until it became clear that only through marriage would Napoleon gain the desired end. They were married early in 1853, the civil ceremony being performed in the Tuileries on 29 January. The service in Notre Dame was either the next day or on 6 February – accounts differ on this, as on so much around this imperial couple. It was a quiet service, not in the sense of being hole-and-corner, but noted for the cool reaction of all present and of the crowds in the streets, doubtful of 'the Emperor's foolish marriage'.

Unusually for the period, the union produced only one child. In 1856, after at least one miscarriage and a difficult labour of 22 hours Eugénie brought forth a boy-child. Christened Napoleon Eugene Louis Jean Joseph, he is usually referred to as the Prince Imperial. As the heir to the Napoleonic Empire he was to be the focus of the hopes and fears of Napoleon and Eugénie.

The *Revue du Souvenir Napoléonien* is a periodical devoted to the two Emperors, Bonaparte and Napoleon III. In three book reviews of 1998 it examined the pedigrees of Josephine, Napoleon III and Charles X, King of France, deposed in 1830. In 'the good old days' the qualification to be of a good family was to have 64 quarterings on one's coat-of-arms, which meant four generations without a commoner in one's family. Napoleon's impeccable credentials were 'proved' by his having 1024 quarterings, from the XVIth century to his birth. So much for poor Mr Ottavi! The Empress Eugénie, however, had only 16 quarterings – as well as being Spanish.

Prosper Mérimée, better known as the author of *Carmen*, on which Bizet's opera was based, obtained from the Spanish heralds a certificate proving her father's impeccably noble birth. He was:

> Don Cipriano Guzmán y Palafox Fernandez de Cordoba, Layos y la Cerda, Viscount of La Calzada,, of Palencia de la Valduerna, Count of Teba, of Banos, of Mora, of Santa Cruz de la Sierra, of Fuenteduena, of Ablitas, of San Esteban de Gormas and of Casarubios del Monte, Marquis of Moya, of Ardales, of Osera, of Barcarotta, of La Algaba, of La Baneza, of Villanuevo del Fresno, of Valdunquillo, of Mirallo and of Valderrabano and Duke of Penaranda.

He was three times a Grandee of Spain of the First Class and the hereditary Grand Marshal of Castile.

The problem was the mother, of whose private life there were lurid rumours and for whom there was not even the excuse of noble birth, her father having been William Kirkpatrick, a bankrupt fruit and wine merchant in Malaga. Although it might be said that a bankrupt Scot was as good as a Spanish grandee any day, a family tree was cooked up ('Maria Manuela Kirkpatrick de Closeburn') so that she could marry a Spanish grandee. Her strengths were in her personal qualities – as well as being a tall, black-eyed, black-haired beauty whom most took to at first sight, she was strong and practical, intelligent and amusing, and of limitless ambition.

Eugénie was a good choice to be an emperor's mate. Winterhalter's glamour portrait could be a photograph taken with a soft-focus lens. Like her mother she was: 'a tall, black-eyed, black-haired beauty' (but who roused fierce jealousy in other women). Like her: 'She was strong and practical, intelligent and amusing, and of limitless ambition'. Unlike most of the other empresses we look at, she took an interest in politics and government and influenced her husband – not always wisely. As when, in 1867, Napoleon began half-hearted attempts at liberalisation of the regime, only to be hampered and deflected by Eugénie.

The Gypsy Empresses

La Ménagerie Impériale was a vicious attack on the Imperial couple. (Ménagerie was a nice pun. It could mean menagery, as in English, but also household). No.1 was a caricature of Napoleon as a tired, shabby vulture sitting on a branch, looking round furtively as he held a naked maiden (labelled 'France') in his talons dripping with blood – an allusion to the thousands punished, deported or exiled for political crimes. No.2 was Eugénie, unflatteringly portrayed as *La Grue* (the crane). She stands on one leg, holding a tambourine in the claws of the other - a reference to her hated Spanish origins. Her hair is tangled and ringletted like a gypsy's. Her heavy earrings emphasise her extravagance and the Egyptian background reminds us of the corruption associated with de Lesseps and the construction of the Suez Canal. Her face is long and pouched, the nose irregular and the eyes heavily lidded.

Napoleon was a moderniser and under his extreme authoritarianism France acquired an overseas empire through a series of colonial conquests which, alas, provided inadequate training for the major conflict to come. In Paris, 20.000 had died of cholera in 1832. A new water supply was engineered. Under Baron Haussmann the quaint medieval slums were cleared away and the network of *Grands Boulevards* created.

> Lined with marvellous mansions, they were laid out to link grand public structures, such as the Opera with the Palais Royal, and they also led to a circle of railway stations that would, in essence, replace the medieval gates to the modern city and that would connect Paris with the rest of France and Europe.

Napoleon was never at ease in Paris and as he went around his country, easing his troubled kidneys at spas and watering places, he was able to supervise a frenzy of commercial and industrial activity, exploitative and corrupt. Trouville, on the English Channel coast, was a favourite summer resort and Boudin (PLATE 4A) captures the atmosphere and spirit of the time to perfection.

The sky is vast, its blue enlivened by fleecy clouds driven along by the stiff breeze which braces the Empress, her ladies and their dogs as they promenade by the sea in their enormous crinolines. (Eugénie did not invent the crinoline, but she gave it respectability and popularised it). We might imagine, looking at this lively scene, that all is for the best in the best of all possible worlds.

In 1870 the bubble burst. Bismarck cleverly manipulated a growing tension between France and Prussia and on 15 July France declared war on Prussia. 'Å Berlin, å Berlin' the Paris crowds were shouting as they escorted their red-pantalooned *poilus* to the Gare de l'Est. Yet only six weeks later the Emperor, Napoleon by name but no Napoleon on the battlefield, found the grey-clad, hymn-singing Prussians surrounding him at Sedan and had to surrender. Ever since, Napoleon has been execrated by all for his ineptitude and for his cowardice in not fighting the situation out to the death. 'No surrender!' is a splendid warcry. It may be, however, that Napoleon showed a degree of compassion higher than mere self-interest. In a letter to Eugénie, after going over his suffering and remorse in leading his army:

> ...to a catastrophe, and that is complete. I would rather have died than have witnessed such a disastrous capitulation, and yet, things being as they are, it was the only way of avoiding the slaughter of 60,000 men...

There may well have been 60,000 Frenchmen who thought, in retrospect, that he had done the right thing for them!

The Prince Imperial, at 9 months old, had been commissioned into the First Regiment of Grenadiers of the Guard. Having received a military training, when Napoleon went off to war, his son went with him. Eugénie insisted that her husband should confine himself to leading his armies in the field while she led a Council of Regency back in Paris.

The war proceeded at a speed which totally discomfited Napoleon and his generals. In brief, on:

4 August, MacMahon's army was crushed at Wissembourg, in Alsace,

6 August, and again at Froeschwiller and Reichshofen Also, on:

6 August, Bazaine was beaten at Forbach. On:

9 August, Strasbourg came under siege. On:

14 August, at Borny, Bazaine was beaten again, and on:

16 August, at Rezonville, and on:

18 August, at St-Privat. On:

19 August, Bazaine allowed himself to be bottled up in Metz and on:

31 August, MacMahon, with a new army, was bottled up in Sedan. On:

1 September, Napoleon and his army surrendered. At the news, on:

3 September, Eugénie was advised to flee the country, while on:

4 September, the Third Republic was proclaimed in the Hôtel de Ville, Paris. Meanwhile, on:

20 September, Paris was encircled and the siege began.

28 September saw the capitulation of Strasbourg, and on 27 October, Bazaine surrendered Metz.

18 January, 1871, Wilhelm I, King of Prussia, was proclaimed Emperor of Germany in the Galerie des Glaces, Versailles, and there took place on: 1 March, 1871, the German march in triumph down the Champs-Elysées.

Eugénie's role over this period was not passive. As Regent she strove hard to hold the administration of the country together from Paris, while harassing Napoleon, MacMahon and Bazaine with advice, some of it sound. With her husband's surrender on 2 September the rage of the Parisian citizenry against their rulers became ferocious. Next day the Prefect of Police warned Eugénie not to remain at the Tuileries in case the mob harmed her and forced her to abdicate.

She agreed to leave the country. There ensued a rather pathetic departure and flight as her fair weather friends melted away. One friend was sent to transfer money to England in Eugénie's name. She and a lady-in-waiting, dressed in concealing clothes and with one satchel of clothes, left the Louvre by a back door. The Austrian ambassador called a cab for them and left them to their own devices. At one Imperialist's house their knocking was ignored. They walked through angry crowds – unrecognised – to another 'friend's' house – with the same result. They sat on the pavement in despair until Eugénie remembered her American dentist, Dr Evans, and summoned another cab.

The women spent the night in Dr Evans' house while he and the Prefect of Police arranged the imperial getaway. Forged passports represented Eugénie as an English invalid, with Evans as her brother, a friend of Evans as her physician and Madame Lebreton, the lady-in-waiting, as her nurse. In Evans' carriage, then a cab, then the train they travelled to Deauville where, at midnight, they went aboard *Gazelle*, the private yacht of Sir John Burgoyne, an English friend of Napoleon, and sailed off to sanctuary in England.

After Sedan, Napoleon and several of his marshals were imprisoned in comfort in Germany, then exiled to Britain. The little imperial family were re-united at Camden Place at Chislehurst in Kent. Eugénie immediately began trying to influence the peace talks which began late in 1870. Already very ill, Naoleon died in 1873. The Prince Imperial escaped from the shambles at Sedan. Many of the French saw him as the new Emperor-in-exile and a coup d'état was planned for the spring of 1873.

Of the other main players in the French debacle Marshal MacMahon bounced back. When the Paris Commune was suppressed in May 1871, it was MacMahon who led the Versailles troops. The French army spent eight days massacring those who had defended the city through the siege. Workers and civilians were shot on sight. Tens of thousands of Communards and workers were summarily executed (as many as 30,000); 38,000 others imprisoned and 7,000 were forcibly deported. MacMahon was Chief of State from 1873 to 1875, when he became the first President of the Republic, from 1875 to 1879.

Bazaine had come up from the ranks to become the Commander-in-Chief of the French Expeditionary force which backed up Maximilian's Mexican adventure. Ordered back to France he showed great lassitude at Metz before giving up the town and with it 173,000 soldiers, 60 generals, 58 regimental colours, 1,570 guns and 260,000 rifles.

He was a popular scapegoat. Sentence of death was passed on him by a military court, then commuted to twenty years imprisonment. In Mexico he had acquired a second wife 38 years his junior and with her energetic assistance he escaped from his island fortress in the Mediterranean to end his days as a poor exile in Spain.

The Prince Imperial was bitter and frustrated as he awaited a call to return to lead his country - which never came. As an outlet for his energies he trained at the Royal Military Academy at Woolwich, passing out in 1875, although, as a foreign prince, he could never hold a commission in the British army.

In South Africa, a British force under Lord Chelmsford had just suffered one of the greatest military defeats of the century at the hands of the Zulus at Isandlwana. Reinforcements were sent out to finish off the war. With them went the Prince Imperial, the handling of whom was another headache for poor Lord Chelmsford, desperately trying to reverse our fortunes on the Veld. The Prince Imperial's position was ambiguous, and he was not popular with the British - officers and men. His end reflected that situation. He was determined in lead a patrol to scout out the enemy. The patrol had to be commanded by a junior lieutenant, but he was in an impossible situation, being overawed by the young aristocrat. Instead of finding the Zulus, the Zulus found them. They were ambushed. The Prince, two troopers and the Zulu scout were speared to death, while the lieutenant and the remaining four men of Bettington's Horse brought the appalling news back to headquarters.

Back in Britain, everyone - from Victoria down - was appalled at this diplomatic disaster, that the son of an ally should have been allowed to wander about and be killed by a marauding group of half-naked savages.

Eugénie was devastated. All her hopes and fears were focussed on the young prince. Now everything had been snatched from her. Until 1875 she had been extravagant but not frivolous. Now she became even more serious, immersed in the memories of her son and husband, growing in piety and continuing her political intrigues.

In 1881 she moved to Farnborough Hill where Berkshire, Hampshire and Surrey meet. Daniel Defoe, in the seventeenth century, described this area.

> Here is a vast tract of land, some of it within seventeen or eighteen miles of the capital city; which is not only poor, but even quite sterile, given up to barrenness, horrid and frightful to look on, not only good for little, but good for nothing; much of it is a sandy desert, and one may frequently be put in mind here of Arabia Deserta, where the winds raise the sands, so as to overwhelm whole caravans of travellers, cattle and people together; for in passing this heath in a windy day, I was so far in danger of smothering with the clouds of sand, which were raised by the storm, that I could neither keep it out of my mouth, nose or eyes: and when the wind was over, the sand appeared spread over the adjacent fields of the forest some miles distant, so that it ruins the very soil. This sand indeed is checked by the heath, or heather, which grows in it, and which is the common product of barren land, even in the very Highlands of Scotland; but the ground is otherwise so poor and barren, that the product of it feeds no creatures, but some very small sheep, who feed chiefly on the said heather, and but very few of these, nor are there any villages, worth mentioning, and but few houses or people for many miles far and wide; this desert lies extended so much, that some say, there is not less than a hundred thousand acres of this barren land that lies all together, reaching out every way in the three counties of Surrey, Hampshire and Berkshire.

So near to London and crossed by the Portsmouth road, the commons and heathland of the Tertiary Bagshot Sands were the favoured haunts of highwaymen in the eighteenth century. The army first arrived in Aldershot in 1854, where it acquired 8000 acres of heathland at £12 per acre. Not merely barracks and parade grounds, but rifle and field firing ranges and other 'danger areas' clutter the modern map. Pubs, brothels and the rat-pit behind an Aldershot hotel absorbed the leisure energies of the other ranks but the area was attractive for officers, serving and retired, to live in.

The Survivor

Land was cheap for building, there was space for riding and golf became a popular sport and social focus.

Anyone who, like the writer, trailed a pike over the Bagshot Sands for two years in the 1950's, will recognise such names as Aldershot, Farnborough, Sandhurst, Camberley, Bisley, Pirbright, Deepcut and Bracknell - all symptomatic of the effectiveness of the armed services, particularly the Army, in occupying territory.

A network of railway lines opened up the area to the civilian population and made it easy to live here yet commute to Waterloo for central London and the City. The infertility of the land was no drawback as it meant that housing plots were cheap, drainage was good and big low-maintenance gardens could be developed almost from scratch using the acid-tolerant plants like conifers, azaleas and rhododendrons.

Eugenie bought over the small manor house of 23 rooms in Farnborough in 1881. There she added another wing of 18 rooms as a memorial to her loved ones and to display her vast collection of memorabilia. She built St Michael's Abbey as a memorial church. The remains of Napoleon and the Prince Imperial were brought there, and she herself was to be buried in the crypt when she died in 1920. Farnborough was the base for the last forty years of her life, her piety increasing in proportion to her years.

The most important reason for choosing Farnborough was its proximity to Windsor, only ten miles away. Queen Victoria and Eugénie exchanged friendly visits and went for companionable drives when they would share their thoughts on widowhood and the vagaries of fortune.

Although Eugénie no longer had a personal interest in the restoration of hereditary monarchy to France she continued to dabble in politics from her ivory tower in Hampshire. Curiously, after the Second Empire collapsed following its defeat in the Franco-Prussian War the royalists became a majority in the National Assembly. First the Comte de Chambord, then Philippe d'Orléans, Comte de Paris had high hopes that the monarchy would be restored till, in May 1886 the French Republic expelled the princes of the former ruling dynasties (except for Princess Mathilde Bonaparte, Napoleon's fiancée of 50 years previously). Strangely, the government must have thought that Eugénie wasn't so bad after all, as their attitude to her returning to France and owning property there eased.

In 1889 Charles White bought Cap Martin and began to sell it off in building plots. At the same time Eugénie began to frequent the Grand Hotel of Cap Martin, at the same time as Sisi., and decided she had to have a villa there - the first big villa on the Cap. Eugénie's niece, born Laetitia Bonaparte and widow of the Duke d'Aosta in Italy, acquired for her aunt a plot of 17,000 square metres. Georges Tersling, the Danish architect responsible for the Grand Hotel, was commissioned to build 'my big green tortoise'. It was to be called the Villa Cyrnos, Cyrnos being Greek for Corsica, in allusion to her late husband's shady past.

Tersling was clearly not a beginner in his profession - he was responsible for at least another 25 villas on the Côte - but this did not prevent Eugénie and Sisi spending many happy hours together deciding how the vision should be brought into being. On the front, in Roman numerals, is the date - 1892 - when construction commenced. In 1895 the work was still not complete, so Eugénie moved into the semi-finished house in order to speed up the workers.

The reason why Cap Martin was undeveloped was that it was an arid, rocky wasteland with pines blasted into weird shapes by the wind and with cliffs all round. Other than for hunting it had no commercial value. Eugénie's head gardener, Jean Pizzi, had a mammoth task in creating an exotic garden from a rocky wilderness. Thirty gardeners laboured for two years blasting rock and building up terraces flat enough and with enough depth of soil for building and planting. Twelve tall palms of different species were brought over the border from Bordighera, each being dragged on a *chariot* - the French use this word today to mean a supermarket trolley – pulled by eighteen horses. They formed a grove called The Oasis. Despite the efforts of her gardeners, Eugénie claimed to love the palms and aloes of which her gardeners were so proud less than the plants that flowered freely in terrain they had chosen themselves.

FIG 6 *Weather vane in the garden of Villa Cyrnos*

Inside, the atmosphere of the house was one of 'a worldliness, smiling and almost young'. There were grand portraits of Josephine and the Prince Imperial and a charming statuette of Sisi, slim and fine, with the heavy crown of her long hair. Eugénie's social life - described by Jean Cocteau as 'the court of Cyrnos' - started with the Emperor and Empress of Austria and Victoria, Empress of India and worked its way down through half of the Kings and Queens of Europe to princes and princesses, Grand Dukes and Duchesses, and even a banker's widow. Government ministers were grateful for her hospitality and interest in affairs. The crowds were so great that Tersling had to build another villa (the Villa Téba, named after her father) to accommodate the stream of guests.

Informally, there were her walks and 'dialogues' with Sisi, at least for a time. She would walk round to see her 'neighbours'. Dressed in black, with a shepherdesses black straw hat, she would show visitors round her garden, pointing out specimen plants with her long black cane. On her own, she would climb to a promontory of rock at the highest point of her property and sit at a round table gazing at the distant blue horizon.

World War I was spent in exile at Farnborough, where part of the house was made over for use as a hospital for wounded officers. After five years of absence, Eugénie returned to Villa Cyrnos in 1919. She was now an old lady of ninety-three and it was clear that this would be her last visit. She personally listed the best plants in the garden and ordered their removal, so that they would not pass into the possession of her heiress the Duchess d'Aosta, for whom Eugénie had little affection. Her head gardener refused to see the destruction of the results of his labours, and resigned. Outside contractors were called in, but the proposal languished and Eugénie moved on to Spain, where she died. Could we imagine the gentle Sisi giving such a splendid display of spite?

Ironically, when Eugénie died and the Duchess entered into her inheritance the first thing she did was to have the whole garden cleared and replanted before selling out to an English World War I captain.

Despite her black eyes and raven locks Eugénie was no gypsy but she was certainly a traveller. And her journeyings may not be over. The proudly republican French have begun again to yearn for some of the trappings of royalty and the 200th anniversary of the birth of Napoleon III saw the beginning of a campaign for the return of his body to France – presumably to lie beside the remains of his uncle, Napoleon Bonaparte. But the Imperial crypt at Farnborough houses the whole Imperial family, Emperor, Eugénie and the Prince Imperial. Should the family be split up in death? Or are they all to be transported to Les Invalides, where Napoleon and his son, the Prince of Rome, lie? But the Empress Marie Louise is back with 'her ain folk' in Vienna. A test for French logic!

CHAPTER 6

Carlota, Empress of Mexico (1840-1927)
The ghostly Empress

POOR LITTLE BELGIUM! As a country, Belgium does not get a good press. When we do hear about it, it is in connection with a paedophile ring, or a major food scandal. Every school has two headteachers, to keep both nationalities, Flemish and Walloon, from each other's throats. Other countries have clear stereotypes. Hans Brinker defends the dykes of Holland, the Frenchman cycles along with his *baguette,* the German has his cigar and his beer – and Belgium has a little boy urinating.

And what sort of country is Belgium, 'the cockpit of Europe', the Piccadilly Circus of marauding armies down the centuries? In the fifteenth century the Low Countries - a conveniently vague term - were, with northern Italy, the most economically active area in Europe, with a great textile industry and powerful cities. When Charles the Bold, Duke of Burgundy was killed in battle, his daughter Mary chose to wed a Habsburg, Maximilian of Austria. As Hendrik Willem Van Loon says:

> From him their descendants inherited the famous jutting Habsburg underlip; from her, a considerable part of what is now Belgium and Holland.

After the Reformation the seven United Provinces in the north broke off to form a republic under a Stadholder, while the rest remained as the Catholic Austrian Netherlands.

Typically, Napoleon upset the apple cart. The Austrian Netherlands were incorporated into France and his brother, Louis, was installed as King of Holland from 1806 to 1810 only to be forced to abdicate because he was more concerned for the interests of his subject people than for those of France. When the map of Europe was redrawn at the Congress of Vienna in 1815 the United Netherlands was created by adding the Austrian Netherlands to the United Provinces so as to have a powerful northern counterweight against the French. (In compensation, Austria received the Venetian republic, the duchy of Milan and other cities in the Po valley, ensuring almost a century of revolutionary struggle and warfare in northern Italy).

In 1830 resentment, liberalism and nationalism combined to deliver the new constitutional monarchy of Belgium. A prince of Saxe-Coburg, uncle of Queen Victoria, was elected as Leopold I. (As Van Loon says: 'He had just refused a similar offer from the Greeks and never had any reason to regret his choice'). Today we see a small country fractured between the Flemings of the north and the French-speaking Walloons in the south but after twenty-five years Leopold's small kingdom was seen as an ideally governed state.

Leopold liked to think of himself as the Nestor of rulers, wielding an influence out of all proportion to his modest kingdom and sought out by the heads of other states for guidance. Charlotte was his fourth child and only daughter. The first child died in infancy. Leopold, Crown Prince and Duke of Brabant was delicate when young. As Leopold II he outraged the civilised world by the treatment of the indigenes of his personal property in the Congo and by the treatment of his family.

Africa had been successively colonised by the Portuguese, Spaniards, Dutch, British and French. The Germans joined in late for 'The Scramble for Africa'. All that was left was the Congo, which fell into the personal clutches of King Leopold II. His Congo Free State (1885-1908) was privately controlled through a dummy non-governmental organization, the *Association Internationale Africaine* of which Leopold was the sole shareholder and chairman. Ostensibly a philanthropic organization, its main purpose was the exploitation of rubber and copper.

> During the decades in which he had run it as a personal fiefdom between five and eight million Africans were reckoned to have lost their lives in the most cruel and exploitative colonial system that would ever be seen in Africa.

In 1908, the Congo Free State was annexed by the government of Belgium. It continued as a colony – the Belgian Congo – until this unhappy territory won a troubled independence in 1960.

His villa-building exploits on Cap Ferrat – in relation to his complex family life - have already been touched on in the chapter on *Belles Demeures*. Leopold's brother, Philip, Count of Flanders, plays no part in this story until Carlota's breakdown in 1886.

The Gypsy Empresses

A tendency to gravity was emphasised when Carlota's mother died. The young princess was then ten. Her education was intense and serious, with her father quizzing her every day. Social appearances were strictly rationed. Only her brothers were permitted to waltz with her. Her sister-in-law, a Hungarian Archduchess, was very kind but her musical taste was not serious - that word again - enough for Carlota.

In 1856, just after the cessation of the Crimean War, the Emperor Franz Josef of Austria sent his brother, the Archduke Maximilian, on a tour of the principal neighbouring Courts of Europe. Of Belgium, Maximilian reported back that:

> I travelled through the whole of Belgium, which can be managed without difficulty in a few hours. It is indeed the most lovely blooming land that I have yet seen; a country possessing all the elements of prosperity and plenty; a fertile soil, rich cities crowded closely together, harbours, the sea, a well laid-out network of railways, commerce and factories. On all sides is manifest a feeling of well-being in which the traveller involuntarily shares; on all sides one sees happy friendly faces; the whole country is well cultivated; forests of factory chimneys, industrial establishments, on a scale which I had never seen before, cover whole stretches of the landscape. Belgium fully deserves the self-chosen name of a model country; this it undoubtedly owes in the first place to the prudent procedure of the King.

While Max's glasses may have been tinted rose by his first setting eyes on the sixteen year old Carlota, there must still have been some underlying truth in his impressions of Belgium.

Two years younger than his brother, Maximilian had to play second string. Franz Josef was industrious and methodical, Max was dreamy yet competitive. He very soon developed a taste for travel. In 1845 he was taken from Venice to Trieste by sea and determined that his future was to be a sailor.

1848 was 'the Year of Revolutions' and in the Austrian Empire there were uprisings political and nationalistic. Archduchess Sophie, the boys' mother, persuaded the ineffectual Emperor Francis I to abdicate, while her husband Francis Charles ('that imbecile!'), younger brother of the Emperor, renounced his claim to the throne, leaving the way open to her son Franz Josef. Pacification was the first priority and this was brutally achieved - Maximilian expressing disgust at the methods used.

After a cruise to Greece and Asia Minor, Maximilian entered the navy as a lieutenant. Fans of 'The Sound of Music' are often surprised that the hero, von Trapp, was a retired captain in the Austrian navy, but the Empire had an Adriatic coast. Venice was still a sizeable, if much decayed, port giving access via the Brenner Pass to the Tirol and Bavaria while Trieste was the main southern outlet of Vienna and much of central Europe.

The navy was in a poor state, but the spirit of reform was in the air and the reformers (North Germans and Danes) proved adept in using Maximilian as a means of winning over the Emperor. Maximilian was able to cruise round the states of the western Mediterranean and Gibraltar and spent three months in the West Indies. The following year it was another round of the Mediterranean, taking in North Africa, Madeira, Portugal and visits to French and British warships. In 1853 Franz Josef was stabbed by a vengeful Hungarian tailor. Maximilian rushed to Vienna, to his brother's side, only to be rebuked for having interrupted his naval duties. Although Maximilian started the thanksgiving fund which produced the Votivkirche which completes the urban splendour of the Ring in Vienna, for the first time, 'the dark shadow of jealousy' had 'fallen between the two brothers'.

Maximilian's next task was to head a mission to Albania, where the Christian minority was being mishandled by the Turkish Muslims. Four years after he joined the navy he was promoted *Marinoberkommandant* with the rank of Rear-Admiral and set to with the task of modernisation to such effect that he was able, next summer, to lead out a fleet of fourteen warships on exercises which ranged from France to Egypt and the Holy Land. When he had joined the navy it had consisted of only three sailing frigates and various small craft. Austria sat out the Crimean War, although her threat of intervention helped to bring about a peace settlement. It was in an attempt to restore Austria's presence that Maximilian was sent round the capitals of Europe and set eyes on Carlota for the first time, while she determined that he was the one for her.

Franz Josef visited Venice and Trieste, approved of Maximilian's activities and promoted him to Vice-Admiral. 1848 was not forgotten, local feeling still rang high and Piedmont-Sardinia - which had fought beside the French and British in the Crimea - was agitating for the unification of Italy. It was time to slip the velvet glove over the iron fist. The Governor of Lombardy and Venetia - General Radetsky, he of the Strauss march - asked to be relieved of his post (at the age of ninety!) and Maximilian was appointed Governor, minus the military command. His initial months were difficult, especially when he accompanied his brother who, despite the public charm of Sisi, was still thoroughly hated.

Maximilian sailed to Lisbon and London, where he stayed at Buckingham Palace and won over a previously-suspicious Victoria and Albert. Then came the wedding in Brussels and the journey to Vienna via the Rhine and the Danube. Charlotte was well received at Schônbrunn. The Archduchess Sophie - the thorn in Sisi's flesh - was *'bien maternelle pour moi'*. The Emperor and Empress were charming. Then it was off to Trieste where Maximilian had had a splendid villa – Miramar – built.

Milan was the headquarters of Lombardy and Maximilian and Carlotta made their state entry on September 6, 1857. Their reception by the general populace was not unfriendly. There was no heavy military presence and both the Governor and his bride won over hearts by speaking Italian well. But, as with the earlier visit of Franz Josef, the nobility and the upper classes boycotted the event. They simply ignored their new rulers, however liberal they might be.

And liberal they were, for their time and background. Maximilian advocated a measure of home rule for the Italian provinces and put forward plans for reform of taxation, education and local government. However, repression was the Habsburg way and everything had to be approved by the Emperor.

Music-lovers will be familiar with the problems Verdi had with the censors. In *Rigoletto* the reckless libertine Francis I of France *('La Donna e mobile')* had to be replaced by a 'Duke of Mantua' lest it be thought a reigning monarch was being criticised. The much-loved Chorus of the Hebrew Slaves in *Nabucco* was clearly an expression of aspiration to liberty and self-government. The last scene of *Don Carlos* is softened in order to show the Emperor Charles V (Franz Josef's remote ancestor) in a sympathetic light. Austrian walls in the north of Italy were daubed with the punning 'Viva Verdi!', which could either have been praise for the composer or support for Victor Emmanuel, **Re d'Italia** – King of Italy.

Franz Josef saw every proposed change as revolutionary mischief. Part of the myth of Franz Josef is the aged Emperor at 4 a.m. working away at state papers, single-handedly holding his crumbling empire together. Most likely he was working on the reports of the *Geheimspolizei* (secret police), whose every detail he attended to. In Italy they were *agents provocateurs*. When Maximilian complained he was very firmly put in his place. Maximilian's reluctance to enforce decrees on making the currency uniform with that of the rest of the Empire and on the extension of compulsory military service was another bone of contention.

PLATE 1A   Menton/Roquebrune – plaque commemorating Sisi's connection

PLATE 1B   Villa Thompson, Nice. Built 1878. Now *Musée des Beaux-Arts Jules-Chéret*

PLATE 2A   Dr James Henry Bennet
in the Menton he helped
to create

PLATE 2B   'Where the lemon trees
bloom'

PLATE 2C   The gypsy stereotype
Aachen style

PLATE 3A   Elisabeth, '98 - the Empress and her City

PLATE 3B   Madame Tussaud's, Berlin - Romy Schneider as Sisi

PLATE 3C   Villa Cyrnos, Roquebrune, 1892

PLATE 4A   *The Empress Eugenie and her Ladies on the Beach at Trouville,*
by Boudin (1824-98)
(By kind permission of Culture and Sport Glasgow (Museums))

PLATE 4B   Praca Dom Pedro IV,
Lisbon. Recycled
statue of Maximilian

PLATE 5A   Russian Cathedral, Nice

PLATE 5B   Her Imperial Majesty in
            Birmingham

PLATE 6A   Outside the Loch Maree Hotel – *Bhan righ Bhictoria* slept here

PLATE 6B   Ardgour – the Queen's profile

PLATE 7A   The Queen's View – looking up the Avon to Ben Avon

PLATE 7B   The Queen's Well in
Glen Mark

PLATE 8A   Menton - Queen's well on
frontier with Italy

PLATE 8B   *L'hôtel Excelsior Regina
à Cimiez c1900*

PLATE 8C   Cimiez, Nice – The gracious
Impératrice des Indes

We have already seen how Napoleon III had grandiose ideas which led him into rather doubtful enterprises. In 1859 he allied himself with Victor Emmanuel of Piedmont against Austria, in return for a promise of the cession of Nice and Savoy. Franz Josef was determined to teach them a lesson and removed Maximilian from his Governership, the civil administration being handed over to General Count Gyulai. Maximilian left for Venice, where he found himself subordinate to the fortress commander, his junior in rank. The Austrian fleet was bottled up in Venice by the French and played no part in the war.

On the plains of Lombardy the Austrian army moved on Piedmont. Napoleon's forces crossed the Alps, fought a bloody battle at Magenta and entered Milan. At Solferino three weeks later, both Emperors commanded their armies in the field, with equal incompetence, their tactics consisting of lining up their troops against the other side and letting them slug it out. (1) Franz Josef wrote:

> Great things were done but fortune did not smile upon us. I am the richer by many experiences and have learnt what it feels like to be a defeated general.

Napoleon III did not have the necessary bloody-mindedness to maximise his bloody victory. He suggested Venetia should become a separate kingdom under Maximilian - but Franz Josef would have none of that. Parma and Lombardy went to Victor Emmanuel, Nice and Savoy became French, Venetia, Tuscany and Modena remained subject to the Hapsburg Emperor. Maximilian was in disgrace. He retired (at twenty-seven) to Miramar and began restoring a monastery on Lacroma, a Dalmatian island Carlota had bought.

He and Carlotta filled in the winter of 1859-60 by visiting Brazil in the Imperial steamer *Elisabeth,* calling in and botanising at Gibraltar and Madeira on the way. The *Elisabeth* was the first Austrian steamship to cross the Equator. The Emperor of Brazil, Pedro II, was a cousin of Maximilian and ruled a country which still practised slavery - on which Maximilian expressed himself with considerable force. Maximilian indulged in a little match-making, suggesting that his younger brother, Ludwig Viktor, could start a new Hapsburg dynasty in Latin America by marrying Pedro's fourteen year old daughter. (2)

Their return to Miramar coincided with the low point in the relationship between Franz Josef and Sisi, which ended when Maximilian escorted his sister-in-law to Corfu, where she began her new life of travels and separations. The relationship between Maximilian and Carlotta was 'not unclouded'. For four years she had done her duty, supporting her husband in the social round of an Admiral, an Archduke or a Governer. At Miramar she wrote and painted. At Lacroma: 'she would bathe, ride, sail, and stroll through the beautiful woods of her fairy island'. But she was not content. She was her father's daughter and wanted to be involved again in matters of great importance.

After four years of marriage, there was no sign of children. Despite their first meeting, the reality of their marriage was more sordid than romantic. Maximilian had loved and lost twice before he met Charlotte. Countess Paula von Linden's father was transferred to Berlin to get rid of her. Princess Maria Amelia of Braganza ('a pure perfect angel') died of consumption at the age of twenty, despite having been taken to Madeira in the mistaken belief that this would better her condition.

Antonio Grill was Maximilian's valet and from him we learn that Maximilian had extra-marital affairs and on one trip to Vienna contracted a venereal disease from a prostitute. This he proceeded to pass on to his wife. In a similar situation Sisi had shown great revulsion and, humiliated, had fled the country and the court, to spend the rest of her life in successive tolerance and escapism. Carlotta, her pride no less wounded, was alienated. They no longer slept in the same bed but kept up the pretence of an affectionate and loving couple in public, 'without seeking to create a public scandal'. (In Mexico, Maximilian's amorous life was to continue. Not only were the ladies of the court his targets, he fathered an illegitimate son on a pretty seventeen-year-old gardener's wife, Concepcion Sedano y Leguiziano).

A difficult situation at home is often resolved by some challenge from outside. A visit in October 1861 by Count Rechberg, the Austrian Foreign Minister, was to change the lives of Maximilian and Carlotta.

The focus now shifts to Mexico, the Audienca of New Spain where a Solemn Declaration of Independence in 1814 led to Spain's acceptance of Mexican independence in 1821. The main architect of independence, Agustin Iturbide, set the pattern for early Mexican history by defeating the greater numbers of the loyal Spanish armies, by being crowned Emperor Agustin II, by abdicating and going into exile in England and by returning to Mexico, where he was executed. Political instability and oppression became endemic and relations with its northern neighbour, the Texan Republic, then the United States, alternated between armed hostility and open warfare. ('Remember the Alamo!')

In 1864 there was a temporary power vacuum in Mexico. The American Civil War meant that attention in the United States was diverted elsewhere. Benito Juarez (3), an extreme Liberal, legitimately became President and at once began a programme of reform, especially aimed at the Church. The Conservatives produced their own President, Miramon, and for four years there was an internal struggle between Juarez in the main port, Vera Cruz, and Miramon in Mexico City. In desperation, Juarez suspended payments on foreign loans for two years, whereupon Spain, France and Britain contemplated intervention.

Paris was full of Mexican exiles and self-styled patriots. Jose Hidalgo was one of these who had known the lovely Eugénie de Montijo years before and was now a regular guest of Napoleon III and his Empress. Napoleon was interested in Latin America – he had once been offered the presidency of Ecuador and he had also toyed with the idea of a canal to link the Atlantic with the Pacific. Hidalgo worked on him to intervene in Mexico and set up a puppet regime. But who should be offered the crown? It was Eugénie who suggested Maximilian. Hence Count Rechberg's visit and the subsequent deputation of four Conservative exiles offering Maximilian the crown.

There was much huffing and puffing in Europe while the French, British and Spanish (from Cuba) occupied Vera Cruz. Marshal Bazaine – a general of no great ability who was later to disgrace himself against the Prussians - led 40,000 French troops against the 20,000 of Juarez, overwhelmed them and seemed to have pacified the country, clearing the way for the new Emperor. (4) In Paris, Napoleon and Eugénie were supportive of Maximilian and Carlotta in public, but doubtful in private. Queen Victoria was friendly but her ministers made it clear that nothing could be done for the young couple. A visit to the Vatican seemed successful - were they not about to go on a kind of Crusade to the New World? - yet once they had arrived in Mexico the papal nuncio proved intractable in opposition to them.

Franz Josef was a disappointment. It is highly improbable that he had the imagination to see that Maximilian was trying to put the clock back by several centuries, to the time when his remote ancestor Charles V ruled over the Hapsburg lands in Austria, the Netherlands, Spain and the Spanish conquests around the world and when he had the Pope arrogantly divide the yet-undiscovered world between Spain and Portugal by the Treaty of Tordesillas. The Mexican adventure was a convenient way of getting rid of his irritating brother, but it would come at a cost - Maximilian had to sign away his and his heirs' right of succession and inheritance in Austria.

At this troubled time young Carlotta - she was still just twenty-four - emerged from her husband's shadow, vigorously attacking Franz Josef and playing a strong part in negotiations while her husband faltered. Finally, in April 1864, at Miramar, Maximilian formally accepted the crown of Mexico. The Imperial oath was administered, the Mexican flag was run up on the castle tower, an Austrian frigate fired a twenty-one gun salute, a Te Deum was sung in the chapel and Carlotta, formerly known as Charlotte, now became known as Carlota. A few days later the Imperial suite embarked on the *Novara*, the frigate flying the flag of Mexico, for their great voyage to claim their Imperial throne. Less than four years later the *Novara* returned to Trieste, this time carrying the dead body of Maximilian.

First impressions of Mexico were mixed. Yellow fever was rampant in Vera Cruz. The roads were bad, as was the food. Yet the Mexicans seemed a 'simple, docile' people, surprisingly well-educated. Maximilian went on long tours of the country when Carlota acted as regent, chairing the council, deputising at Sunday audiences with the public, visiting schools and charitable institutions, She wrote to Eugénie showing how she was following her 'good example'. As time went by it became clear that Maximilian was well-meaning but indecisive, too concerned with the trappings of rule rather than its business. At the same time, Carlota aroused resentment by becoming more and more involved in matters that were, strictly speaking, no concern of hers. It was obvious too, that the picture that had been painted in Europe, of a populace eager to welcome the young couple, had been exaggerated, if not untrue. A Carlota Colony set up to resettle Confederate refugees did not prove viable.

In April 1865 'The War between the States' ended. Lincoln had never recognised Maximilian as Emperor and his successor, Andrew Johnson, remembered the Monroe Doctrine of 1823, that attempts by European countries to colonise in the Americas would be regarded as acts of aggression. Seward, the American Secretary of State, reminded Napoleon and Leopold of Belgium of this and informed Juarez's man in Washington accordingly. Caches of guns and ammunition were 'lost' or 'mislaid' just over the Rio Grande. The forces of Juarez took new heart and sporadic resistance developed into another civil war. On 5 February 1867 Bazaine and his force marched out of Mexico City, leaving Maximilian supported by a small Imperialist force whose maintenance would no longer come from French sources.

Briefly, there was a bloody little civil war. Maximilian considered abdication, but fought on. He was betrayed, captured and surrendered. A military court found him guilty of promoting invasion and usurping supreme power. On 19 June 1867, within a square of 4.000 troops Maximilian and two of his generals were executed by firing squad. In January 1868 the coffin was deposited, after much solemnity, in the *Kaisersgruft* of the Kapuzinerkirche in Vienna.

Edouard Manet, the leading artist of the French Impressionist school, painted 'The Execution of Maximilian and Generals Miramon and Mejia' immediately after the event. In it we find ourselves looking over the shoulders of the firing squad in the act of firing at a dignified Maximilian, flanked by his generals. Manet clearly refers to Goya's great execution scene *Third of May, 1808* and to the Crucifixion. Maximilian wears a sombrero with a bright broad brim which is almost a halo. He and Miramon are holding hands to give each other courage and Miramon's hand is bleeding, an allusion to Christ's wounds on the Cross. Behind the firing squad a rather detached sergeant cocks his musket. His duty will be to supply the coup de grace once the squad have carried out their orders.

Manet turned out a small study in oils, a lithograph and three large paintings in eighteen months, making changes as he went along. In July 1867 his first version had the firing squad and the sergeant in exotic Mexican uniforms and sombreros. These were painted over to suggest French uniforms. Manet reworked the sergeant, giving him the features of Napoléon. Manet was criticising his own government. Frenchmen were responsible for Maximilian's death, not Mexicans.

Public exhibition of the pictures and the sale of prints in France were forbidden by order of the Emperor Napoleon III's censor. They remained rolled up in Manet's studio till after his death in 1883, after which they ended up in London, Boston, Copenhagen and Mannheim. Thus any French person who wants to study this French artist's view of French history must venture abroad to do so. Napoleon still has his revenge!

Going back to Carlota, on 9 July 1866 she had left Mexico, not for safety or as an exile, but to go to Europe to plead Maximilian's cause with Napoleon III and Pope Pius IX. She was received with coolness and discourtesy. Eugénie tried to save her husband from an unpleasant interview by visiting Carlota at her hotel, but did not deflect her from her purpose. Twice Carlota had an audience at St Cloud. The French Emperor was unwell and ill at ease. Carlota read his letters back to him. He squirmed and gave evasive replies. He wept and looked helplessly at his wife, who cut short the interview by inviting Carlota to her own apartments.

Napoleon called at the Grand Hotel to terminate the whole affair. Carlota flew into a rage, Napoleon walked out and sent a formal note refusing any further help to Maximilian.

Carlota's visit to the Vatican was catastrophic. For some time she had been showing signs of disturbance. In Rome her collapse was to be complete. From Paris she wrote a long rambling letter full of hate to Maximilian. Napoleon sent her on her way to Miramar in a special train. Joy at her return to Miramar was negated by bad news from Mexico. Worried, Carlota set off for Rome. At Bolzano she felt unwell and said she had been poisoned by Napoleon's spies. She thought she saw the commandant of the Mexico City town guard playing a street organ in disguise. In Rome she had an audience with the Pope, from which she returned depressed, and two days later he returned her visit. Two days after that, clearly unwell, she was driven to the Vatican and demanded to see the Pope.

Disturbing his breakfast, there was an emotional scene as Carlota stuck her fingers into a half-finished cup of chocolate, exclaiming:

> This at least is not poisoned. Everything they give me is drugged and I am starving, literally starving.

The Pope's daily routine was in tatters as Carlota insisted - who could deny an Empress? - that he did not leave her side. At lunch she ate from someone else's plate. After lunch she took a goblet to the Trevi Fountain and drank from it, then bought a glass of lemonade from a street vendor before returning to the Vatican where she announced that she would spend the night. This was a sensation, for no woman in known history had spent a night in the Vatican, but the Library was transformed into a bedroom for two - for no Empress could prepare for bed or get up in the morning without a lady-in-waiting. She now made a will and wrote farewell letters, including three affectionate lines to her husband.

Carlota was manoeuvred out of the Vatican when the Mother Superior of the Convent of St Vincent de Paul invited her to visit the orphanage and assist at the feeding of the poor children. Carlota was driven there incognito and put on a good performance for the five hundred children. In the kitchens she was offered some of the orphans' stew to taste. With a look of terror she said to the Mother Superior, 'You see the poison? They have forgotten to polish the knife', which had a speck of rust on it. She knelt and gave thanks for her life having been saved. Then she plunged her arm into a boiling cauldron and began to attack a piece of meat, saying: 'I felt so hungry and they can't have poisoned this morsel'.

Back at her hotel her state of mind became more serious. All her food had to be cooked in her room and tasted by a cat before she would eat it. She would not undress at night or go to bed. But the telegraph wires had been busy and her brother, the Count of Flanders arrived to take her to Miramar. Carlota tried to escape to Vienna in disguise and plead for her husband with Franz Josef. Instead Professor Riedel, brain specialist and director of a mental hospital, came from Vienna to set Carlota up in the pavilion with the windows screwed down. There she painted, read and played the piano until the muddled soliloquies poured out. Her physical condition improved while, by the end of 1866, she was said to be completely imbecile and her condition hopeless. It could be said that her life had ended at the age of 26. The sixty years of life remaining to her will not take long to describe.

Early in 1867 Carlota showed some signs of improvement. Her physical health was good. She no longer had wild illusions about her husband. She read, she wrote, she did needlework. Her family, however, resented her strict isolation at Miramar. Her brother Leopold took custody of his sister and took upon himself her maintenance. Queen Marie of the Belgians fetched her from Trieste, settled her in a royal castle at Tervueren and treated her with great tenderness. She took the news of her husband's death well, consoled that he had faced death bravely. For ten years the world saw nothing of Carlota, but servants' gossip told of lonely nights spent talking, laughing and weeping. During the day she had a room full of strange objects, including a life-size doll of Maximilian, to which she would talk for hours.

A fire in her wing of the castle forced a move to a castle just outside Brussels - Bouchout - which Leopold bought for her and provided with 'an establishment befitting an ex-Empress of the Belgian royal house'. For almost fifty years there were periods of calm, broken by wild outbursts of destruction - although anything reminiscent of Maximilian was spared. She had some consciousness of what she had been and would speak of 'one'. She was appreciative of the services others did for her. She was punctilious in her dress. She was conscious of the days of the month - she had a ritual with a boat on the first day of the month - and of anniversaries, although she got relationships mixed up.

The first month of the First World War was notorious for the burning and sack of Louvain. Carlota must have heard the rumble of the guns, but otherwise the war passed her by. A notice on the castle gates said that the castle was occupied by the sister-in-law of 'our revered ally the Emperor of Austria' and commanded all German soldiers 'to pass by without singing and to leave this place untouched'. One patrol did force their way in to find Carlota at the table, while another company commander vainly tried to billet his men in the castle just before the Armistice.

Without knowing it, Carlota outlasted them all. The Romanovs and Hohenzollerns disappeared. The Habsburg legacy was broken into four new republics. Napoleon and Eugénie's French Empire had been blown apart forty years before and even Eugénie was dead. The insubstantial Carlota slipped away early in 1927, bronchial influenza developing into pneumonia. She was buried in the crypt of the Belgian royal family at Laeken, while her beloved Max is with his ancestors in Vienna.

As Empress of Mexico Carlota left a faint footprint in a long life of enduring melancholy; but is she out of place in this catalogue of Gypsy Empresses? She was a good, hard-working, earnest girl who had the misfortune to fall in love with an unsettled and unsatisfactory man. In the song it is the lady in the manor who runs off with the gypsies. We can see Carlota as the one who follows the romantic Max and takes all the blame upon herself.

At Miramar, near Trieste, the young couple in effect developed their own version of the Riviera. Leopold, her brother, led a spectacular life between Nice and Monaco. He made sure that his sister was properly cared for - but made jolly sure that she was not going to queer his pitch on the Mediterranean! Carlota and Sisi were sisters-in-law with the same kind of problem - the betrayal of innocence by powerful men thirled to the double standard. Sisi chose the escapist way of unhappily wandering until she was stopped by the assassin's blade. Carlota's sense of duty helped to knock her off balance, leading to fifty years of occasional violence, but with long periods of apparent acceptance. Who can say which was the better fate?

The search for an illustration for this chapter was frustrating. There are photographs of Carlota, but one little old lady in black in an open landau is very much like another. However, behind PLATE 4B, we have a suitably muddled and contorted story which matches Carlota's Imperial existence.

One of the main squares of Lisbon is the Rossio or Praca Dom Pedro IV, which is dominated by a great column which is, according to the plaque at its base, dedicated to King Pedro IV (who was also Emperor Pedro I of Brazil - and fortunately beyond our territory).

Maximilian and his circle concentrated too much on the trappings of the Empire and not enough on good government. A fine statue of Maximilian was commissioned and was on the way to Mexico when the skipper put in at Lisbon, to learn of the execution and the pointlessness of the voyage The statue was unloaded and lay at the dockside till it was hauled up to the top of the column, where it was transformed into Pedro IV. At that height, who could tell the difference? And no doubt a great deal of money was saved.

We are used to revolutionaries tearing down the symbols of hated despots, but this twisted tale must be unique in recycling a misguided despot and making him the centre of admiration in a foreign capital. I do not suppose Carlota ever knew of this and she certainly had no sense of humour, but if she had realised her late husband was up there on a pedestal she would have supposed he had earned his reward.

End Notes

1   Henri Dunant (1828-1910) was a Swiss banker with interests in Algeria who made his way to Solferino to present to Napoleon III a flattering book he had written. He arrived after the battle to find 38,000 dead, dying and wounded scattered about the battlefield, uncared for. Nothing had been learned in the Crimea. Dunant organised the local population and took over churches and other buildings as temporary hospitals. His book *A Memory of Solferino* aroused international concern and in 1863 the International Committee of the Red Cross was set up, with Dunant as one of its five members.

Dunant's wobbly finances meant he was partly sidelined and it was not until 1897 that his contribution was properly recognised. Maria Feodorovna, Tsarina of Russia ('the sad fiancée') was a generous supporter and in 1901 he shared the Nobel Peace Prize with a French pacifist.

A visit to the headquarters and museum of the International Red Cross in Geneva is at once depressing and inspiring. Depressing because of the scale and frequency of 'Man's inhumanity unto man'. Inspiring because of the constant stream of idealistic service released by Dunant's reaction to the horrors of Solferino.

2   When Maximilian became Emperor he proposed that Ludwig Viktor (1842-1919) become Crown Prince, in the absence of a son. The 'frivolous' Archduke Ludwig Viktor, to quote Montgomery Hyde:

...became addicted to members of his own sex in a manner which would not perhaps have provoked comment in ancient Greece but which resulted in his banishment from the Imperial Court of Austria.

Ludwig Viktor never married.

3   Benito Juarez (1806-72) was a most remarkable character, the second full-blooded Indian (as he was described at the time) in the whole of Latin America to make it to the top. As he said of himself: 'a man who came out of the dark masses of the common people', he was orphaned at the age of three and at twelve was illiterate and could speak only Zapotek. He was adopted by a wealthy tradesman, became a lawyer and successful politician and served five terms as President. He was hated by the Church and the great landowners and has become one of Mexico's national heroes, not least because he threw out the foreign Imperialists.

4   Marshall Bazaine (1811-1888) rose from the ranks and held every rank in the army. He served with competence and great courage in France's colonial wars, the Crimea, at Solferino and in Mexico. After the initial disasters of the Franco-Prussian War Napoleon resigned as Commander-in-Chief and appointed Bazaine in his place. The task was too big for him and he allowed the Army of the Rhine to be bottled up in Metz. After a siege of seventy days Bazaine surrendered his force of 173,000 men, 60 generals, 58 flags, 1570 guns and 260,000 rifles. After the war he had to carry the can for the collapse of France and was sentenced to death for treason, commuted to twenty years imprisonment.

Bazaine was luckier in love than in war. In North Africa, as a colonel of thirty-six, he fell for his Spanish landlady's daughter, Maria de la Soledad Tormo, a pretty seventeen year old, the favourite of the regiment, who had to be sent back to school before the authorities would approve the match. She followed him to the Crimea and northern Italy, but her poor health meant she did not go to Mexico. Indeed she died in rather odd circumstances. For a time Bazaine was prostrate, but cheered up when he found another seventeen year old, a brunette called Maria Josefa de la Pena y Barragan y Azcarate, commonly known as Pepita. She had no money but her uncle had once been President of the Republic. Unfortunately, her father was a supporter of Juarez, which caused problems. But Carlota quite took to her and said so in letters to Eugénie.

After Bazaine's trial he was imprisoned on the Ile Ste Marguerite, off the Riviera coast. Pepita organised his escape. Ropes and a harness were smuggled in and the 63-year old climbed down the 300-foot cliffs to his wife in a boat below. The family went to Genoa, then London, before settling in Spain, where Bazaine was highly regarded. The Madrid winters were destructive to health. Pepita took the children back to Mexico and Bazaine died alone and in shabby circumstances.

CHAPTER 7
The Empresses of Germany

ON 18 JANUARY 1871, a new German Empire was proclaimed in the Hall of Mirrors at the Palace of Versailles. King William I of Prussia accepted the title of German Emperor. In the early hours of 10 November 1918, William II ('Kaiser Bill' to our forefathers) crossed the Dutch border and left his country forever, signing an instrument of abdication on 28 November. The German Empire therefore lasted a mere 47 years and there were only three German Kaisers. Each had his Empress. A stereotypical view of German women, especially Prussian, is of *Kinder, Küche und Kirche* (children, kitchen and church). Did the Empresses all conform or could any one of these let her hair down and qualify as a Gypsy Empress?

But first we must examine what is, or was, meant by Germany and the Germans. The Frankish Charlemagne brought most of Western Europe under his control and on 25 December 800 was crowned Holy Roman Emperor. The eastern part around the fifteenth century became 'The Holy Roman Empire of the German Nation'. This developed into a complex mélange of princely states, church lands with prince-bishops, and free imperial cities. By the eighteenth century there were over three hundred authorities in Germany, each with its own capital, court, currency and laws. Overall was the Emperor, by now almost always a Hapsburg, but he was elected by the seven Electors and was therefore subject to a degree of control. Austria, or the Hapsburg lands, was the senior partner and defender of Europe from Muslim invasions until the eighteenth century saw the rise of Prussia as a counterweight in northern Germany.

Napoleon started the process of unification when he swept across Europe, repeatedly defeating Austria, Prussia and the lesser states in battle after battle, effectively destroying the Empire and setting up the Confederation of the Rhine, which became the German Confederation of 39 states in 1815. A Customs Union of 1834 demonstrated some of the advantages of cooperation and unification and all the German-speaking territories – with the exception of the Austrian Empire and Switzerland – were united under Prussian leadership to form the German Empire.

Augusta of Saxony-Weimar (1811-1890)
A superior being

IN MARCH 1888 the Emperor Wilhelm I of Germany, King of Prussia, lay dying on his narrow camp bed. Around him was his immediate family circle; his Empress, Augusta, in a wheelchair, his daughter Louise, Grand Duchess of Baden and his grandson, Willy, who was to succeed him within the year as Wilhelm II. Louise brought from his desk a miniature of Elise Radziwill, who had died of a broken heart – or tuberculosis – in 1834. The portrait was placed in his feeble hands and the Grand Duchess:

> ...watched his fingers close gently round it as a look of peace came to his face.

The Polish Radziwills were considered inferior to the Hohenzollerns of Prussia and Wilhelm was ordered to look elsewhere for a bride. In 1829 he married Augusta of Saxe-Weimar Eisenach, one of the more advanced states, politically speaking, of the German Confederation. The couple were ill-matched, although they did, eventually, develop a grudging mutual respect, their duty to the state resulting in only two children, well below the average for a great family of the time.

For Wilhelm high rank meant a total commitment to militarism, he was a 'dour reactionary Prussian soldier prince'. Drill, parades and manoeuvres were to be more important than the good administration of his lands and people. He was an unimaginative and remote father. He served a long apprenticeship, becoming Regent when his older brother, Friedrich Wilhelm IV, suffered a succession of strokes. In 1861 he succeeded as King of Prussia and in the following decade - aided and abetted and bullied by Bismarck - reorganised the army and defeated Denmark, Austria and France. As Emperor he presided over a Germany growing fast in industrial strength and international influence.

Augusta came from a very different stable. She was fourteen years younger than her husband, and vivacious with it. Goethe had been her tutor and from him she had acquired a love of literature. She had been given an excellent education and had a wealth of intellectual interests. She was a free-thinker with liberal tendencies and a sense of religious toleration. This fitted ill with:

> The bigotry, anti-Semitism, anti-Catholicism and generally narrow outlook of the philistine Berlin court.

At six feet tall and with a stentorian voice - her nickname was 'Foghorn' - she had a presence, but she learned very quickly that the best way to a trouble-free life was to conform to type, to argue with her husband when she must, but make the best of her situation.

Her innate liberalism and intellectual interests ensured that their family life was notoriously fractious but with no positive outlet for her undoubted talents Augusta's life style sank into a preoccupation with meddling and the free use of her sharp tongue.

As a mother-in-law to Vicky, she interfered with her family life, and. like many another grandmother, did her best to drive a wedge between Vicky and her firstborn, Wilhelm. Vicky's first three children were put out to wet nurses at Augusta's insistence. It is surely no coincidence that relations between Vicky and her three eldest were not good, while the remaining five, whom she nursed herself, all grew up well-integrated. There were occasions when Augusta would draw Vicky aside for some friendly advice and both ladies detested (and were detested by) Bismarck, but reconciliation was never permanent.

Augusta was no Gypsy Empress. She seldom left Germany, and then usually 'on business'. Although court tittle-tattle was her main preoccupation, she ceased to stay in Berlin after the social season any longer than court etiquette demanded, preferring to move alternately between Weimar and Baden, or her country place in Koblenz. But she was not escaping. There was no informality in these peregrinations. Rather was she demonstrating an alternative lifestyle for a great lady.

Empress Frederick/Victoria of Great Britain (1840-1901) Ninety-nine days

PRINCE FRIEDRICH WILHELM NIKLAUS KARL (1831-88), son of Emperor Wilhelm I and Empress Augusta and Crown Prince of Prussia, Crown Prince of the German Empire and Kaiser Friedrich III, also known as 'Fritz', has always appeared to me a sad figure – a nineteenth century embodiment of the American principle that 'nice guys come second'.

As we have seen, his father Wilhelm I was a Type B Hohenzollern, austere, thrifty and a workaholic. He was revered, if not loved, as a character who resisted the installation of decadent hot baths in the Berlin palace. Who seldom spoke in public and rarely ventured outside his kingdom. Who marked the labels on bottles to restrict the sly drinking of the servants. Who wiped the wet nib of his pen on the dark blue sleeve of his uniform jacket, which was made to do long service. Who appeared at his study window every day at the same time to superintend the changing of the palace guard.

Some of this was deliberate image-building and there was a theatrical tinge to his relationship with Bismarck. Their relationship was stormy as Bismarck used every trick in the book to impose his will on his master; as Wilhelm said - 'It is hard being Emperor under Bismarck'. But Wilhelm could be quite cunning in allowing himself to appear to have been bullied into some action he had really wanted to make in the first place, but had been reluctant to risk public antipathy by initiating it himself.

From childhood the handsome, red-haired Fritz was generous, unselfish, even-tempered, and like his father he was quiet and serious-minded.

Fritz's home life was bedevilled by family quarrels. His father was insistent on a military education but his mother contrived for him to attend the University of Bonn, the first Hohenzollern prince to go to university (and graduate). His English tutor, Copland Perry, had a great influence on him. Augusta was an Anglophile and early visits to Britain gave Fritz an early admiration for the comparative openness, safety and liberalism of British society. In the year of the Great Exhibition (1851), the Prussian royal family visited London. The Queen's eldest child, also called Victoria, was brought into the circle. She was a bright child of ten who took Fritz (then nineteen) in hand at the Exhibition, leaving his parents to quarrel. The initial attraction and respect grew into something deeper and in 1858 the couple were married in St James's Palace - which did not please the Prussians. (It was as the happy couple made their way out of the chapel that Mendelssohn's *Wedding March* was given its first public airing). Victoria and Albert became his mentors - which did not go down well back in Berlin, either.

Fritz would have liked to have studied government and statecraft but was instead compelled to follow a military career – which he conscientiously did. His father became Regent and, in 1861, King of Prussia. Fritz was now Crown Prince, and would remain so for 27 years. He need not have waited so long - at one stage there was a deal of discontent with William, who threatened to abdicate. A military junta were going to depose him and put Fritz in his place. He declined to be involved and told his father so - only to be berated for plotting behind his back!

In marrying Fritz the young Vicky moved from a sheltered family life in which she was a natural leader into being the youngest of several princesses,

> ...almost all dull and vacuous and filling their time with gossip and dinner parties until childbearing took over.

Victoria and Albert wrote to her every day, giving her good advice about her behaviour, and they expected her to reply with the same regularity. No wonder the Prussians were suspicious of English (1) interference in their affairs, particularly when Vicky unwisely lectured them on the superiority of institutions in her home country. Vicky complained to her mother that her children were pitied for having a mother with *'unglücklichen englischen Ideen'* and *'unpreussischen Gesinnugen'* (unfortunate English ideas and un-Prussian views). Fritz's loyalties were also suspect, particularly after the death of Albert, when he deputised for Victoria in Britain when she and her children were too prostrated by grief to carry out their duties.

In their private life they were probably as happy as any royal couple can be. One measure of this is probably the comparison between the two generations. Victoria and Albert, of whose uxoriousness there is no doubt, in the course of 17 years had nine children, all of whom lived well into adulthood. Vicky and Fritz, in 13 years, had 8 children, of whom two unfortunately died young.

Part of their chemistry was the similarity of their views - Vicky's expressed clearly and trenchantly, Fritz's more shyly because of the need to keep his nose clean with his mother, his father and, increasingly, Bismarck. Back from a three-week trip to Berlin in January 1865, Charles Lyell (2) - Darwin's best friend and conservative critic - recounted how he had engaged the Princess Royal of Prussia 'in an animated conversation on Darwinism' and found her 'very much au fait' at the *'Origin'* and Huxley's book, the *'Antiquity'* etc etc.

Fritz and Vicky were systematically isolated by Bismarck and the German press. Some of their complaints could be justified, others were simply inventions. At the same time, Fritz was deliberately kept out of the limelight and given duties where he had no decisions to make. In 1868 he went to Rome, to the princely marriage of the Italian Crown Prince. He represented Prussia at the opening of the Suez Canal in 1869, where he met Emperor Franz Josef (but no Sisi!), Emperor Napoleon and Empress Eugenie. (Vicky took two of her children to Cannes for a holiday). (3) They began taking holidays, usually in north Italy, Florence and Venice. Much time was spent in 'England', where the relaxed way of life at Balmoral suited the growing family.

As a soldier, Fritz was more than competent and was popular with those under his command. The decorations he won in Denmark, Austria and France seem to have been deserved. In the first - mobile - phase of the Franco-Prussian War he was in command of the Third Army, which achieved two major victories (although he lost 10,000 men in a day at Froeschwiler). At the siege of Paris it was decided that his unit should bombard the city into submission. Fritz opposed this but had to do what he was ordered to do.

For three weeks from 5 January 1871, three or four hundred shells arrived every day, at random and with no attempt to single out military targets. This marked 'the beginning of the Germanic technique of war by *Schrecklichkeit*'. Ninety-seven Parisians were killed, 278 were wounded and 1400 buildings damaged. The culprit was the same model of Prussian gun that had been proudly displayed in the heart of the city in the great exhibition of 1867, held on the *Champ de Mars*. The bombardment outraged Europe and achieved no tangible success. (4) When Fritz learned that shells had exploded among a church congregation, he exclaimed, 'Such a piece of news wrings my heart'.

At last, seventeen years after the siege and the declaration of Empire, old Wilhelm died. How ready was Fritz, a fifty-seven year old, to take on the burdens of government? In February 1887 Fritz's voice went and it was clear there was something very wrong with the Crown Prince. Six doctors were called in and, although they differed, a cancerous growth in the throat was their conclusion. For political reasons - for no German would want to have to carry the can - someone from outside was needed and a London-based Scotsman was chosen. Morell Mackenzie was well-qualified, had written textbooks on nose and throat diseases and was fluent in German. Victoria's physician, Sir William Jenner, agreed that the Scot was clever but 'greedy and grasping about money and tries to make a profit out of his attendance'. The medical men did not settle into becoming a useful team. Treatment of cancer was at an early, even primitive, stage and there were disagreements and botched procedures – even drunkenness.

Vicky probably made a mistake in trying to keep her husband's illness concealed. She did not want him to read about his illness in the papers His public appearances were cut to the minimum and carefully stage-managed. She would read documents to him and, if he nodded assent, guide his hand in signing them. What would once have been spoken had to be written on a pad. Once he had become Kaiser, the pressure from Bismarck increased. Frederick could not stand and address a group in public or speak to his ministers; therefore he was not fit to be Emperor and should stand down or be replaced by his son, now Crown Prince. Naturally, Wilhelm was of the same opinion and disgraced himself by swanking about while his father was still alive!

In an attempt to achieve some comfort in his last year, Vicky and Fritz travelled to quite an extent. Partly it was an attempt to escape the suffocation of Berlin, partly a quest for a congenial environment, and partly an attempt to keep Mackenzie to themselves. In the summer of 1887 they spent the summer in London and at Osborne. They moved to the Fife Arms at Braemar and commuted daily to Balmoral, a regime which seemed to make Fritz stronger. He contrived a lunch invitation for Mackenzie, who was knighted in the drawing-room on 7 September. Public clamour in Berlin forced them back - but they managed to take in the Tirol, Venice and Lake Maggiore en route. In November 1887 they discovered San Remo on the Italian Riviera, where the Villa Zirio was ideally placed but could not provide even an amelioration of his troubles.

On 9 March 1888 Fritz received a telegram informing him of his father's death. He arrived in Berlin and did not leave it for the period of his short reign. At the beginning he did his best, but was gradually overcome by the cancer. Queen Victoria made a special journey from London to console her dying son-in-law.

Willy, now Wilhelm II, wasted no time in showing who was now boss. His father's funeral was hurried through and a thorough search was made for incriminating papers. Vicky was curtly informed that she must get out of the Friedrichskron palace, and then the Villa Liegnitz. Fortunately she had money of her own and bought an estate of 250 acres in1890, near the Rhine in the forested Taunus. There she built Friedrichshof and lived the life of a country lady in a country house, 200 miles from Berlin, which she visited as rarely as possible and as a painful duty for a few state occasions.

Vicky still loved to travel and, for example, had to be summoned back from Italy to attend the funeral of the other Dowager Empress, Augusta. Again, there was a hurried journey to Greece for the birth of her daughter Sophie's (Queen of Greece) first child. Vicky loved Paris and made a semi-official visit there in 1891. This was a kind of pilgrimage to places her husband had occupied during the siege, but 'her nostalgia got the better of her discretion'. She went to Versailles where the German Empire had been proclaimed and to Saint-Cloud, which had been destroyed by artillery under his command. There was such a storm of chauvinism in the press that she was almost forced to flee to England.

In the period from September 1898 to May 1899 Vicky spent substantial periods of time in London, then Breslau, back to Balmoral, then on to Bordighera on the Italian Riviera for the cold weather, then Florence, then Venice and back to Friedrichshof. When at Balmoral she had learned that she had inoperable spinal cancer and in May she was unable to attend her mother's 80th birthday celebrations in London. In July she learned of the death from cancer of the throat of her brother 'Affie', Duke of Edinburgh and Saxe-Coburg-Gotha. On 22 January 1901 Queen Victoria died at Osborne. Vicky could not leave Friedrichshof, far less travel to England for the funeral. Bertie, the new King, or King-Emperor, to be pedantic, paid her a private visit a week later, to be followed by Queen Alexandra and a string of relatives over the next few months.

Even for the great ones of the time there was little palliative care except for increasing doses of morphia.

> Sentries on duty at Friedrichshof asked to be moved further away, so they could not hear her screams of agony.

The Dowager Empress died on 5 August 1901, with lengthy instructions amounting to no fuss. For once, her son the Kaiser behaved properly and there was a grand funeral at Potsdam, where:

> ...he and Bertie were united in their grief for the sorely-tried mother and sister, and for once nobody could doubt the depth of his feeling as he arranged the wreath on her coffin at the altar and fell to his knees, placing his face in the folds of the pall as he silently broke down.

Was Vicky a Gypsy Empress? Hardly. Like her mother, she travelled a great deal, on official duties - which often merged into family visits - and for pleasure. Often her visits were part of the conventional leisure pattern of the upper crust - Florence, Venice, Paris - but sometimes there was a definite purpose of escape. She took her dying husband to San Remo in an attempt to rehabilitate him, only to have to take him back to Berlin for his imperial ninety-nine days.

Empress Augusta of Schleswig-Holstein (1858-1921)
Kinder, Küche und Kirche

A RICH SUPPLY OF "QUOTABLE QUOTES' was generated by Wilhelm, the 29-year old who succeeded his father as Wilhelm II in the 'Year of the Three Kaisers'. Edward VII, his uncle, said he was 'the most brilliant failure in history'. Martin Kitchen, a most balanced historian, said he:

> ...was highly talented but superficial, a neurotic braggart and romantic dreamer, a militaristic poseur and passionate slaughterer of wild animals, a father of seven children and an enthusiastic womaniser, who was happiest in the exclusive circle of his homosexual and transvestite intimates.

Bismarck, the 'Iron Chancellor' whom many would regard as the architect of the German Empire and who was dumped by the new Kaiser (marked by *Punch* with the famous cartoon 'Dropping the Pilot'), said that Wilhelm wanted every day to be his birthday. Others carried on the jest and said he wanted to be the bride at every wedding, the stag at every hunt, and the corpse at every funeral. My mother, who had Higher German, whose job before she married was foreign correspondent for an Aberdeen shipbuilder, and whose Hamburg pen-pal disappeared about 1938, explained to me that the Kaiser had 'a tucky airm' and that this was the basis for many of his problems. He was always photographed from his good side and the left hand was firmly on the hilt of his sword.

For his birth Queen Victoria sent Dr James Clark to Berlin, where he was joined by two eminent German doctors. Mrs Innocent, the English midwife, forecast trouble but the eminent gynaecological trio were taken by surprise and the birth was bungled. Wilhelm was left with a withered arm - a terrible handicap for one so much in love with things martial and dressing up - and a hatred for everything English, including, as we have seen, his mother. (Yet, as so often happens, his relationship with his grandmother was not at all bad).

An early foretaste of his style of behaviour was given on 10 March 1863, in St George's Chapel, Windsor, at the wedding of the Prince of Wales and Alexandra of Denmark. Fritz was the best man and young

Willy attended in Highland dress. Bored by the service, he drew the dirk from his stocking and threw it on the floor. When his uncles, Arthur, Duke of Connaught (aged twelve) and Leopold, Duke of Albany (aged nine), remonstrated with him, he struck back by biting them in the legs.

The criminal code established in 1871 made male homosexual acts an offence and a series of spectacular trials revealed how close Wilhelm sailed to the wind. His favourite, Prince Philipp zu Eulenberg und Hertefeld (known in the inner circle as 'she') had a gay coterie, many of them close to the Kaiser. Eulenberg was charged with perjury and 'the Kaiser's tottering reputation suffered yet another setback'. At the height of the crisis Wilhelm went off hunting with another friend – Carl Furstenberg.

> During one evening of jollification the worthy chief of the Civil Cabinet, 56-year old Count Dietrich von Hürselen-Haeseler, died of a heart attack while dancing in front of the King-Emperor in a ballerina's tutu. This terpsichorean transvestism was greeted with a mixture of ribald humour and outrage.

In public life he was determined to show who was boss. 'Only one person can be master in the Reich, I cannot tolerate anyone else'. 'I shall destroy anyone who stands in my way'. 'A soldier must be ready to shoot his own parents'. He surrounded himself with cronies and placemen, like many another despot. All this might have been tolerated had he been consistent, but Wilhelm was incapable of ruling effectively. He changed his mind. He rushed in - he was nicknamed 'William the Sudden'. His surface belligerence often melted into sullen acceptance. For half the year he travelled, slept late, spent most of the day at table, or strolling, or in the social whirl. Franz Josef spent his time anchored to his desk, signing every trivial document. Wilhelm frittered his time away. It is no surprise to learn that his generals tried everything possible to keep this militarily incompetent 'supreme warlord' from leading them into battle.

After unification and despite his ministrations, German industry and commerce were booming. Germany acquired an international presence, established colonies and alliances. After Russia's defeat by Japan in 1904, Germany was confirmed as Europe's leading land-based power and began an arms race with Britain. Queen Victoria was very annoyed at German support for the Boers in South Africa, and told Wilhelm so. Other 'incidents' heightened the tension until, in summer 1914, trouble in the Balkans spread and the Great Powers, with varying degrees of eagerness, honoured their treaty obligations, mobilised their armies and joined in the fray.

To his credit, Wilhelm did not enter whole-heartedly into mass conflict. He wanted power and prestige and had hoped to get these by frightening the lesser nations. Instead he had to support Franz Josef's arrogant bullying of Serbia and was persuaded that it was too late to stop the superbly-organised invasion of Belgium. By the end of August 1914 it was already clear that the nations were caught in a trap. There were to be no lightning victories, only deadly attrition. In Britain we see the Battle of the Somme as the extreme of horror, but, in fact, it was a bloody sideshow designed to distract the Germans from their summer-long assault on Verdun.

The Kaiser was the Supreme War Lord, whose name was signed to every order of OHL (*Oberste Heeresleitung,* or Supreme Headquarters). It was obvious, from August 1916, that Germany and Austria could not win the war. Hindenburg and Ludendorff, the heroes of Tannenberg on the Russian front, took over the High Command and the Kaiser was relegated to the background. In the autumn of 1918 Germany collapsed. Their armies were in retreat. The sailors of the great fleet that Tirpitz had built mutinied and the unrest spread to the big cities.

All was confusion. On 9 November Prince Max of Baden jumped the gun in announcing the abdication of the Kaiser. Next day a republic was proclaimed and Wilhelm sought refuge in neutral Holland. An Armistice took effect on 11 November.

In the many metres of learned books on Wilhelmine Germany, Bismarck, and the inevitability of World War I there is scarcely a mention of Augusta of Schleswig-Holstein-Sonderburg-Augustinberg ('Dona') 'a plain, pious, but even-tempered young woman' three months older than young Willy. Like some others of his kind he had been besotted with another, in this case his mother's niece, but she was ruled out because of the 'haemophiliac taint' in the family. When he began to court Dona there was little enthusiasm for his choice. Dona was not aristocratic enough for the Berliners, neither was she pretty or even rich.

Willy's sister Charlotte found her 'silent, uncommunicative, very shy and a poor figure beside her more lively sister'. She was concerned that Willy was 'strangely cool', and showed little affection for her or enthusiasm about the engagement. Fritz thought similarly and thought Willy was 'not truly committed' to the marriage. His mother recalled her own early days and thought that the Berliners had hated her and might therefore take to a

Princess ' bred, born and educated in Germany'.

> More spite, ill-will, backbiting and criticism of the unkindest sort, she
> never can have to endure - than I have gone through for twenty-two
> years.

Kaiser Wilhelm threatened to forbid the marriage, but support
arrived from an unexpected quarter. Dona's father died of cancer early
in 1880 and Bismarck became her advocate. He approved of this simple,
unambitious woman. By now exhausted from ceaseless verbal battles with
Augusta and Vicky he was relieved to find someone who would not be a
challenge and on personal grounds supported Dona:

> ...whose evident lack of cleverness placed her in a different class from
> the regrettable tradition of intelligent Hohenzollern consorts.

Given the treatment Vicky had had at the hands of her mother-in-law, one
might have expected change in the next generation, but this was not to be.
Vicky had a reputation for managing the lives of others, but Dona was not
going to be managed or patronised.

'Ditta' was Vicky's oldest daughter, 'a social butterfly at the head of
Berlin's "smart young things"'. When attempts were made to draw Dona
into the family circle, she was effortlessly upstaged by Ditta, who made no
attempt to conceal her disdain for her slow and stupid sister-in-law. Vicky's
silver wedding was celebrated with a *tableau vivant,* at which Dona missed
a vital cue and shocked with a tight dress which showed off her pregnancy,
her pale face and scarlet arms. Worse, she refused to wear a dress Vicky
had given her. Vicky did try at first to be more welcoming than her mother-
in-law had been, but Dona was having none of it. After the birth of her
first son, Wilhelm, she refused clothes that would have helped her to get
her shape back. Dona's case was that there was no point in trying to get
her shape back only to lose it again, as her husband intended to safeguard
the imperial succession. Crude and cruel, as Vicky had lost two sons.
Acceptance was made with the utmost reluctance.

As Vicky lay dying, five of her children sat at the bedside. Vicky did
not want Dona to stay and she went to Kiel to meet the Kaiser who had
been cruising on his yacht in the North Sea. Publicly he berated her for
leaving Vicky to die alone before rushing off to Berlin to join his siblings.

On the subject of the succession, the Crown Prince (mocked in *Punch* cartoons as 'Little Willie', a chinless wonder) was:

> ...a narrow-chested, willowy creature with the face of a fox who did not at all resemble his five sturdy brothers whom the Empress at annual intervals had presented to her husband.

And no one did more to bring the German Empire to a disastrous end than the husband Dona worshipped.

Life in exile at Doorn was quiet. It is unlikely that Augusta blamed her husband for the agonies of the First World War and the revolt of the German people against their Emperor, but the shock of exile and abdication and the changes in their lifestyle must have had their effect. There was also family trouble. Her sixth child, Joachim (1890-1920) married Princess Marie-Auguste of Anhalt. The marriage broke down, Joachim committed suicide and Augusta collapsed.

Dona was no gypsy. Wilhelm's life was much more than the diplomatic round of official and family engagements. Whether it was escapism or not he had interests which took him off the beaten imperial track. He would have liked a place on the Riviera and in 1904 failed to purchase the Chateau Grimaldi, Dr Bennet's former home, just over the Italian border from Menton. For obvious reasons, his presence so near France would not have been welcome.

Yet Dona in her own way was quite successful. Despite being the second choice and a very mixed blessing socially, she made a nice comfortable life for herself. She did her duty as a bearer of children and it was not her fault that there was nothing, eventually, for them to inherit. In return she had wealth and position.

Here ends the Tale of the Three Empresses, but I cannot resist a postscript, since Hermina Ida Louise Frederick Reuss was such an interesting character. She was the daughter of a minor prince and married a Silesian prince. In 1922 she was a 35-year old widow with five children, one of whom sent the ex-Emperor birthday wishes. In November 1922 Princess Hermine of Reuss and Wilhelm were married at Doorn, after which she was known as the 'Quotation Mark Empress'.

Hermine was a handsome woman, who was never quite accepted by the Hohenzollerns.

> A healthy, good-humoured woman with an easy stride, who does not take too seriously the pompous courtesy titles sometimes proclaimed at

her approach by Netherlandic butlers in the vicinity of Doorn...Actually Princess Hermine is a strictly practical woman who stipulated in her marriage contract that she should be allowed every year a vacation away from the Netherlands - in Germany. (*Time* magazine.)

In 1927 she wrote her memoirs up to that date – *An Empress in exile: My Days in Doorn.*

Wilhelm, of course, was not allowed to dabble in politics, or even to leave the Netherlands. Hermine was therefore very useful and one gets the impression she enjoyed stirring things up. In Berlin she insisted on staying in the old palace of Wilhelm I on Unter den Linden, taking with her from Doorn two of her Mercedes. In the twenties and thirties there was some feeling in Germany for the restoration of the Empire and Hermine busied herself in diplomatic circles. In 1933 she visited Hitler, whom the monarchists thought might favour their cause, and had to face embarrassing questions about financial support of the Nazi party.

Anna Anderson was one of the women who claimed to be Grand Duchess Anastasia of Russia, and probably the most plausible of them.. The old ex-Kaiser Wilhelm II sent Hermine to visit the claimant in a German sanatorium. (One wonders what qualifications Hermine had for the role of private eye). No statement was issued, but from such an august quarter as this, silence was assumed to mean assent.

The marriage lasted almost twenty years. On Wilhelm's death in 1941, Hermine moved back to Silesia. In 1945 the Russians took over her palace and imprisoned her in a camp for displaced persons at Frankfurt an der Oder, where she died in 1947. I think she would have been pleased that she was buried in the Antique Temple of SansSouci in Potsdam, beside the Empress Augusta Victoria, Wilhelm's first wife.

End Notes

1   It is an irritating weakness of some of our most respected historians that they seem unable to differentiate between England and Britain. This is especially true in relation to Victoria and Vicky, to the extent that one can find some passages worse than ambiguous. While original German documents may have used *Englisch* loosely, there is no excuse for a British writer, for example, to lump together Balmoral, Edinburgh and England.

2   Charles Lyell (1797-1875), influential Scottish-born geologist. His *Principles of Geology* (1830 - 12 editions) was read by Darwin on the *Beagle* voyage, and

changed his life. More conservative than Darwin, his advice was valued above all others. Lyell disseminated the principle of Uniformitariaism, that 'the present is the key to the past'. He divided the geological record into time periods, mainly based on fossils.

He was created a Baronet and was buried in Westminster Abbey.

3 A German newspaper story said that Fritz contracted a venereal disease on this Egyptian jaunt, which developed into the throat cancer which killed him. This story has never been substantiated and surely must fall into the same category as the gossip about Queen Victoria's relationship with John Brown – which had the same German source.

4 At the same time as the city was under fire the German artillery was bombarding the ring of forts defending the city. Several of these were put out of action – but at the cost of several hundred Prussian gunners hit by French counter-battery fire.

CHAPTER 8
The Russians

Alexandra Feodorovna, Empress of Russia (1798-1860) Diplomacy in the sunshine

THE CRIMEAN WAR was a mess. Of course, all wars are a mess, but the Crimean out-messed most other wars by a long chalk. The original source of the trouble lay in squabbles between Greek and Latin monks in Palestine as to who should hold the key of the church of Bethlehem, but, stripped of all excuses, the Crimean War was fought to keep Russia out of the Bosphorus. The Russians supported the Greeks while the French, the British and the Sultan of Turkey supported the Latins. Later, Sardinia joined in to secure a place at the peace table.

The Turkish fleet was destroyed at Sinope in the Black Sea. Russia and Turkey fought it out in the Danube Principalities of Moldavia and Wallachia until the Tsar withdrew his troops when Austria threatened to intervene. The war should have ended here, but the flywheel was now turning and could not be stopped. French and British troops and ships had arrived in the area and it was decided that they should be used to capture Sebastopol, the base of the Russian Black Sea Fleet.

'The whole story of the campaign reads more like comic opera than war', writes Major LL Gordon in *British Battles and Medals*. Some comic opera when the British expeditionary force was well supplied with right-footed boots and summer clothing. Lord Cardigan commanded the famous Light Brigade from his yacht *Dryad* lying in Balaklava Bay. After the Charge, Lord George Paget, who coolly rode through the whole affair with a cheroot in his mouth, and thirty-eight other officers, sent in their papers, citing 'Urgent Private Affairs', and fled from the savagery of the Russian winter to London, leaving the troops under their command to starve and freeze.

The British were often dependent on the French leftovers for food. The death rate in the hastily converted hospitals was 88%. Four men died from disease to every one killed by enemy action. The final humiliation came on 8 September 1855 when the French captured the Malakoff, the key to Sebastopol, which was evacuated the next day. The parallel British attack on the Redan failed miserably.

Still the war ground on, with a new tsar, Alexander II, as bloodthirsty from his St Petersburg refuge as his predecessor, repeatedly sending Prince Gorchakov, the man on the spot, letters urging decisive action. The butcher's bill for this so-called comic opera was the longest for any war between Waterloo and the Somme, including the American Civil War. Probably 500,000 Russians died of disease, wounds, starvation and cold - nobody bothered to count them. The French support systems started off well, then collapsed. They may have lost 100,000. We lost 22,000. Even the late-coming Sardinians lost 2,000 while at least as many Ottomans died as French.

Once again, however, Austria intervened, threatening to join the Allies if Alexander refused to accept their demands. On 16 January 1856 the Tsar accepted the four main demands of the Allies, the third being 'Neutralisation of the Black Sea'. This meant that Russia could no longer have a Black Sea Fleet, nor could Russian warships pass through the Dardanelles. What was an aggressively imperialist world power to do?

In October 1856 the *Carlo Alberto*, a three-masted steamship of Victor-Emmanuel II, King of Piedmont-Sardinia and the Tsar's erstwhile enemy, dropped anchor in the bay of Villefranche. A year before, 15,000 Sardinians had been fighting in the Crimea. Now, politics and strategy dictated that Russia must secure a toehold in the Mediterranean and on board was Alexandra Feodorovna, Empress of Russia, at whose disposal Victor-Emmanuel had put his vessel.

Before the 1850s Russians were turning up in small numbers on the Riviera. Gogol, the writer, had a romantic season in Nice with a Countess Vielgorsky from December 1842. Alexander Herzen, author of the bible of nihilism which was to threaten the Tsars for over half a century (*Des idées révolutionnaires en Russie*), was a consumptive exile who moved round Switzerland, London - and Nice, where he was buried. The same forces drew Russians to the Riviera as they did others from northern Europe – the sun, the light, the mildness of the winters. (1) They had even recruited British sailors at Villefranche to train their own. But after 1856 an additional force operated for them, adding a permanent population to the erstwhile winter transients - *les hivernants*.

The Empresses of Russia could scarcely be called gypsies. Rather the opposite since despite their German and Danish Lutheran upbringing they became more Russian than the Russian aristocracy themselves, abandoning their cool and rational origins for all the excesses of an illiberal church and state. Yet, as we shall see, they also joined in the winter movement south, with thousands of their compatriots in their wake.

How Russian were these Empresses with the magnificent names and splendid titles? Alexandra Feodorovna and Marie Alexandrovna were German princesses, respectively Charlotte of Prussia and Maria of Hesse. Dagmar of Denmark (younger sister of Alexandra, who married the Prince of Wales, to become Queen Alexandra and Empress of India) became the 'sad fiancée' of Nicholas, the half-German eldest son of Alexander II. When the Tsarevich died in 1864 at the age of 21, she married his brother, Alexander, changing her name (to Maria Feodorovna) and religion when he became Alexander III. Thus the offspring of this union (the oldest of whom was to become Tsar Nicholas II) were half Danish, a quarter German and only a quarter Russian.

My own experience of the Russians at play abroad is limited to the second and third acts of Johann Strauss's *Die Fledermaus* in which Prince Orlofsky gives a party to which all the principal characters are invited. *Fledermaus* is a light-hearted study in deception, in which no-one is quite what he or she appears to be. Orlofsky is immensely rich, young and awkward. His part is usually sung by a contralto - on my recording the magnificently-named Birgitte Fassbender - much better than Cooper! He welcomes everyone to his party, saying they should enjoy themselves - '*chacun à son goût*' - at the same time telling them that, if they do not drink in time with him, he will throw a bottle at their heads. Properly sung, there is a real undercurrent of menace when Orlofsky holds the stage.

As the party proceeds Eisenstein makes a fool of himself by imagining that a beautiful stranger is his wife's maid (which she is). She mocks him publicly by asking him (*Mein Herr Marquis*) how someone with such beautiful arms as she could be a lady's maid? His wife pretends to be a Hungarian countess and brilliantly sings a czardas of her homeland. (This is the number of which Andre Previn said, on being asked how he would like to die, if he had a choice: 'conducting Kiri Te Kanawa singing *Klänge der Heimat*'). Eisenstein then tries to seduce her (his wife!), losing his watch in the process. Orlofsky leads a sparkling number in praise of champagne, which flows freely. To a languorous slow waltz everyone embraces everyone else, swearing eternal brotherhood and sisterhood. 'Coherent expression seems out of place'. From using the familiar *Du*: 'In their efforts to do justice to the toast, they resort to "Duidu" and "la, la, la'". Then silence is broken as Orlofsky brings in the ballet dancers, then challenges the partygoers to do better with the luscious *Fledermaus* waltz. The clock strikes six, Eisenstein goes off to jail, the guests help each other from the stage and the curtain comes down.

Act 3 takes place in jail. Adèle, the maid, has ambitions and demonstrates how good an actress she is in three stunning songs, as a simple country girl, a Queen and as a French Marquise with a young lover. In the closing moments - a reprise of the toast to King Champagne - Frank, the prison governer, who sees himself becoming the protector of Adèle, finds himself gently pushed aside as Orlofsky takes her under his wing. All froth and nonsense, of course, but there must be a grain of recognisable truth in there for it to have been acceptable to a Viennese audience in 1874.

Of the Russians at home it was said, in 1890:

Foreign observers noted a carnival atmosphere among the crowds at St Petersburg dances and receptions, a spirited gaiety that distinguished the high-born Russians from the decorous, ponderous Germans or the homely albeit ceremonious British. The Russians had style, bravado, dash; their mansions, their clothing, their banquets, the very livery of their servants had a splendour that was almost gaudy by comparison with the high society of Western capitals. It was, in part, a lavishness of scale; everything in Russia was large, in keeping with the vast land itself - the fortunes, the aristocratic estates, the style of living. Extravagance and profligacy, among the aristocratic class, were all but taken for granted.

When this brilliant society fled the ferocious winter of Russia for the mild sunshine of the Riviera it is not surprising that the relaxed warmth of the south released further displays of hedonism, where they would not be under the scrutiny of judgmental do-gooders. In this they were not entirely successful. Among the crowds of servants and other hangers-on were anarchists like Herzen and other dangerous plotters. (1)

The attraction of Villefranche for the Empress had little to do with the climate and much to its status as the best natural harbour along the Mediterranean coast of what is now France. From Genoa to the mouths of the Rhone the mountains tip straight into the sea. A counter-clockwise current cleans out the bays and moves sediment westwards. West of the Rhone its deposits are spread along a coast of sandbars and lagoons, where former ports, like Aigues-Mortes, are silted up or new artificial ports must be created.

Villefranche is, quite simply, the best anchorage in the 300 miles between Genoa and Marseille, being deep and quite well-protected by headlands. Today it is the main destination for cruise ships, from which fleets of tenders land tourists who take the train along the coast to Nice, Monaco and Menton. As early as the 16th century it had an international importance. A famous meeting was arranged between the Emperor Charles V and Francis I of France. Unfortunately, the ship prepared for the meeting was grossly overloaded with decorations and signalling guns. The crowds of representatives were similarly overloaded and as they processed on to the ship and the saluting guns began to fire it began to sink at its moorings. Imperial and royal dignity suffered as the grand assembly found itself awash up to the knees and protocol was abandoned in the scramble for the quayside.

Villefranche was more than a safe anchorage. In the eighteenth century the Counts of Savoy added breakwaters, an impressive citadel and all the infrastructure of a port and naval base – ropeworks, warehouses, even one of the world's first dry docks. Sailing vessels, like Nelson's navy, could spend many months afloat without ever touching land but galleys were still used in the Mediterranean. Accordingly, in the Darse at Villefranche there are still the rows of barracks where the motive power of the galleys - slaves and prisoners - were kept between voyages.

So Alexandra Feodorovna, Empress of Russia emerged from her cabin to savour the mild October air and admire the ochre walled town of Villefranche piled up against the mountain slopes. She had never been a beauty and at fifty-eight looked ten years older. She was worn out by the journey and was unwilling to submit herself to the rigours of a grand processional entrance to Nice. But she was to be the first of many great lady visitors to the Riviera and was persuaded to show herself in an open carriage, preceded by an escort of carabiniers and followed by seventeen coaches filled with local dignitaries and members of her suite. The baggage train followed, over the recently made-up road.

On the Promenade des Anglais in Nice the recent war was forgotten. The welcome was triumphal. The tiredness and ill-temper of the Empress vanished. A dawn fanfare aroused the crowd. A delegation of ladies presented her with an enormous bouquet. The Empress was touched. She spoke to the ladies in French, asking them about their activities, telling them of the pleasures of being a grandmother, enquiring about the economic situation of the town. She was anxious to choose which vases in which to set the various flowers she had received. In a few minutes her audience was eating out of her hand and Nice had adopted her as *'son impératrice'*.

Charlotte of Prussia was nineteen when she married Nicholas I, her senior by only two years. The young Nicholas bore no resemblance to his ancestor Ivan the Terrible; he was a romantic who read Goethe and played the piano rather well. The young couple brought together the two nations of Prussia and Russia, both worn out by the wars against Napoleon. As Tsar, Nicholas was hardened by having to deal with uprisings and an attempt to depose him. His energy was inexhaustible. As well as 'numerous examples of unacceptable conjugal behaviour', he was responsible for seven Imperial pregnancies. Yet Alexandra Feodorovna realised that she had made a real love match! As Astolphe de Custine wrote in *Lettres de Russie:*

> He watches after her, prepares her drinks, insists she swallows them like a nurse; when she is back on her feet again he kills her with hustle and bustle, holidays, trips, with love.

Just before his death in 1855 Nicholas wrote to his wife:

> If I am sometimes demanding, it is because I look for everything in you: happiness, joy, repose…I would have liked to have made you a hundred times happier…

Nevertheless, both had a strong sense of duty and Alexandra Feodorovna supported her husband despite his occasionally misplaced energy. In 1856 she was, strictly speaking, the Dowager Empress but she was an eminently suitable negotiator for her country.

In her 'free' time in Nice she set the pattern for later noble visitors to the Riviera. Her presence was the big event of the season. The newspapers reported her every move and listed those from the *Almanach de Gotha* who came to call on her. She liked to walk on the coastal road, armed with a black-and-white umbrella to protect her pale northern skin from the autumn sun. Some bold young people came very close, just to see what an empress looked like and the municipality had to pass an ordinance forbidding people from importuning the wintering empress. In view of later events on the Riviera it is interesting to note that this anxiety about security did not come from Alexandra Feodorovna. Far from St Petersburg she found any slight deficiencies in Nice insignificant.

On this first visit she lived in the Villa Avigdor, on the Promenade des Anglais. Abraham Avigdor was the banker responsible for the affairs of the Russians along the coast and, looking ahead to her grandson's persecution of the Jews a generation later, was clearly perfectly acceptable to the Empress.

She was almost happy, surrounded by her children, some grandchildren and her sister-in-law, of whom she was very fond, in spite of her progressive ideas, and who had rented a villa in the town. They made excursions into the countryside around. They climbed the hill of Cimiez, to the Franciscan monastery. (By the end of the century Cimiez had become a very high-class suburb indeed). They went on trips in a little boat of the Sardinian navy, usually landing in a bay or on an island and climbing to the nearest hill or shrine. Off Cannes, on the Île Sainte-Marguerite they distributed food and tobacco to Arabian prisoners from the war in Algeria. At the end of their visit twelve of the prisoners were set free as a result of the Tsarina's intercession. Everyone praised her humanity.

Alexandra Feodorovna's presence had revealed so many Russians in the area that she devised a grand project - Nice needed to have an Orthodox church. The municipality agreed. Alexandra bought a plot of land and brought in an architect from Moscow to start the work. With him was an Orthodox priest who blessed the foundations and terrified the local children with his unkempt beard, long moustache and immense black headgear.

Meanwhile, diplomatic progress was being made. On 1 March 1857 Grand-Duke Constantin sailed into Villefranche at the head of a little Russian squadron. As if by chance, Victor-Emmanuel also arrived to pay his respects to the Empress. His main preoccupation was the unification of Italy and the guarantee of Russian neutrality if and when there was confrontation with Austria-Hungary, which had received the Venetian republic, the duchy of Milan and other cities in the Po valley at the Congress of Vienna. He therefore offered the Russian admiral the port of Villefranche as a base for a Russian fleet, with the port buildings as storage for equipment and coal.

The Russian crews astounded the Villefranche people by their giant stature and their inextinguishable thirst, often ending in drunken brawls. Anger succeeded astonishment when the body was found of a sailor who had been beaten to death by corporal punishment. A delegation took up the matter with the Tsarina, who took it up with her son, Alexander II, who rapidly issued an ukase that all corporal punishment in the armies must cease.

In spring 1857 her daughter-in-law, Grand-Duchess Helen Pavlovna, took a notion to start sea-bathing - till then unknown on the Riviera, where the sea was where fish were caught. Wooden bathing-machines enabled ladies to make the transition from land to sea and to bathe in complete modesty. Another brick was added to the leisure edifice of the Côte d'Azur!

Alexandra Feodorovna returned to Russia as the days lengthened. Her health was much improved. Her children had had a marvellous holiday in the sunshine. Her diplomatic mission had been successful. She promised to return.

She kept her word. In 1859 she returned, the last stage of her journey being by the steamer *Svetlana* from Marseille to Villefranche. This time she stayed at the Villa De Orestis, belonging to the Countess De Orestis, whose maiden name (Tihatchef) betrayed her Russian origin. The Orthodox church was now completed. At its inauguration more turned up than could be accommodated within it, although Alexandra Feodorovna herself was unable to attend. Politically, the situation was delicate. Victor-Emmanuel was on the point of handing over to Napoleon III of France the County of Nice, in exchange for his support in helping Italian unification. The people of Nice were in a ferment – for or against annexation? What would happen to the Russian base? Who would guarantee the security of the Empress? The departing Sardinians? The municipal guard of Nice? Napoleon gallantly stepped in and provided a company of Zouaves, the colourful colonial infantry from Algeria. All was well and the good folks of Nice voted the right way when they had their chance of a referendum.

An exhausted Alexandra Feodorovna was taken back to St Petersburg to die six months later. Her last acts in Nice were to contribute generously to the Holy Cross hospital, the local savings bank and to the needy. The local notables received gifts and the future of the Russian church was assured. Her visits to the Riviera and the succeeding Russian influx had given a new impetus to tourism and to the local economy, in addition to the benefits brought by the presence of the Russian fleet.

Marie Alexandrovna, Tsarina of Russia (1824-1880), An inconsolable *mater dolorosa*

THE RUSSIAN ORTHODOX cathedral in Nice is a splendidly polychromatic mass which erupts upwards in a cluster of onion domes. Over to one side, at the edge of the extensive property, is a slightly decayed little chapel with a disintegrating plaque which tells us that, on the very spot where the altar now stands, was the funeral couch on which died on 12 April 1865, at the age of 21, Nicolas Alexandrovich, eldest son of Emperor Alexander II. It tells us also that the chapel was consecrated on 26 March 1869.

Marie Alexandrovna, his Tsarina mother, was devastated and spent the rest of her life sorrowing for him and for the lost love of her husband. For her the Riviera was changed from a place for family pleasures to a morbid misery.

The nineteenth century Tsars showed a refreshing originality in their choice of brides. Not for them the Hapsburg way of marrying land

FIG 7 *Here lay the body of the Grand Duke Nicholas*

or making dynastic alliances. The Tsars and Russia were big enough to go their own way, they could marry whom they willed - so long as they were of royal blood and converted to the Russian Orthodox church. The young Alexander toured the courts of Europe in search of a bride worthy of him. At their first encounter he fell for Marie of Hesse, a fifteen-year-old blonde with turquoise eyes, with all the sparkle of youth. There was some ambiguity about her birth - she was the outcome of an adulterous relationship of the Grand Duchess of Hesse - but this did not seem to upset Alexander's father.

Alexander proved to be an active Tsar, celebrated as the liberator of the serfs. He abolished corporal punishment in the forces, reorganised the administration, education and the law, while fighting always on two fronts - against the reactionaries and the nihilists. Marie Alexandrovna was thirty-five before she became acquainted with the south of France. By that time she had had eight pregnancies and the most recent birth had been very difficult. She was so anaemic that her doctors feared for her life and forbade further intercourse. 'What a relief!' says Martine Gasquet in *Les Femmes à la Belle Époque*. No longer need she fear the huge silhouette drawing aside the curtain of the bedchamber; not the act itself, but its terrible consequences. Her mother-in-law, Alexandra Feodorovna, had for so long sung the praises of the Mediterranean coast - its beauty, its perpetual spring, the kindness of its people, its marvellous gardens, the relaxed protocol - that the Tsarina decided there was no better place for a family holiday, where Alexander could join in and earn his pardon for causing her so much suffering.

On 21 October 1864 the Imperial party arrived at Nice by the newly opened railway. On a miserably wet day the Tsar demonstrated the private nature of the visit by wearing civilian dress, while the Tsarina must have looked quite special enveloped in a large white cashmere cloak. The assembled crowd saluted the 'liberating Tsar'. Alexandra Feodorovna had recommended the Villa Peillon, one of the biggest and finest of the Nice villas, with frescoes and a theatre, with gardens, a Chinese aviary and glasshouses, complete with bananas. 'A terrestrial paradise', says Gayraud.

Napoleon III paid a visit to welcome the party to France, cementing good relations between their countries while strolling round the grounds with Alexander. For two days the eyes of Europe were fixed on Nice. Alexander indulged in a frenzy of activity, reviewing French troops, visiting barracks, questioning the soldiers about their daily routine and maintaining regular contact with the Tuileries in Paris. Napoleon and Marie Alexandrovna took tea together, she dressed magnificently for various official functions and Napoleon, unprepossessing but with a way with the ladies, invited her to dance at the Prefecture ball. A splendid start to her holiday, away from the formality and spite of the Russian court.

But this was a tricky time, politically speaking. Napoleon left. Alexander played with his children for a few days, then returned to St Petersburg. Next to the Villa Peillon was the Villa Bermond, linked by a suspension bridge and even more splendid than Peillon. The daughter-in-law of Empress Alexandra Feodorovna, Grand-Duchess Helen Pavlovna, had appeared on the Riviera at the same time as the Empress led her diplomatic mission to Villefranche. The Grand-Duchess took Bermond for two spells when she made it the highest point of Riviera society, but also opened it up to the locals with a fireworks display and an open air ball attended by thousands. A refreshed Marie and her entourage now moved into Bermond to await the arrival of her eldest son, Nicholas.

The Villa Bermond was one of the oldest villas (c1820) on the Côte. Four storeys high and with four pavilions around it, it was also one of the biggest. At 19 hectares, the park around it was the biggest agricultural holding in Nice, with ten thousand fruit and olive trees. The greenhouses, if placed end to end, would have measured four kilometres and were filled with bananas, sugar cane and cotton plants. The villa had its own stables, a piggery and an oil mill employing twenty sharecroppers.

The expected 21-year-old Tsarevich Nicholas was refined, intelligent and fragile, so fragile. As part of his training to be a sovereign he toured Europe, visiting friendly courts and examining the latest inventions and industrial processes - in which he had a genuine interest.

After a fall from his horse he was slow to recover. The doctors talked of rheumatism and were reassuring. The Empress continued to worry. In Denmark Nicholas became engaged to Marie Dagmar, daughter of Christian IX, then moved to Nice, to the sumptuous Villa Diesbach. Every day mother and son met for excursions to the hill country in a landau, for the exotic spectacle of the olive harvest. Despite the tranquillity Nicholas was tortured by every bump in the road. He suffered terrible pains in his back. He was compelled to leave his villa and move to Bermond, where his mother could look after him. Soon he was unable to stand upright. He reviewed a parade from a wheelchair. He was confined to bed, and in a fever. On Easter Sunday he could not attend Mass, nor receive the compliments and embraces of his family. During the night he became paralysed down the right side.

Doctor Zdekauer, summoned from Moscow, diagnosed cerebro-spinal meningitis. The Empress did not leave his bedside. Marie Dagmar hastened from Denmark to be by him and to support his mother. He noticed his brother Alexander and asked him to: 'Come quickly and embrace me'. According to one authority he had Alexander and Dagmar brought to his bedside, where he insisted that they should marry after his death. Alexander II arrived by special train from St Petersburg - a journey of 85 hours.

The funeral cortege was headed by the Tsar and Alexander, now Tsarevich, followed by French cavalry and marines, Cossacks of the Russian Imperial Guard, infantry of the French Imperial Guard, and a huge crowd. Mass was held in the little church in Nice. The body was put on the frigate *Alexander Nevski* at Villefranche and taken to Cronstadt, while the family returned to St Petersburg.

Marie Alexandrovna retreated into a solitude surrounded by holy icons. Her only wish was to weep and pray and repent of her sins which must have been so great because of the ways in which God had punished her, while Alexander (at 48) found himself a new happiness three times a week with 18-year-old Catherine Dolgourouki, with whom he started a new family.

The Empress swore never to return but Dagmar ('the sad fiancée') helped her with a new project - a memorial devoted to the memory of the late Nicholas. Alexander proposed to buy the Villa Bermond but Bermond was disinclined to give up such a lucrative property. Eventually he was persuaded into selling the villa and 15,000 square metres of the land. Some of the buildings were demolished to make room for the commemorative Byzantine chapel, 20 metres high and dedicated in 1869, complete with the plaque with which we came in. (The rump of the Bermond land was divided up and then sold in 1899. The luxury Hôtel du Parc Impérial was built, only to be converted into a lycée after the First World War).

The Church of Saint-Nicolas and Sainte-Alexandra in the Rue Longchamp in central Nice was by now far too small for the Russian colony so Tsar Nicholas and the Dowager Empress had the Villa Bermond demolished and a splendid new cathedral built (PLATE 5A), to be officially opened and dedicated in 1912.

Almost a century later, it was at the centre of some controversy. Just before the work was complete Nicholas gave the bishop of St Petersburg - who would be responsible for the operation of the cathedral - a 99-year lease on the building. This lease expired on 31 December 2007. In February 2006 a bailiff, sent by the Russian Embassy in Paris, appeared, with the intention of listing the assets and furnishings of the cathedral. A churchwarden of the religious association managing the church shut the door in the bailiff's face. In November the Russian Federation came back with a demand for the contents, the building itself and 3000 square metres of land in the high-class Tsarevich quarter of Nice.

Moscow's argument, relayed through Paris, was logical. The French Republic had recognised that the USSR was the successor to the Russian Empire. At the collapse of communism France had recognised the Russian Federation as the successor to the USSR. Therefore the Russian state was within its rights in taking back the land and the building.

For the locals, Alexis Obolensky established that, under French law, a murderer could not inherit from his victim. In addition, the land and Villa Bermond belonged personally to the Emperor and it was therefore Monsieur Nicolas Romanov who had transferred the property to the Russian community, and not Nicholas II, Tsar of Russia.

The decision of the tribunal was to award the property to the Russian state, arousing some popular feeling in Nice. Peevishly, the *Nice-Matin* wondered whether the Russian state would take the cathedral, stone by stone, back to Russia. And would the Americans take back the *Quai des Etats-Unis?* And what about the *Promenade des Anglais?*

To come back to our narrative, the Empress did return, fifteen years after her son's death. In 1874 she was persuaded to winter in San Remo, on the Italian Riviera, and from October 1879 till January 1880 she took the Villa Des Dunes in Cannes. The billiard room was converted into an office. Two rooms were made into a boudoir and another two into a private chapel.

'The visit of the Empress did not pass unnoticed' says Gayraud, ironically. The Imperial train of twelve coaches ornamented with the Imperial coat-of-arms pulled into the station at Cannes as the Mediterranean squadron pounded out a hundred-gun salute. Seventeen coaches were required to transport the Empress, her two sons, her doctors, her pharmacist, the Court equerry, the arch-priest, priests and choristers, her hairdresser, her chamberlain, her chef, footmen and various other servants. Nine railway wagons followed with the baggage and Imperial wardrobe. Around Des Dunes various other houses and apartments were rented to accommodate others in her train.

During her stay the Empress received a stream of dignitaries and nobles, local and from the courts of Europe. She also invited humbler visitors, like the flower-sellers of Nice. She felt well enough to organise several receptions, notably the presentation of gifts to her entourage around the Christmas tree and at the Russian New Year. She made the usual excursions and received a special dispensation from Pope Leo XIII to visit the monastery of Saint-Honorat, normally forbidden to women. It is likely that she visited the chapel in Nice but I have been unable to find any record of this.

In view of what was to happen in St Petersburg in 1894, it is not surprising that the Empress's presence in Cannes posed a security problem for the local authorities. A few weeks before her arrival known anarchists and dissidents were swept up and expelled from the area. Twenty policeman were continually on duty in the villa and its grounds.

Maria's health - the excuse for her visit - had not improved and she began to plan for the return to St Petersburg. She picked up an old copy of the *Journal du Littoral,* left in a reception room, knowing that it would not contain good news. (One cannot believe that, in a well-conducted *ménage,* such a document was left lying around by chance). The newspaper contained an explicit account of Alexander's exploits back in St Petersburg and his 'conjugal life' with Catherine Dolgourouki, with whom he was now living shamelessly. To the Countess Tolstoy she said: 'I can pardon the offences he inflicted on the sovereign, I cannot take it upon myself to pardon the tortures he has inflicted on the spouse'.

Broken, in every sense, she returned to Russia, where she died three months later, on 9 June 1880. God had abandoned her. She could fight no longer. She could only wish that He would reunite her with her son Nicholas. In a final display of insensitivity Alexander, impatiently awaiting her death, asked her to bless his children born out of wedlock!

As she lay dying in the palace, almost alone, her last moments were disturbed by the clatter of the feet of the Imperial bastards, whose quarters were in the floor above.

Martine Gasquet sums up Marie Alexandrovna very well: 'Decidedly, she had been spared nothing'.

Maria Feodorovna, Dowager Empress of Russia (1847-1929)
Sad *Fiancée* and Dowager Empress

DAGMAR IS ONE of my favourite names. Had my third child been a girl she would have been christened Dagmar. She would have been blonde, cool, beautiful and intelligent – everything a woman should be, but in a self-confident understated way. It is not surprising, therefore, that I approach Dagmar of Denmark in a positive frame of mind.

Her father, King Christian IX (1818-1906), in his long life presided over a changing nation. Denmark had been quite a substantial power controlling access to the Baltic till it made the mistake of siding with Napoleon. Nelson destroyed the Danish fleet and fortresses. In 1863 Bismarck's Prussia flexed its muscles by destroying the Danish army and annexing Schleswig and Holstein. Yet, by the end of the century, Bishop Grundtvig's 'mission statement' - 'Few people with too little and even fewer with too much'. - was beginning to win through. As Van Loon said of Denmark in 1933 - in a world deep in recession: 'while few people have three overcoats, none go without'.

Dagmar - commonly known as 'Minnie' - was the fourth child of Christian IX. The eldest succeeded as Frederick VIII of Denmark. Alexandra married the Prince of Wales, later Edward VII. Thus she became Queen Alexandra and Empress of India. Brother William was elected by the Greek National Assembly George I of Greece in 1863, at the age of seventeen, avoiding assassination for almost fifty years. (2)

We have seen how Dagmar was engaged to Nicholas, the Tsarevich, and when he became seriously ill, hastened to his side in order to nurse him and support the Empress. The support became friendship which lasted until the latter's death on 9 June 1880. On his death bed Nicholas blessed the union of Dagmar and his brother Alexander. Dagmar became again a fiancée of the heir to the crown of Russia, a condition that was to last seven years, until they were married and Dagmar had adopted a new name and a new religion.

Forty days after the death of his Empress Alexander II married Catherine Dolgourouki. She and Dagmar were to fight a long campaign as

Catherine sought to regularise her position in society. Dagmar refused to forgive her for her loose behaviour - and excluded her. The future Alexander III was more amenable. He was happy to see his father's happiness and thought that his mother's love for his brother and her grief were overdone. Yet he allowed his oldest son to be named Nicholas.

The happiness proved to be short-lived. On 1 March 1881 the Tsar was returning to the Winter Palace in St Petersburg when his coach was ambushed. When he got out to attend to the wounded lying in the street a second bomber threw another bomb at his feet and he was ripped apart. This was the sixth assassination attempt he had faced. Ironically, earlier in the day he had signed a new constitutional order which would have brought in some kind of representative government. The order died with his murder. His son, now Alexander III, who watched him die, was not going to tolerate terrorists or revolutionaries. He would be a stern, if loving, father to the Russian people.

Alexander III had many attractive features. He was big - six feet four inches tall - and intimidatingly strong. His exploits were the stuff of reminiscence. His style was simple, that of the Russian landowner who loved everything Russian. He wore the peasant uniform of blouse and boots. His shirts were patched. After his father's death he moved the administration to Gatchina, a garrison town and summer resort an hour by train from St Petersburg. The Gatchina Palace was as magnificent as any palace could be, but Alexander located himself, his family and his core staff in the Arsenal, an adjoining quadrangle and ate and slept in rooms which had been intended as staff quarters.

> An Emperor who washed in cold water, wore patched clothing and had a boiled egg for breakfast, was not likely to find fault with a nursery regime in which jam on the bread at tea-time was presented as a treat.

In these Spartan conditions he devoted himself to directing the progress of his country towards parity with the industrialised West, not the least of his achievements being to keep Russia at peace for his thirteen year reign. His main precept was to preserve the foundations of the family and the state and he showed a good example by having a happy marriage and being a marvellous family man with his many children.

Like many a big man, Alexander doted on his dainty wife. Dagmar had come from a modest court but with her change of name and religion came a change in lifestyle. She preferred the splendid marble of the Anichov Palace in the Nevsky Prospekt in St Petersburg. She dressed beautifully and covered herself in magnificent jewellery. Her mission was to charm all who met her - and she succeeded. She loved dancing and her appearance at Winter Palace balls was a blaze of glory, crown jewels, diamonds and all. No gypsy she! Although she did travel a great deal and clocked up a fair amount of time in Cannes and Nice, heading up the Russian colony. She visited Queen Victoria at the Hotel Regina, making sure that Catherine Dolgourouki, by now Princess Yourievski, would not be invited to tea.

Alexander would have preferred to have worked at his desk, but could deny his wife nothing. He attended events, morosely, and did his best to be gracious, while fidgeting to be off, on occasion turning off the lights himself when the ball had gone on too long to suit him.

In one respect, out of a misplaced patriotism, Alexander did his country a great disservice. There were four million Jews in Russia. What to do with them? The Jews are a most irritating people. They see themselves as a chosen people, which means the rest of us - even Christian Emperors - must be (in Jewish eyes) their inferiors. They attach enormous importance to their holy books and the law, which means that they have developed great experience in nit-picking and advocacy. Thus, David Daiches (1912-2005), son of an Edinburgh rabbi, described in *Two Worlds: An Edinburgh Jewish Childhood* how, on a late Saturday afternoon in winter, he was sent out to find a Gentile who would come in and light the gas lamps for the family. Saturday was the Sabbath, the Sabbath was to be kept holy, presumably turning on a light was work, and therefore an unholy act, but it was acceptable to God for a Jew to implicate a non-Jew in an unholy act. And was it not work to persuade a passing Gentile to do this small act? And there are so many legalistic jokes, many of them wryly told by Jews themselves.

Yet the qualities in Jews that irritate us - their forensic abilities and entrepreneurial skills - are the same qualities that help them to achieve an influence in society out of all proportion to their numbers. Jews comprise about 0.02% of the world's population, yet they have received 129 Nobel Prizes, many more than countries with massive populations. As Ray Soweto writes in *The New Dawn*:

> The Jewish Religion Men would no doubt like to attribute the achievements of their people to Old Testament teaching and studying of the Torah. The fact is that almost all the outstanding Jewish composers,

musicians, writers and scientists, understandably, rejected their traditional religion.

To go back to *Belles Demeures en Riviera, 1835-1930*, it is quite astonishing to see how many extremely rich Jewish people owned villas on the Côte d'Azur in the 1890s, and how, earlier, Alexandra Feodorovna had been happy to use a Russian Jew's villa in Nice. (A recent example. Mrs Thatcher's Cabinet at one point had seven members who had been born into the Jewish faith).

Jews have a long history of being regarded as dissidents within a Christian state and of being a convenient pressure valve for popular tension. Alexander was determined to create a Russian nation out of disparate elements and to stamp his authority on it. Among the nihilists and revolutionaries were many clever Jews, while among the mass of poor Jews were many who found it difficult to reconcile their allegiance to God with the demands of a militaristic theocracy. The Jews were a vast, under-utilised store of intellect, energy and cohesiveness.

Alexander treated this resource by bringing back state anti-Semitism and the pogrom. Tens of thousands of potentially highly enterprising people fled or were driven out of Russia. Britain, the United States and other liberal countries benefited enormously from this influx, initially of cheap labour and then, as they matured in their new surroundings, of high intellect. (3)

Alexander III should have learned from history, and especially from the example of Louis XIV, 'the Sun King'. Henri of Navarre (1553-1610), a Protestant, converted to Catholicism in order to become Henri IV of France, one of their best kings. As he said: *'Paris vaut bien une messe'* - Paris is well worth a mass. He did not abandon his fellow-believers, introducing a measure in 1598 - The Edict of Nantes - which guaranteed religious tolerance. Louis XIV, Henri's grandson, was a good dancer in his youth. Otherwise he had little to recommend him, almost bankrupting his wealthy country through costly building programmes and foreign wars. Louis ditched a fleshly mistress in favour of his children's pious former governess, who was pious enough to have her adultery condoned by the Jesuits, who proceeded to manipulate the King through her.

1685 saw the Revocation of the Edict of Nantes and the beginning of the persecution of the Huguenots. (The same year saw, in Britain, the intensification of the persecution of the Covenanters by James VII and II, begun under Charles II). Billeting of troops, confiscations and judicial murders forced many Protestants (perhaps 400,000) to flee to Britain, Prussia, the Netherlands, Switzerland, the French colony of Canada and the Cape of Good Hope in southern Africa. The Huguenots were thoroughly imbued with the Protestant work ethic and were wealthy, industrious and innovative. They were a great loss to France while many industries and work practices new to Britain and these other countries came with the Huguenots.

Ironically, Alexander III gave to his Empress on Easter Sunday 1885 a jewelled enamelled egg, which opened to reveal a golden 'yolk', complete with hen. The Imperial couple were delighted and the presentation of ever-more-elaborate and costly jewelled eggs became an annual Easter tradition, continued by Nicholas II. The irony was that the eggs were produced in the workshops of one Carl Fabergé, the descendant of one of Louis' persecuted Huguenots. A total of 50 Fabergé eggs was presented to the Imperial family, of which 46 are known to survive, useless symbols of a degrading and tyrannical regime.

Alexander II and Alexander III make us wonder about the mysterious workings of heredity. Both the first-borns were rather weak and weedy, while the subsequent sons were good physical specimens with strong characters. The doctor who brought Alexander III's Nicholas into the world thought he should be shot and as the child grew into manhood he proved to be rather unsatisfactory, as the perfect Imperial family began to crumble. His father had little respect for him and Carolly Erickson suggests that he was all but prevented by his father from preparing for his future role as tsar. His education was poor and he lived:

> ...the feckless life of a young officer with very light military duties, staying out too late at night, drinking too much, whiling away his days socializing and his nights in dining, gambling and flirting.

When he was seventeen Alexandra of Hesse-Darmstadt had been smitten by him, but Alexander and Dagmar found her unsuitable and Alexander decided it was time for his son (at twenty-two) to have a mistress. Matilda Kchessinsky was a rising star at the Imperial Ballet School and after two years 18 English Prospekt, a two-storey house owned by Rimsky-Korsakov, was rented for them in her name. (4) Nicholas was besotted by her until, in 1894, his parents came round to Alexandra and Matilda had to go. (The Empress did try to block an appearance by Matilda in a new ballet at the Bolshoi). Neither Kchessinsky's love life nor her career suffered by her association with the Tsarevich. In the chapter on *Belles Demeures* she - by then Princess Krassinsky-Romanovsky - figures as the owner of the Villa Alam. Alexandra, who was to be so difficult in the matter of changing her religion, showed a remarkable tolerance in welcoming back her errant Nicholas.

The death of Alexander in 1894, at the age of forty-nine, came as a shock. He had always enjoyed superb health. He was huge, strong, and seemingly indestructible. Yet his health weakened, he collapsed in September and his unready heir, Nicholas had only a matter of weeks to condition himself to the task of ruling the vast and chaotic Russian empire.

The Dowager Empress

WITH THE DEATH of Alexander, Maria Feodorovna's life entered a new phase. She had become Tsarina at the age of 34. She had been Tsarina for 13 years. Now, her son had become Tsar Nicholas II and had married Alexandra of Hesse-Darmstadt ('The Funeral Bride') 25 days later, making her his Tsarina. Maria Feodorovna was now the Dowager Empress and was to be such for 34 years - giving her life a nice symmetrical touch.

Her first year of widowhood was full of family incident. Alexander III died on 1 November 1894 and his son Nicholas immediately became Emperor. A week after his father's funeral, on 26 November, Nicholas married Princess Alexandra. The coronation took place in May 1896 when, perhaps significantly, Nicholas on a white horse led the procession of soldiers, bands and notables, the gilded carriage of the Dowager Empress immediately followed by that of the new Empress.

Maria Feodorovna was to play a dual role as Dowager Empress. Although she was still young and active, she was now the head of an important family full of complexes and all at a difficult age (Nicholas 26, George 23, Xenia 19, Michael 16, and Olga 12).

Nicholas was a model family man, with all the domestic virtues, but, as in many another family, his wife and his mother did not see eye to eye. As a ruler he was inept, with the capacity for doing the wrong thing - or nothing - in any crisis.

Grand Duke George Aleksandrovich has made little impact on history. As a child he outshone his older brother, but he was consumptive and he spent most of his time in the Caucasus where it was hoped the mountain air and the smell of the pines would prolong his life. That issue went unresolved as he was found, one day in 1899, lying dying beside his motorbike, leaving Michael as heir presumptive.

Despite the example of Catherine the Great (another German) Paul I in the eighteenth century - who hated his mother - had ruled that no woman could take the crown. Therefore Xenia, like Nicholas's four lovely girls in the next generation, could not succeed. She was unhappily married to her second cousin ('Sandro') and, having borne him seven children, discovered that he was keeping a pretty young American as his mistress. At Biarritz (not the Riviera!) he planned to elope with her to Australia and buy a farm near Sydney! Sandro confessed all to Xenia, who got her own back by taking a lover for herself, the married 'Prince F', whose identity has never been established. She remained on good terms with her mother and helped to bring about a reconciliation between the Dowager Empress, brother Michael and his morganatic wife Natasha. After the death of the Dowager Empress in 1928 her property in Denmark, Hvidore, which she had shared with the Dowager Queen Alexandra, was sold. King George V and his sisters waived their rights and the proceeds of the sale were divided equally between Xenia, Olga and Michael's son George. Xenia's latter years (from 1936 to 1960) were spent in London, in Wilderness House, a small mansion provided by the British Crown.

I often think that the character of Count Danilo Danilovich in Franz Lehar's *The Merry Widow* was based on Grand Duke Michael Aleksandrovich, for two days 'His Majesty the Emperor Michael II'. Michael was everything his elder brother Nicholas was not. Like Danilo Michael was tall, handsome, charming and good-natured. He was a good linguist, a competent musician - even composer - and patron of the arts. He had all the military virtues and had a good World War I. He was also one of the richest young men in the world and was to spend much of his life in Cannes, near, but not too near, Nice, the Russian core of the Riviera.

Michael had also a propensity - like Count Danilo - for getting into scrapes and was to exile himself from his family by marrying what was, in Russian terms, 'a penniless lass wi' a lang pedigree'.

Rosemary and Donald Crawford in *Michael and Natasha* summarise his love life thus.

> Well-meaning though he was, it sometimes seemed as if Grand Duke Michael did little else but write letters of regret. Between 1903 and 1905 he was apologising to Princess Beatrice of Great Britain, in 1906, to Princess Patricia of Connaught, and in 1907 to Alexandra Kossikovskaya, long-time lady-in-waiting to his younger sister Olga. While he could not apologise to everyone, of course, among those who would have expected him to do so were a furious Duchess of Saxe-Coburg-Gotha, an outraged Grand Duchess of Hesse-Darmstadt, an indignant Duke and Duchess of Connaught, a bewildered Buckingham Palace, an enraged Vladimir Kossikovsky, and even the discomfited country priest whom he had bribed to conduct an illegal wedding.

The Dowager Empress had a part to play in these imbroglios. Dina, the lady-in-waiting 'with more brains than beauty', was, by normal standards, perfect for Michael. Yet she was not of royal blood and

Michael's parents forbade the match. The Dowager Empress dismissed Dina and took Michael off on holiday with her to Denmark. Michael and Dina planned a secret marriage in Russia, then Michael went ahead to Italy, where Dina would join him. The secret service were put on to the pair and at Odessa Dina was taken into custody and sent back to St Petersburg, later retreating to England, beaten and 'blaming the Dowager Empress for the destruction of her life'. Whether by chance or design, the cruiser *HMS Minerva* was in Sorrento and was put at Michael's disposal till he rejoined his mother in Denmark before moving to the Crimea to stay with his sister Xenia.

In the midst of this the news appeared in the London *Observer* that Michael was to marry Patricia, daughter of Arthur, Duke of Connaught, Queen Victoria's favourite son. It seemed that the Dowager Empress and her sister, Queen Alexandra, had been match-making when on holiday together - in Denmark again, of course. There was much fluttering in the royal and imperial dovecotes, but the two great ladies sat tight, professed ignorance and the fuss subsided.

Michael now fell for Madame Nathalie (Natasha) Wulfert, twenty-seven years old, beautiful, charming, clever and at ease in a social circle which included the composer Rachmaninov and the greatest bass singer of the time - of all time? - Chaliapin. She was also a divorcée with a four-year-old daughter. Her husband, Vladimir Wulfert, was from a German military family and was a Lieutenant in His Majesty's Cuirassier Regiment, a crack regiment known as the Blue Cuirassiers. The Dowager Empress was colonel-in-chief of the Blue Cuirassiers and took a keen interest in 'Les petits bleus de Sa Majesté'. She visited the sick in the regimental hospital, turned up at services in the garrison church and talked to troopers in the barracks. And her son Michael was a squadron commander in the same regiment!

For her the situation was impossible. Although at that time divorce was rampant in the upper echelons of Russian society, a divorcée was just not acceptable in the Imperial circle. Also, she had already had trouble with Olga and 'was likely to be enraged on discovering that the wife of another officer had become involved with her son'. The honour of her favourite regiment was tarnished yet again and the scandal deepened when Wulfert challenged Michael to a duel - a challenge the latter could not accept because of their difference in rank. Forty-eight hours later Michael was no longer a Guards officer and was transferred to Orel, 650 miles south of the capital, as colonel of the run-of-the-mill Chernigov Hussars.

Over the next two years Michael could not have spent much time at his post, as he flitted from one watering-hole to another. In one episode, the Imperial family were living in their yachts in Copenhagen while Natasha was installed in the Royal Suite of the Hotel d'Angleterre in the city. The Dowager Empress would leave the *Polar Star* at noon and be back on board at 6 pm, allowing Michael to slip away to the Royal Suite.

On the Riviera the favoured focus of the Romanovs had been Nice. Michael favoured Cannes, because it was on the Riviera yet far enough from Nice to be considered as exile. His wanderings took him to Scotland where, partridge-shooting, he observed golfers on the Old Course at St Andrews. The result was the foundation of a golf club at Cannes, the fourth oldest in France. It took Monte Carlo some time to catch up. It was 1911 before the *Societé des Bains de Mer* commissioned Willie Park Junior of Musselburgh, twice Open Champion, to lay out the Monte Carlo course.

The details of the marriage read more like high comedy than tragedy and Michael's relationship with his mother was to become severely strained. Matters came to a head in 1910, when Natasha found that she was pregnant. Now began a curious kind of race, in which she tried to divorce her husband before the child was born. Bureaucracy and the Church were less than helpful and the little boy was registered as George Wulfert, necessitating the later backdating of the divorce date and the 'doctoring' of his original certificate of birth and baptism.

Natasha was now twice a divorcée, which did not endear her more to the Dowager Empress - although she did urge Nicholas to be more flexible in dealing with his brother, who was now allowed to travel abroad incognito with Natasha. From Paris they went to Cannes, for two months in the Hotel du Parc, always under the surveillance of Okhrana, the secret police. Returning to Russia, Natasha was cut by society, including the officers of the Chevalier Guards, of whom Michael was now colonel and of whom the Dowager Empress was also colonel-in-chief! Michael had promised not to marry Natasha, but three years of 'humiliation and insult' forced him to renege on his promise.

The events of 1912 are reminiscent of an operetta of the period and would be highly amusing on the stage. But real people were involved, so that, beneath the superficial comedy of the blundering secret service outwitted by the clever lovers, there is a dark layer of stupidity, prejudice and ignorance.

For a wedding to be valid in Russia it would have to be in an Orthodox church. The Okhrana would have three weeks notice of such an event and interception would be possible. In September, Michael and Natasha took the international train to Berlin with their Opel touring car as part of the baggage. Twelve days later they moved, with their baggage, to Bad Kissingen, where Natasha was admitted to a sanatorium and Michael jovially took the waters. At every stage the Okhrana followed and reported back to St Petersburg. Michael telegraphed Berlin, booking eight tickets from Frankfurt-am-Main to Paris. The Okhrana having booked their tickets, Michael announced that he was going to drive to Cannes via Switzerland and Italy, leaving his staff to travel by rail. A postcard to his brother (intercepted by the secret police) confirmed his intention. A week later the various parties reassembled at the Hotel du Parc in Cannes and for several weeks the Okhrana kept an eye on the Orthodox church in Cannes (founded by Alexander III, Michael's father, in 1894) and the church in Nice founded by Marie Alexandrova.

The Okhrana had been outwitted. Michael and Natasha had driven to Vienna, to an accommodation address prearranged for the Bad Kissingen period. They were perfectly validly married in a Serbian Orthodox church by a priest whose fee was equal to two months income and who owed no loyalty to Russia.

Before the Okhrana discovered what had happened, Michael had confessed - by letter - to his brother and his mother. The Dowager Empress was horrified - 'It has completely killed me!' Nicholas for once - probably with Alexandra at his side - acted decisively. Michael's estate and funds were to be taken into the guardianship of the Tsar. Michael had been nominated as Regent for the Tsarevich in the event of Nicholas's death. He was now divested of this responsibility. He was granted eleven months leave of absence from his regiment and relieved of his command. In 1910 Michael had represented Russia at the funeral of Edward VII. In June 1911 he was to represent Russia at the coronation of his cousin King George IV, when it was announced from St Petersburg that he was unable to travel 'for health reasons'.

He and Natasha retreated to Cannes where they found banishment gave them liberty as well as being a punishment. In June 1913 the Dowager Empress and Xenia were staying with the Dowager Queen Alexandra at Marlborough House, her London residence. Michael had two conversations with his mother, which went well. Then it was Natasha's turn to face the music. This must have been unpleasant for her, but at least it gave the Dowager Empress the satisfaction of administering a thorough tongue-lashing to the woman who had wrecked everything for her.

Olga was Maria Feodorovna's youngest child. She would say she was 'tricked into' marrying Duke Peter of Oldenburg because her mother wanted to keep her close to home and not live abroad as the wife of some foreign royal. Duke Peter wanted position and Olga's money, much of which went on the roulette table - some of it on their wedding night when Olga wept and the homosexual Peter gambled the night away. Olga turned to a commoner, Captain Kulikovsky of the Blue Cuirassiers, for consolation, seriously disturbing 'Olga's formidable mother' the Dowager Empress - who just happened to be the colonel-in-chief of the Blue Cuirassiers and was enraged at the insult to her regiment's honour. (5)

Instead of banishing Kulikovsky to Siberia, or worse, scandal was avoided by having him appointed as aide-de-camp to Duke Peter, living in his house. Fifteen years later, Olga divorced the Duke and married Kulikovsky, now a colonel, scandalising the Imperial family, who, while their armies were being slaughtered and the population at home were on the brink of revolution, were more concerned about an archaic Imperial law. After 1919 Olga and her husband remained in Denmark. After the Second World War they moved to Canada. Kulikovsky died there and Olga moved in with a Russian couple who lived over a barber's shop in Toronto, where she died seven months after her sister.

Domestic problems there were in abundance yet the Dowager Empress was also, to some extent, the mother of the nation. In a parliamentary democracy she would have been shuffled off to the sidelines, but as the mother of a feeble autocrat, loved or admired by many of the people, she had a great deal of informal power and could attempt to use it. Nicholas was the focus of political problems for the twenty years leading up to the First World War, but at his shoulder were two women at loggerheads, his Empress and his mother, the Dowager Empress.

Alexandra of Hesse-Darmstadt (1872-1918) was the sixth child of Princess Alice, Grand Duchess of Hesse and thus a grand-daughter of Queen Victoria. Although she became Empress I do not think of her as a Gypsy Empress. She did not have the temperament. She had the coolness and distance of the congenitally shy and fended off embarrassment with her regal bearing. Yet she could be impetuous and overbearing and showed, on occasion a streak of levity, even frivolity, which could get her into trouble. In her latter days, one of the charges laid against her was that she had taken up gipsy music and played hostess to a gypsy orchestra on Thursdays! Nor was she a wandering escapist. She travelled a great deal, as any Empress must, but her travels were generally with her husband, performing their joint duties, or visiting her pack of relatives, scattered round the courts of Europe.

Alix was serious and thoughtful as well as beautiful, and this showed up early in her relationship with Nicholas, the Tsarevitch who was to become Nicholas II. Nicholas and Alexandra were cousins and by the time she was thirteen (and he was seventeen) she knew that she loved him. As we have seen, Alexander III and Maria Feodorovna were not inclined in her favour and were happy - indeed insistent - that Nicholas broaden his experience. Minnie told her sister that the heir to the Russian throne could never marry the youngest daughter of an undistinguished grand duke, particularly as she was too hard, was lacking in grace and tact and did not have the gift of making people like her. Alix turned down at least two suitors until, in 1894, when she was a mature twenty-two, the Tsar and Minnie dropped their objections to her as a suitable match for their son.

A new problem arose. The Romanovs had made it a practice to marry into minor German princely families rather than incur alliances with other major powers. The three immediately previous Empresses had been Protestants who had changed their names and religion in order to conform with Russian law. But:

> Alix now clung to her Lutheran faith with the tenacious fervour of a martyr in Roman times being sent into the arena to face the lions.

Both parties were in despair until Alix's older sister Ella came up with a solution. She had married Serge, Nicholas's uncle, to be faced with the same problem of conscience. She had formally adopted the Greek Orthodox faith but had not been obliged to abjure her Lutheranism. Other German princesses had done the same and Alix now felt able to follow their example. Serious and honest as she was, it is difficult for us, at this distance, to judge whether having her cake and eating it adversely affected her perception of herself. What is regrettable is that, having conformed to Russian expectations on the surface, she appears also to have swallowed their beliefs on autocracy and believed her husband semi-divine, although life with him must have indicated otherwise.

What was expected of an Empress was fairly straightforward. She should be beautiful and gracious. She should preside benignly over a number of charitable causes. She should be of good breeding stock, producing, at least, 'an heir and a spare'. Alix tried hard, but she had to work through a weak husband of pretty low intellect and under the close scrutiny of his mother. In 21 years, much could go wrong - and did.

This is not the place for a detailed academic analysis of the complexities and horrors of the period from 1896 to 1917. Maria Feodorovna was on the fringe of great events where family and national issues overlapped and a snapshot of some of these will convey enough for us to empathise with her situation.

The coronation of Nicholas II and his Empress on 14 May 1896 was a great occasion, although it was clear that the court had considered Alix both foreign and provincial and that the crowds had somehow picked up the same feelings. An enormous crowd at the public festival at Khodynka Field (attracted by the promise of free beer and mead) got out of control. There was a stampede and many were killed and injured. The authorities were totally incompetent and it took several days to remove the dead and injured - while the normal activities of a national occasion, parades, dancing, eating, a speech by the Tsar and the blessing of delegations of peasants, went on nearby. Blame was liberally apportioned. 'Muted antagonism' arose between Minnie and Alix. The workers came out on strike and the Tsar was called 'Bloody Nicholas'. Alix was 'The German Bitch' and miscarried.

The same summer Alix launched a charitable project - 'Help Through Handwork'. Women from the aristocratic and merchant classes were to embroider garments which would be sold to support needy families. She was also going to set up a school for nurses and housemaids. Unfortunately, those who joined in did so for the wrong reasons. Worse, Alix discovered that, in Russia, most charities were headed by the Dowager Empress. Whatever she tried to do, Minnie stood in the way. A diplomatic tour of Europe with her husband was not a success. She fell out with her cousin Willy - Kaiser Wilhelm II, whose armies were soon to smash their way into Russia and precipitate that country's collapse. Victoria found she had become distant and unapproachable. Alix hated Balmoral; the Scots took exception to her costly gowns and were affronted that she did not choose tweeds.

Alix was under tremendous pressure - some of it self-imposed - to produce the desired heir. Four daughters were produced at two-yearly intervals but, however delightful they might be, they were of no value for the perpetuation of the Romanovs. When a son, Alexis, eventually came along it was very soon apparent that there was something seriously wrong with him. In fact, he was a haemophiliac and his pitifully short life of fourteen years was a succession of illnesses, crises and temporary recoveries. The birth of a Tsarevich should have been good news (although it could have meant 'another of the same'), but once it became known that he was so fragile Alix was blamed yet again for her shortcoming. (6)

In desperation, Alix thrashed around in all directions, seeking support and reassurance in a society becoming increasingly hostile as Germany and Russia inched their way to war. Nicholas was no help. A loving husband and father he might be, but he was weak and his Empress had to provide him with backbone. For example, in 1907 the royal yacht *Standart* was cruising in the Baltic when she ran on to rocks and began to sink. Nicholas took out his watch and timed the rising water line as the crew launched the lifeboats and filled them with food and water. The Empress got her children into the lifeboats then went back to the cabins, collected all the valuables and dragged them to the waiting lifeboats, the last woman to leave the sinking ship.

Father Gregory (7) was one person Alix could lean on. Unsavoury in many ways, he seems to have been able to help the ailing Tsarevich, even saving his life through prayer on one occasion. Thus he came to have great influence over the Empress, which did not please Maria Feodorovna. Still, at sixty-five, bustling and charming, one afternoon in 1912 she sailed into action, dismissing Alix's ill health and blaming her for ruining 'both the dynasty and herself' by her relationship with Father Gregory. The dignity and authority of the throne were being undermined. Father Gregory must be sent away. Nicholas said little, but Alexandra mounted a spirited defence, so much so that Minnie recognised that Alix was blind to the dangers of the situation, while Nicholas was passive.

As an absolute monarch Nicholas had total responsibility. He had courtiers and advisers and a Duma, the token beginnings of a parliament - but he had the power. Yet he knew he was unfit to use it. On his father's death he had wept: 'I know nothing of the business of ruling'. His choices were unfortunate - sometimes, it has to be said, acting on the advice of his wife. Time and time again he would be bullied into a decision one day, only to change his mind overnight. Yet he could be obdurate to the point of self-destruction.

In 1895, after many petitions, there was a big meeting of the nobility and city delegates. The time was ripe for change, the country had come through famines and epidemics and could now look forward to fairer taxation, broader rights and better representation, a slow progression towards reform. Instead Nicholas delivered a short speech maintaining 'the principle of autocracy just as firmly and unflinchingly as it was preserved by my unforgettable dead father'. His speech-writer had used the phrase 'unrealisable dreams'. For whatever reason, nervousness or hubris, this came out as 'senseless dreams', turning eager hopes into dismay.

Russia was a major military power with aggressive ambitions in the Balkans, the Caucasus, Central Asia and the Far East. In the east Siberia had been acquired in 1880. The capital, Vladivostok, was eventually at the end of a long railway link from Moscow - 9288 Km. Even by today's electrified system the journey still requires over 6 days.

Russia was a great land power with problems of maritime access. As well as fleets based on the Baltic and the Black Sea a totally separate Pacific fleet was needed to keep an eye on the emerging Japanese. (8)

We have seen how the Black Sea fleet was relocated at Villefranche and how this was a main cause of the Russian presence on the Riviera. How competent was the Russian navy? How did they conduct themselves when faced by opponents they despised and belittled?

Rather than an extended discussion I have chosen to quote a series of extracts from *The Pageant of the Century* (Odhams Press Ltd, London, 1933). Unedited, these represent a British view of the Russo-Japanese War and convey well the succession of hammer-blows to the pride of the Tsar and his people.

The Russo-Japanese War revealed the corruption of the Tsarist administration and was provoked by...the cavalier treatment of Japanese protests. St Petersburg was so slow in replying to Tokyo that the Japanese declared war and inflicted severe defeats on the Russian forces.

8 February 1904: Outbreak of war between Japan and Russia. Admiral Togo's squadron makes a midnight attack on Port Arthur and torpedoes three Russian warships.

24 February 1904: Japanese attempt to block entrance to Port Arthur by sinking steamers.

6 March 1904: Vladivostok bombarded by the Japanese.

13 April 1904: Russian battleship *Petropavlovsk* blown up by a mine outside Port Arthur harbour. Admiral Makaroff drowned.

The Russians

Flagship of the Russian fleet, the *Tsarewitch* was engaged in the naval battle, disastrous to Russian prestige, outside Port Arthur. So drastic was the Japanese assault that the vessel was severely damaged, but succeeded in escaping to Tsingtao [then under German, neutral, control], where she was disarmed. The Admiral lost an arm and the casualties on board amounted to no fewer than 400 men and 100 officers.

13 July 1904: Russian Volunteer Fleet seizes P and O steamer *Malacca* in the Red Sea.

16 July 1904: British steamer *Allanton* seized by Russian fleet.

20 July 1904: Russian Vladivostok squadron commences a raid on Japanese shipping and on 23 July sinks the British vessel *Knight Commander.*

21 October 1904: Russian Baltic Squadron fires on Hull trawling fleet while fishing on the Dogger Bank. Steam trawler *Crane* sunk; other vessels badly damaged. War scare.

Under the alleged belief that the Gamecock Trawling Fleet of Hull was a squadron of Japanese torpedo boats, the Russian Baltic Squadron, under Admiral Rojdestvensky, opened fire. The warships added another stain to their record by rendering no assistance.

The Dogger Bank outrage almost induced Britain to declare war.

12 January 1905: Japanese enter Port Arthur.

9 March 1905: The Russian Ambassador pays the North Sea incident indemnity of £65,000.

15 March 1905: Sir Charles Hardinge hands the Russian Government a claim   of £100,000 for the sinking of the *Knight Commander.*

After 21 October the brave boys of the Baltic Squadron worked their ageing and decrepit ships round… and into Far Eastern waters, wasting three months in Madagascar while the seas were scoured for cargoes of coal. Having arrived, on:

> 27-28 May 1905: Admiral Togo annihilates the Russian Baltic Fleet
> in the Sea of Japan, sinking or capturing almost every vessel. 8,000
> prisoners taken.

This sorry catalogue of disasters is put in some sort of context by incidents at home in Mother Russia. In the same period, from 8 February 1904 to 28 May 1905, *The Pageant of the Century* records:

> assassination of Governor-General of Finland [then part of Russia],
> assassination of Minister of the Interior in St Petersburg,
> assassination of Russian Chief of Police in the Caucasus,
> assassination of Grand Duke Sergius of Russia in Moscow,
> attempted assassination of the Tsar,
> 'Bloody Sunday' - massacre of strikers in St Petersburg, hundreds killed
> and wounded,
> massacres in Warsaw [also part of Russia at that time],
> another General Strike in St Petersburg (no casualties),
> Gorki arrested in Riga [also in Russia then].
> Tsar grants freedom of worship in Russia.

Too little, too late?

In the next few months came peace with Japan, more assassinations and the naval mutiny immortalised in Eisenstein's film *Battleship Potemkin*. On 25 October there was widespread disorder reported throughout Russia. The British Ambassador was unable to leave St Petersburg by train, owing to a railway strike. The Tsar consented to a manifesto offering civil liberties and a popularly-elected assembly. Sometimes known as the 1905 Revolution, this is seen by some historians as significant. In the event, when popular protest had subsided, the concessions were modified or never activated. Between 1906 and 1914 the Tsar attempted to rule as he had always done.   For me, the condition of Russia at this time was summed up by an exhibition in the Queen's Gallery, next to the Palace of Holyroodhouse in Edinburgh. Here articles from the Queen's collections are made accessible to the public. One year it was the Fabergé eggs which were on display. They are, of course, exquisitely crafted from enamel, precious metals and jewels. Whether they are beautiful is a matter of personal taste - one is reminded of Vladimir Putin's recent outburst against the gross excesses of the new Russian oligarchs. They serve no purpose other than the glorification of the persons who commissioned them and passed them around a very select circle. They disgusted me. Looking at them I could only see the rotting hulks of the Baltic fleet on its way to destruction in Asian waters, or the massacres of destitute workers driven crazy by oppression.

The Great War (as it was called when I was young) was a catastrophe for Russia, her ill-equipped and badly trained armies inferior in every respect save numbers and - for a period - stolid courage. Minnie returned to Russia from London via Germany, but her train was attacked by hostile crowds in Berlin. She was given safe passage to neutral Denmark and continued via Sweden and Finland. Minnie, her daughters, Alix and her daughters did what Empresses do in wartime. They set up hospitals, they trained as nurses, they visited the wounded and even worked regular shifts until their health suffered. (9)

Nicholas, as Tsar, was, by right of birth, in charge of the whole operation but, in practice, Grand Duke Nicholas Nikolaevich was Supreme Commander, struggling with the task of defending Mother Russia, earning the respect of the French, the British and even his German opponents. Alexandra determined that Nicholas would do a far better job. Nicholas appointed himself Supreme Commander. Grand Duke Nicholas was removed, as was the disastrous war minister Sukhomlinov. Effectively, Alexandra acted as Regent in St Petersburg while Nicholas moved to Stavka (Supreme Headquarters) at Mogilev, 450 miles south of the capital. Minnie, worn out by her efforts in trying to widen Alexandra's opinions and to correct her judgment, left the capital for the south.

Nicholas's military competence was limited to saluting troops, reviewing parades and handing out medals. Stavka ceased to be a train and was moved to a comfortable mansion house. Michael observed that his brother's routine was to sit down every day, chain-smoking, to read Alexandra's long letters of instruction, letters beginning 'be firm...you are the master, the Autocrat'. Fortunately, there was also a General Alexseev, who had risen from the ranks and was highly competent.

Michael had a good war. Too good a soldier to waste, he was kept at a distance by the Imperial court but given command of the unfashionable Savage Division, then the 2nd Cavalry Corps, and was promoted to lieutenant-general, adjutant-general and Inspector-General of Cavalry. He received various gallantry awards. These are usually 'given out with

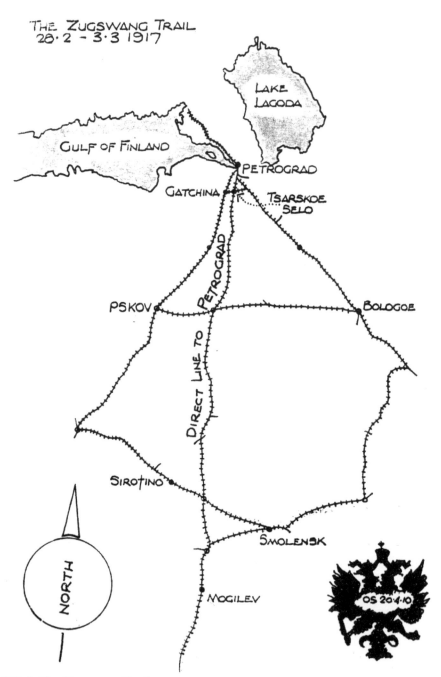

THE ZUGSWANG TRAIL
28·2 – 3·3 1917

LAKE LADOGA

GULF OF FINLAND

PETROGRAD

GATCHINA

TSARSKOE SELO

PSKOV

DIRECT LINE TO PETROGRAD

BOLOGOE

SIROTINO

NORTH

SMOLENSK

MOGILEV

OS 20·4·10

FIG 8 *The Zugswang Trail*

the rations' to aristocratic officers, but there is no doubt that Michael served within the sound of the guns, had others killed around him and was esteemed by those who served under him.

'Zugswang' is a term used in the game of chess. Despite general impression, this is a game of rapid movement as each player moves purposely to defeat the other and the onus is to move faster than one's opponent. Occasionally, however, as the game nears its end, one player will deliberately waste a move in order that his opponent has no option but to move into a worse position. This is Zugswang and Nicholas's movements in the three days 28 February - 3 March 1917 are worth examining with this concept in mind.

On 28 February the Russian Revolution was in full turmoil. Michael was in Petrograd, Alexandra and her children were in the New Palace at Tsarskoe Selo, 20 miles from the city. With a black coat over her nurse's uniform she walked among the troops defending the palace, praising their loyalty. Nicholas was at Stavka, at Mogilev, and determined to get back to the capital and the family. 'Every hour is precious' read Michael's telegram. Leaving the main line clear for the force that would crush the revolutionaries, his train (10) set off at 5 am on Tuesday on the 650 - mile, 27 - hour journey, a journey on which the Tsar was totally out of touch - no mobile phones, no radio - with whatever government still remained. The country was leaderless.

100 miles short of Petrograd, the train was stopped because of revolutionary troops ahead. The train returned to Bologoe and headed west along a branch line to Pskov, headquarters of the Northern Army (a journey of 321 miles and 15 hours), arriving at 7 pm on Wednesday. At Tsarskoe Selo a worried Alexandra sent a telegram to 'His Imperial Majesty' asking Nicholas for news, only for it to be returned, marked with blue pencil: 'Address of person mentioned unknown'.

Nicholas spent 30 hours at Pskov, in touch with the world again. In those thirty hours telegrams whizzed in all directions at twenty words per minute, the outcome being the abdication of Nicholas (and Alexis) at 11.40 pm on Thursday, although the manifesto was timed as of 3 pm, that being the time when Nicholas had decided to abdicate. Back in Petrograd, Michael had gone to bed on Thursday night thinking that next day he would be Regent, not a bad outcome for a supporter of constitutional monarchy. Instead, he woke on Friday morning to find that, from 3 pm on Thursday afternoon, he had been His Majesty Michael II, Emperor of All the Russias, King of Poland, Grand Duke of Finland etc. etc.

Nicholas now resumed his incommunicado journey back to Mogilev (420 miles, 19 hours). At Sirotino he remembered that he had omitted to tell his brother that he was the new Emperor and sent him a telegram at 2.56 pm addressed to 'Imperial Majesty, Petrograd'. By the time he had arrived at Mogilev at 8.20 pm on Friday 3 March Michael had signed a manifesto which said he would only assume the Supreme Power 'if such be the will of our great people'. With time in short supply this was, in effect, an abdication.

For three days Nicholas had been trundling round his domain. Great events were being played out around him and he - the Supreme Commander - was unable to influence them. Was this Zugswang? Did he expect a rabbit to be pulled out of the revolutionary hat? Was it just sheer stupidity? Or was it a public denial, a ducking of responsibility in the hope that something would turn up?

What eventuated for Nicholas and his family was extinction. Michael was discharged from military service. He applied to go to Britain, but was denied. George V was not prepared to give sanctuary to the Romanovs, despite the links of family and friendship. The downfall of Nicholas was welcomed, particularly by the British left. Michael was arrested, imprisoned and exiled to Perm in the Ural Mountains. At approximately 2 am on Thursday 13 June Michael and his secretary were murdered in a wood just outside the town. They were buried on the spot and their clothes burnt.

Nicholas turned up at Tsarskoe Selo in the imperial train on 9 March, to be reunited with his family, who were now effectively prisoners. As long as they were near Petrograd they could be a focus for counter-revolutionary activity, so they were moved to Ekaterinburg. There were rumours that Michael was leading armies in Serbia and Czech troops fighting for the White Russians were supposed to be nearby. Therefore early on Thursday 18 July Nicholas and his family were taken downstairs to a basement room and murdered. In a touch of savage irony, poor little Alexis, the cause of so much anxiety to his parents, did not die from a fall or some internal bleeding but suffered the same violent death as his parents and sisters. He may even have outlived them by a few seconds.

The Dowager Empress was fortunate not to have been a witness of these terrible events. In the spring of 1916 she left Petrograd for Kiev, where her daughter Olga was serving in a hospital. Minnie was worn out by the struggle to control Alexandra and the insidious influence of Father Gregory. She had tried to lecture to her son, only for her feelings to run away with her. He would then stand on his dignity and remind his mother that he was the Emperor.

In September 1917, after the deaths of the Imperial family and Michael, the Dowager Empress was ordered by the revolutionary authorities to leave for the relative safety of the Crimea. At Livadia, the Imperial palace near Yalta, a Black Sea town which served as a kind of Russian Riviera, the Dowager Empress gathered around her a little court of her daughters Olga and Xenia, the Grand Duke Nicholas Nicholaevich (formerly Supreme Commander) and his brother Peter. For eighteen months they lived comfortably but uncertainly as the war with Germany stumbled to a halt, to be followed by bloody revolution and a menacing civil war.

The revolutionary authorities announced that she was the first member of the Imperial family 'to be allowed to go abroad' whenever she pleased 'whether to England, Denmark or Finland' and 'Grand Duke Michael would be next'. (Michael had been in his unmarked grave for three months by this time).

Despite George V's reluctance, in April 1919 *HMS Marlborough* arrived to take his aunt, the Dowager Empress, to Britain. She refused to go, unless the British were prepared to take the Romanov family members, a flock of retainers and various other hangers-on along with her. The decks were awash with Russians as they were brought into exile.

For a while, Minnie shone in London society. She spent much time with her sister Alexandra, also a Dowager Queen and Empress, both in Britain and (later) in Denmark. She and her daughters lived on what they could earn from the sale of their jewellery and on the charity of their Danish and British relatives. Minnie took up photography, at which she proved more than competent. But Minnie and Alexandra began to get on each other's nerves and Minnie returned to her native Denmark where her nephew Christian X was now king and allowed her a wing of his palace. There were constant arguments about money and electricity bills. Her relationship with her daughters was now satisfactory and, as we have seen, when Minnie died her estate went to Olga, Xenia and Michael's son George. (11)

As for Michael's morganatic wife, Natasha, there was a degree of reconciliation. On 26 July 1919 Natasha met the Dowager Empress in Alexandra's London home, Marlborough House. This was a happy occasion. The Dowager Empress was impressed by Natasha, now known as the Countess Brasova (from Michael's estate of that name). 'What a beautiful woman, she is so pretty I had quite forgotten' was her reaction. Natasha's comment was: 'She was rather nice to me'. And Minnie fussed over her grandson George.

The legacy did George little good. Some of it went on a new car, a Sports Chrysler. After his finals at the Sorbonne he and a Dutch friend set off for Cannes, skidded off the road and hit a tree. The Dutch boy was killed instantly and George died without recovering consciousness. He was buried in the fashionable cemetery at Passy, in Paris, where his mother bought two plots.

In January 1952 an impoverished old woman of 71 died of cancer in the charity hospital of Laënnec in Paris. She claimed to be a Princess Brasova but her faded birth certificate said she was plain Nathalie Sheremetevskaya, and that is what was written on the death certificate. But the word got round the dwindling Russian community in Paris and she was buried next to her son in Passy.

Dagmar, Minnie, Maria Alexandrovna, the Dowager Empress never accepted that Nicholas, his family, and Michael were dead. When a memorial service on their behalf was organised, she refused to attend. By the 1920s there were many questions being asked about the fate of the Tsar and his family. It was suggested that the youngest daughter - the Grand Duchess Anastasia - had survived and claimants came forward claiming to be her. Sokolov, a professional legal investigator, was employed to clear up the mystery and the Dowager Empress contributed to the project. He reported that he believed the entire family was dead but produced a box of relics which included a charred emerald cross which the Dowager Empress had given to the Empress Alexandra. The Dowager Empress refused to see Sokolov, or to receive his dossier, or his box of relics.

In 1928 she was angry with her daughter Olga for seeing the sick woman who claimed to be Anastasia, but relented enough for her last public action before her death to be the giving of permission for an investigation of the claim. (12)

Katia Dolgourika /
Catherine Yourievski
The Shadow Empress

THE ABOLITION OF SERFDOM was not the unmixed blessing one might imagine. Serfs worked the great estates and had therefore to be cared for - up to a point - in the interests of efficiency. Once the serfs were freed the landowners could employ the workers they needed and get rid of the lazy, the sick and the old. Landowners received payments in compensation for the loss of their tied workers and in many cases this money was squandered 'on mad nights which have passed into legend' and not ploughed back into the estates. Thus many established families fell on hard times.

The Institute Smolny was set up to give the daughters of poor nobles a free and appropriate education. As at the Imperial court, French was the language in use, history, drawing and music the main elements of the curriculum. One of the Dolgourika family had been among the founders of Moscow but the abolition of serfdom had shattered them. Informed of their situation, Alexander II 'the liberating Tsar' personally permitted two young sisters, Katia and Moucha to enter the Institute Smolny. At sixteen the uniform of the boarders complemented the startling beauty of the young Katia. Her long blonde hair was piled high on her head in the Russian style. She carried herself like a dancer and her look had the arrogance of her ancestors. Like the other girls at the school, her knowledge of the court was confined to crumbs picked up at the family dining table or to dormitory chatter out of earshot of the supervisor.

In 1865, Alexander II was 47 years old, still handsome and vigorous. Marie Alexandrova, worn out by multiple pregnancies and lost in a religious torment at the loss of her first-born, was declared out of bounds for carnal purposes. At the Institute Smolny the girls talked to Katia about Alexander's latest conquest, Alexandra Yourievski, a distant relative of Katia; hoping to pick up some juicy items of gossip.

One April morning the Tsar was crossing the park of the palace at the same time as the young boarders of the Institute Smolny. His eyes met those of Katia and 'he received a shock such as he had never before experienced'. This young girl was his for life, of that he was absolutely certain. (My authority for this is Martine Gasquet, who has a tendency to gush). He enquired the girl's name, realised he knew her family and several times invited her, suitably chaperoned, to various official functions where his attention to her could not be missed. Soon he was writing passionate letters - in French - to her every day, just as he had done with the fifteen-year-old blonde Marie of Hesse 25 years previously. After a year Katia became his mistress. First a separate entrance was created for her which she used three times a week. Then she was moved into the palace and allocated quarters away from Alexander's other family. There Katia and her growing family began to feel hemmed in by what they thought was excessive security - although Alexander's end showed how vulnerable these people really were.

Alexander paid the occasional token visit to his unhappy wife, usually on some business matter that had to be discussed, like the blessing of his bastards. Dagmar took the part of her shamed mother-in-law and opposed Katia at every turn. Alexander saw the death of his wife as a relief and a release, losing no time in marrying Katia and legitimising their children. This was a morganatic marriage; however long her pedigree Katia was not of royal blood and could not be Empress, although moves were being made when Alexander was assassinated.

That put an end to her social pretensions. She was not allowed to attend Alexander's funeral and proceeded to move into a self-imposed exile in Nice. Her life was in tatters, she had been humiliated - but she was immensely rich and threw herself into a frenzied social life. She bought houses, furnishings, motor cars, she clothed her staff in black and gold. As compensation for being unable to become Empress she had been created Imperial Highness and had the arms of the Romanovs painted on her special railway coach in which she wandered round Europe.

Members of the Russian colony abroad were less hostile than the Imperial court. Princess Yourievski was seen in all the right places, in the Bois de Boulogne in Paris, at regattas in Cannes, at the races in Nice. Her daily routine in Nice was to drive in her open coach, her coachmen in white blouses and black breeches, her faithful dogs at her feet and a black-and-white lace parasol in her hand. She would admire the courageous bathers before returning to her pine villa, with its golden samovar on a precious marquetry table, to read and reread fourteen years of letters from the late Alexander.

Although she was not invited to the dedication of the new cathedral, she had her little triumphs. Two of her children were married in the original Orthodox church in the Rue Longchamp, where the guest list was of the greatest distinction. Every year, on the anniversary of the abolition of serfdom, she gave a great dinner in memory of her husband. Everyone - with one exception - was there, from her late husband's Grand Ducal brothers downward. The exception was Maria Feodorovna, who remained intractable towards the woman she considered had helped to destroy Marie Alexandrovna. She may also have been jealous of Katia's beautiful children, who were admired by all as being so Russian (although their father's mother was German).

After she had turned fifty Katia settled for a quiet and almost banal life in Nice. The great events that turned the Russian upper classes topsy-turvy - the Great War, the Revolution - were very far away and she did not allow herself to be affected by them. Members of her family who had fled Russia moved in with her, in her nice villa, Mon Plaisir, but she took no part in the kind of charitable activities undertaken by other rich Russians on the Riviera - setting up schools, clinics and the like for the exiles. Far from the intrigues and court of Tsarskoe Selo she died on 15 February 1922, at the age of 75.

By way of an epitaph I would refer back to Alexander's statement - in French - at the time of their marriage:

> It is a private person and not an Emperor who remedies a fault... committed by him and repairs the reputation of a young woman.

How can we measure celebrity? Katia was the subject of two films of that name. Danielle Darrieux, the great French star, played her in 1938, while Romy Schneider, who specialised in fragile heroines including, as we have seen, the Empress Sissi - several times - was in the 1959 version.

End Notes

1 On the Hotel Oasis, Rue Gounod, Nice, formerly the Pension Russe, are three plaques, in French and Russian, recording the fact that Tchekhov (in the winters of 1897, 1898, 1900, 1901 and 1903) and Lenin (in 1911) had resided there.

2 This unhappy country had just deposed its King Otto. George's nomination was suggested and supported by the United Kingdom, the Second French Empire and the Russian Empire.

George's 50-year reign (the longest in modern Greek history) was characterized by territorial gains as Greece established a place in pre-World War I Europe. Two weeks short of the fiftieth anniversary of his accession (during the First Balkan War) he was assassinated. In sharp contrast to his own reign, the reigns of his successors were to prove short and insecure.

3   My sweeping generalisations on the Jews are firmly based on my recollections of a Glasgow primary school during the Second World War. I was fortunate in having in my class a French refugee, one from the Channel Islands, and six or eight Jewish children, with such splendid names as Sylvia Mendelssohn and Maurice Bromberg. At the time one did not think of such things, but I decided they must have been refugees from Hitler's Germany. Much later I realised that they could not have been recent immigrants, but that they probably came from families who had fled from Russia around the turn of the century and ended up in the Gorbals. By 1943 they were moving upwards socially and our area was a staging post on the way to Newton Mearns.

4   Rimsky-Korsakov (1844-1908) was one of the Russian composers known as 'The Mighty Handful', who took Russian national and folk music and grafted it on to the European classical tradition. His music has 'a powerful dramatic impulse, with much rhythmic force and a vivid sense of orchestral colour'. An amateur in the best sense, it is yet another comment on the effectiveness of the Russian navy that Rimsky-Korsakov was a naval officer. His First Symphony was the first symphony composed by a Russian and was composed aboard ship, at sea and while stationed off Gravesend in Kent.

5   Although Olga was younger than Michael by four years, this incident took place earlier (1903) than Michael's problem with the Blue Cuirassiers (1908). The recollection of Olga's misbehaviour in front of her favourite regiment would have done nothing to sweeten the Dowager Empress's temper when she learned of her favourite son's entanglement.

6   On 13 February, 1904 Alexandra learned of the death of her four-year-old nephew, Henry, after a fall on the head. Alexei was born on 30 July, 1904. These events were not unconnected. Haemophilia – 'the terrible illness of the English family' - affects males but is transmitted through the female line. Alexandra and her sister Irene were carriers, and their brother Frederick died at the age of three. Their mother, Alice of Hesse, was a carrier and her brother Leopold struggled through a short life, dying at 33. Their mother was Queen Victoria, the carrier whose numerous progeny and dynastic marriages spread the family curse around half the crowned heads of Europe.

7   I have given Father Gregory his correct name and title rather than use the more familiar Rasputin or the Mad Monk, in the hope that the reader will start with an open mind. Rasputin (1869-1916) was a Russian mystic - a *strannik* (religious pilgrim) or a *starets* (monk-confessor). He was a psychic and faith healer, whose partial success with the ailing Tsarevich may have had some basis in sound medical practice e.g. he took him off aspirin, an anti-coagulant, which must have lessened his proneness to bleeding. Hypnosis would also have helped the young man to relax. The doctrine of attaining divine grace through sin fitted in with the frenetic behaviour of the Russian upper classes and proved popular with society ladies. His revelations were listened to by Alexandra and led her into unpopular political actions while her husband was at Army Headquarters.

Rasputin's behaviour further undermined respect for the Tsar and aroused the opposition of the nobility. His murder was characteristically confused and mysterious. It could be said he was thrice murdered. He was poisoned, shot four times, once in the head, clubbed and castrated, wrapped in a carpet and thrown into the River Neva, where he was drowned.

To quote an important search-engine:

> There has been much uncertainty over Rasputin's life and influence, for accounts of his life have often been based on dubious memoirs, hearsay, and legend.

8   At the Battle of Tsushima half of the Japanese warships were Clyde-built and most of the remainder were built in Japan from British plans. A few years ago, in Kelvingrove Museum, Glasgow, there was an exhibition of the links between Japan and Scotland in the nineteenth century, as Japan was rapidly preparing to catch up with the European industrial powers. From Japan came a delightful collection of lacquered boxes, textiles, ceramics and prints of Mount Fuji. Glasgow sent machines and engineering drawings. Which party had the better of the exchange?

9   One of the writer's more enjoyable memories is of the time he spent as a guest of Queen Alexandra's Royal Army Nursing Corps in a military hospital in Aldershot. Sadly, both of these fine institutions have been dispensed with by our slimmed-down Army.

10 There were actually two trains, another, carrying his suite, had left an hour earlier. In the interests of clarity I shall refer to the two trains as if they were one. Railway enthusiasts will easily imagine the chaotic problems faced by engineers and signalmen as these juggernauts trundled round the winter countryside.

11 The last meeting of the sister Dowager Empresses was in 1923, when Albert, Duke of York (later George VI) married Elizabeth Bowes-Lyon in Westminster Abbey. I almost feel an emotional link with these two ladies, as George VI once waved to me in Wendover, Bucks, and one day in Dundas Street, Edinburgh, Elizabeth, by then Queen Mother, smiled sweetly to me as I stood outside the New Town Conservation Committee's premises, holding a giant piece of hardboard.

12 In chapter 7 I describe the visit of Princess Hermine of Reuss, Kaiser Wilhelm II's second wife to investigate the claim of Anna Anderson.

CHAPTER 9
Victoria, Empress of India (1819-1901)
Our own dear Queen

MORE THAN A CENTURY after her death Victoria is still with us. Her long reign coincided with a period of hectic change and rapid growth in almost every aspect of British society - industry, agriculture, commerce and trade, urban development, public health, the Empire – and as a figurehead she is still associated with these changes. (PLATE 5B)

In Edinburgh a landmark statue of the young Queen sits on the Royal Scottish Academy, supervising the latest excavations in Princes Street while, at the 'Foot of the Walk' in Leith, where five main routes converge, her mature persona became the traditional rendezvous for young Leithers.

Victoria Street, an atmospheric 'City Improvement' has become almost a photographic cliché for conservation, while the Queen's Drive opened up the less accessible side of Arthur's Seat to the nineteenth century public.

The Queen and the Prince Consort visited the Royal Botanic Garden in October 1861. From the edge of the terrace south of Inverleith House excellent views of Edinburgh in silhouette from Murrayfield to Arthur's Seat are obtained and this area became known as 'The Queen's Views'. Later, trees were planted there by HRH The Prince of Wales, HRH The Duke of Edinburgh, the Prince of Hesse and Lord Palmerston, former Prime Minister and spokesman for the campaign to keep the Garden closed on the Sabbath.

In the nation's capital the Victoria Embankment tamed the vagaries of the Thames and gave the city an attractive promenade. The Victoria and Albert Museum provided a secure home for the treasures of the nation and an inspiration for designers - for example, it has two rooms full to the brim of the best Persian carpets, sent home by the Royal Engineers officer responsible for constructing the electric telegraph system in what was then Persia. Convenient for Buckingham Palace is Victoria Station, a splendid gateway to the Continent. (By contrast, on the old road north of Bridge of Orchy, the Victoria Bridge replaced the eighteenth century bridge of the military engineers).

Most considerable towns and cities have a hospital or infirmary associated with Victoria. Edinburgh has the Royal Victoria Hospital, pioneer of tuberculosis treatment: Glasgow has its Victoria Infirmary, as has Kirkcaldy.

In Glasgow the grand processional way of Victoria Road leads up to the Queen's Park, while in Aberdeen Victoria Road was the main artery of the developing fishing suburb of Torry, in contrast with the splendid granite 'West End' terrace of Queen's Crescent and the vast villas of Queen's Road, thoughtfully punctuated by a fine statue of the Queen (although she was only moved here in the 1960s, from the city centre).

Even on the Continent her presence is felt. There are umpteen Hotels Victoria, although she could only have slept in a fraction of those that used her name. Brig is a kind of railway crossroads in the Swiss Alps, where the east-west route from Paris and Geneva up the Rhone to Andermatt, the Grisons and Austria is crossed by the route from northern Europe through the Lötschberg Tunnel and on to Milan through the Simplon. Here we find the Victoria-Terminus Hotel and on the Lötschberg line, approaching Brig from the north, in the words of *Muirhead's Blue Guide to Switzerland*:

> ...the line passes through the short Victoria Tunnel pierced through a rock offering an unflattering but undoubted resemblance to the profile of Queen Victoria.

Fame indeed!

In the lonely places she loved the Queen left her mark. (PLATE 6A) If one stands on the shore of Loch Leven by Glencoe village and looks west to the hills of Ardgour, the silhouette of the sleeping Queen is plain for all to see (PLATE 6B). Just outside Tomintoul the Queen's View (PLATE 7A) looks up the valley of the Avon to the multiple tops of

FIG 9 *Victoria and John Brown at Tomintoul (Noted and adapted by Olrig Stephen)*

168

Ben Avon. Here, on 5 September 1860:

> We came upon a beautiful view, looking down upon the Avon and
> up a fine glen. There we rested and took luncheon.

Just outside Ballater, in Glen Muick, a wordy roadside plaque and cairn commemorate the occasion when the Queen, when out driving:

> …met the 1st Battalion Gordon Highlanders, who, in camp at Glenmuick,
> were to be presented with new colours by His Royal Highness The
> Prince of Wales.
> Sir Allan Mackenzie had the honour of presenting Lt Colonel Downman,
> the Commanding Officer The Battalion, at Her Majesty's special desire,
> then marched past her and embarked for South Africa shortly afterwards,
> where Lt Colonel Downman and a large number of his officers and men
> laid down their lives for their Queen and country.

A strange mixture of spontaneity and formality. One wonders what memories of the incident the rank and file carried as they lay dying under the withering fire of the Boers at Magersfontein or of enteric fever in some makeshift field hospital.

At Fettercairn is a grandiose memorial arch and nearby, in remote Glen Mark, is the Queen's Well. (PLATE 7B) This marks a stopping-point in the Second Great Expedition to Invermark and Fettercairn, when the Royal party stopped 'to drink some water out of a very pure well, called the White Well'. This was, in effect, almost the end of Phase I of Victoria's travels. As the plaque on the well records:

> Her Majesty Queen Victoria and the Prince Consort visited this and
> drank of its refreshing water on the 20th of September 1861 The Year
> of Her Majesty's Great Sorrow.

A month later the Last Expedition to Loch Callater and Cairn Lochan ended with a beautiful moonrise and the Queen's reflection - 'Alas! I fear our last great one!' (expedition).

The irony was that Albert's death came as a result of typhoid, but not from drinking Highland water!

Time and time again, in everyday talk, we refer to Victorian values or Victorian attitudes – usually simplistically, as in Victorian values good,

Victorian attitudes bad. But still they hang over us.

Much of Victoria's travel was the necessary business of a reigning monarch - 'showing the flag' or 'embodying effective sovereignty'. But much was also for pleasure and escapism. Her activity divides neatly into three phases - life with Albert, retreat into the isolation of widowhood, and an Indian summer when the pleasures of family and the search for a more kindly winter brought her out of her shell again.

For one who was to embody all the virtues of rectitude and respectability, Victoria's beginnings were distinctly unimpressive. Although George III's royal brood-mare Charlotte of Mecklenburg-Strelitz had produced fifteen children for him, it looked in the early nineteenth century as though the Hanoverian line might die out. His family was fertile enough, producing fifty-six offspring between them, the problem was that only one of the grandchildren - Charlotte (1796-1817) - was legitimate. By all accounts an estimable person, she died five hours after giving birth to a still-born son, after fifty hours in labour, precipitating a succession crisis and an unseemly race for an heir. The Duke of York dismissed his mistress, the mother of his ten children, returned from Brussels and acquired a Duchess, Victoria Maria Louisa of Saxe-Coburg. The result - in 1819 - was the girl we know as Victoria, baptised Alexandrina Victoria.

Even the name - her mother's - was suspect. It was quite new in Britain and was certainly not one that was current among the Protestant princesses of Europe. Mother's influence was oppressive. It was only immediately after Victoria learned that she had become Queen that she ceased to sleep in the same room as her mother and could free herself from her continual plotting.

Because of her long life, her large family and the dynastic marriages made on their behalf, Victoria had links with most of the ruling families in Europe at a period when she was one of the few constitutional monarchs in a continent of very limited democracy. Many of these links were political, a consequence of her responsibility as Queen to provide alliances which would advance her country's influence.

Others were, however, personal. In many cases the relationship went beyond political duty and dynastic marriage to actual friendship, particularly in Victoria's later years.

There could, however, be tensions. For example, Victoria's eldest - and probably favourite - daughter, also Victoria, married Prince Frederick William of Prussia who became Emperor of Germany. He 'popped the question' when at Balmoral, through the medium of a piece of lucky white heather. Their son was 'the Kaiser' or 'Kaiser Bill' who led his people into the First World War. As a family member he could be, on occasion, a loyal and even admiring grandson, yet the two nations embarked on rivalry with destructive consequences.

During the Boer War Queen Victoria was particularly incensed when told that fifty German officers and non-commissioned officers had landed at Delagoa Bay and were on their way to the Transvaal. She instructed Lord Salisbury:

> ...to remonstrate at the presence of so many German officers and men with the Boers. It is monstrous.

She herself wrote to the Kaiser, and in reply he assured her that no regular serving officers were in South Africa - which was not true.

In some respects Victoria differed from the other Empresses we have looked at. Victoria was British by descent. She was unique among the empresses in that she was Queen in her own right. There was no ambiguity about her succession - however hastily contrived - while neither of the preceding Kings - her uncles George IV and William IV - had left legitimate issue.

The other Empresses married their empires. Victoria's empire was created for her. What we called the Indian Mutiny lasted from 10 May 1857 until 20 December 1858, when Sir Colin Campbell, later Lord Clyde, announced that the last rebel had been driven out of the country. On 2 August 1858 the authority of the Honourable East India Company was transferred to the Crown but it was not until 1 January 1877 that Victoria was proclaimed, on Disraeli's advice, Kaisar-i-Hind, Empress of India, by simultaneous proclamations in Delhi, Calcutta, Madras and Bombay.

Bahadur Shah II was the last Mughal Emperor. The loot from the suppression of the Mutiny was auctioned off at Delhi, where Major Robert Tytler bought the Emperor's crown, which he then offered to Queen Victoria. It is now in the Royal Collection. It could be said, therefore, that Queen Victoria had become Empress by right of conquest - and there was the crown to prove it!

In 1926 George Macaulay Trevelyan - born in 1876 and therefore an active Victorian - summed up Queen Victoria in terms with which some traditional contemporary historians would still agree.

> Victoria was possessed in a high degree of queenly instincts and dignity,

but they were softened and popularised by a mind and an emotional nature of great simplicity. In herself she was not very different from her female subjects in humble stations of life - except that she was also a great Queen. She was not at all an aristocrat; the amusements and life of the aristocracy and their dependents and imitators meant little to her. She was above the aristocracy, not of it. With the other side of her nature she was a simple wife and widow-woman, who would have. been at home in any cottage parlour. So, too, the intellectual and artistic currents of the age flowed by her unnoticed - except when Prince Albert was there to instruct her. The common people understood her in her joys and sorrows better than they understood those who stood between themselves and her, raised on the platforms of aristocracy or of intellect.

One can only warm to a queen who, on her accession, took a solid engagement 'to maintain the Established Church of Scotland' and who, in the face of Episcopalian pressure, wrote:

> The Queen will *not* stand the attempts made to destroy the simple and truly Protestant faith of the Church of Scotland.

Yet, when she stayed in certain Scottish country houses a short service was arranged to be taken in private when the parish minister was known to be long-winded. On the other hand, when Principal Caird, a former blacksmith, preached a famous sermon of forty-five minutes at Crathie where other men must not exceed twenty, the Queen 'took this with good humour' and said drily, 'When English dignitaries and clergy can preach as well... will let them go on as long as they like.'

Victoria's filmography is, as one would expect, extensive. Her 'walk-on' parts must have run into the hundreds, while I remember three outstanding films where she was centre-stage. *Sixty Glorious Years* was a tour-de-force, for Anna Neagle, till then a young actress playing light society comedies. This was the first major film in which the heroine aged visibly in appearance and behaviour and was enormously popular. Anton Walbrook played Prince Albert (too smooth?) while Gordon McLeod (who he?) was John Brown. Despite the name, McLeod was born in Devon and never surfaced again.

A very young Andrew Ray in 1950 played *The Mudlark*, based on a true incident. A homeless vagrant who keeps alive by scavenging the banks of the Thames at low tide, contrives to get into the royal presence, to convince Her Majesty that her people need her and she must show herself to the nation. In 1875 London, young Wheeler, who lived by scavenging, found a cameo of Queen Victoria which he thought so beautiful he risked his life to save it. Possessed of a desire to see the Queen - 'the mother of all England' - he slipped past the Beefeaters and wandered about Windsor Castle, just when a state dinner was in preparation. Meanwhile, Prime Minister Disraeli (Alex Guinness) was struggling hard to persuade the Queen to end her long seclusion and he and The Mudlark cooperated to bring this about.

'In *The Mudlark* (1950), Dunne was nearly unrecognizable under heavy makeup as Queen Victoria', says a search engine. Irene Dunne, an American with five Oscar nominations under her belt, was 52. She had been in some fine films and was trying to prolong a long career - but this was not the role for her. On the other hand, Finlay Currie was superb - as he always was - as John Brown. If you wanted honesty and dependability, reinforced by a strong Scots voice (he was from Edinburgh) Finlay Currie was your man. In *Quo Vadis* he was Saint Peter. In *Ben-Hur* he was one of the Three Wise Men. He was an aged, wise senator in *The Fall of the Roman Empire*. His last part was of the old minister in *Brigadoon*.

Popular culture – including films like these - has familiarised us with the dark period of Victoria's early widowhood and her consequent withdrawal from the world. Billy Connolly in *Mrs Brown* (1997) was a surprise for some as John Brown. More Glasgow shipyards than Royal Deeside, he managed to give a performance of integrity and engage our sympathy for the loyal servant who is dumped by Victoria (Dame Judi Dench) when the time comes for her to move on.

One representation of Victoria has been denied to me. One Bond, in 1968, wrote *Early Morning*, which had the distinction of being one of the last plays to be banned by the Lord Chamberlain. Methuen declined to publish it because of the declaration in the Foreword: 'Everything in this play is true'. Bond's Queen Victoria first rapes then has a lesbian relationship with Florence Nightingale and the production - had it taken place - would have been awash with kilts and bad Scots.

And so to New Year's Day, 1868, when there appeared a slim volume under the leisurely title of *Leaves from the Journal of Our Life in the Highlands*. Victoria was now a widow of seven years standing, had been going over her old journals and been persuaded to write them up for publication. Despite her apprehensions, the book was a great success. Anything by a reigning monarch should sell but by 1880 she had earned over £30,000 in royalties and provided for gifts 'of a charitable nature'.

The public loved *Leaves*. It is a happy book, letting the reader get behind the façade of royalty to a simple world of marital love and family life in the open air, where we are on familiar terms with all concerned. Without deep analysis or great originality she loves with schoolgirlish enthusiasm the Highlands and the Highlanders. Of Balmoral she writes: 'Every year my heart becomes more fixed in this dear Paradise'. Albert learns Gaelic and wears Highland dress every evening. Family, servants and tenants build a cairn to mark the completion of Balmoral and celebrate with a bonfire, dancing and whisky. A torch-light ball at Corriemulzie was led by seven pipers, with sixty Highlanders and sixty others dancing 'pretty nearly alternately'. Surely no mother of nine children living as she did could be unaware of the symbolism of Highland dancing, of adult men cavorting around, arms upraised, representing *Caber Feidh*, the antlers of the stag, and the leap of ecstasy as the stag completes the sexual act.

The book did, however, cause offence, especially close to the Queen. Too much attention was said to have been given to the Queen's servants, who were treated 'as if they were as interesting as gentlemen' and 'on the same footing'. The Prince of Wales accused his Mama of not mentioning his name once in the book - to be crushed when she said it appeared five times! By contrast 'Brown' makes his first appearance on page 55, where he rates a lengthy and eulogistic footnote. Which also gives details of his family. He was the second of nine brothers – three of whom had died. Two were in Australia and New Zealand, while two were living in the neighbourhood of Balmoral.

> The youngest, Archie (Archibald) is valet to our son Leopold, and is an excellent trustworthy young man.

On page 56 Brown is portrayed in his kilt, cap in hand, seated with a dog at his feet.

Back in London the courtiers and politicians hated the heartiness of Balmoral and resented the Queen's easy relationship with what they considered to be their inferiors.

Victoria's 'cheerful democracy' is best summed up for me in Figure 10 which shows the Queen and Prince Consort fording the Poll Tarff on their Third Great Expedition in October 1861. The ford was very deep 'and after heavy rain almost impassable'. The Queen asked for Brown '(whom I have far the most confidence in)' to lead her pony and the Duke of Athole took the other side.

What a splendid sight the royal party must have made –

Sandy McAra, the guide, and the two pipers went first, playing all the time…We came very well through, all the others following, the men chiefly wading.

FIG 10 *Crossing the Poll Tarff* (From *Leaves from the Journal of Our Life in the Highlands.* 1868 edition, by kind permission of the National Library of Scotland)

In the original, the caption is very full, continuing as follows:

> With portraits of The Prince, The Queen, Princess Alice, Prince Louis of Hesse, Lady Churchill, General Grey, C.Stewart (Guide), Eneas Rose and J.Macpherson (Pipers), J.Brown (leading the Queen's pony), Sandy McAra, D.McBeath (leading Princess Alice's pony), J.Morgan (behind Prince Louis), Peter Robertson (behind General Grey), Jack McAra (leading Lady Churchill's pony), J.Smith, J.Grant (Head-keeper), A.Campbell, G.McHardy (other Guide), Jack Robertson, John Stewart, and Robert McNaughton.

Everyone gets a mention (except for the Duke of Athole, on whose land they were!), with his or her correct title. And what an array of romantic Highland names – McAra, Rose, Macpherson, McBeath, Grant, Campbell, Stewart and McNaughton. Yet no commentator has pointed out how the most famous name of all - John Brown - sticks out like a sore thumb as banal Lowland Scots or Sassenach. How could this be?

In 1851 John Brown's father, also John Brown, was 60 and had the small farm of the Bush, above Crathie, described in the Census as of 20 acres plus 100 acres of hill pasture and employing labour. John Brown was 24 and resident on the farm. No occupation was given for him, so, presumably, he was the 'labour' on the farm. This was the year in which John Brown entered the Queen's service permanently.

In the 1861 Census there were only two persons resident in the 16 rooms of Balmoral Stables on Census night – one of them being 'John Brown, 33, Servant. Groom. Born Crathie.' His royal mistress would have been far off at Windsor or Osborne at this time. So much for his constant presence at the Queen's side! (Fig 9)

John Brown Senior was born at Crathie (in 1791), like all his children. How did there come to be an even earlier Brown at Crathie before the end of the eighteenth century? On Deeside there were no Highland Clearances in the Sutherland style, with mass evictions, house-burnings and authoritarian intervention; but a similar set of agricultural improvements were made more gradually, transforming a community agriculture into a land of small farms tenanted by sheep farmers from the Borders. By the 1850s only the Lowland name remained. By then the Browns had been assimilated into the traditional Gaelic-speaking culture of Deeside.

Queen Victoria rode through Glen Tilt to Deeside and wrote cheerfully in her journal about the 'beautiful scenery', yet just seventy-five years earlier Thomas Pennant thought the pass 'the most dangerous and the most horrible' he had ever travelled. Between these two came the evolution of the general appreciation of scenery to which we are heirs. While the Queen's pleasure was quite simple and uncomplicated, it was genuine. About the worst criticism she could voice was: 'No pudding and no FUN'.

In the early days of Robert the Bruce's struggle to establish himself as King of Scotland he fought a little battle against the MacDougalls in 1306 at Dalry ('the field of the king') near Tyndrum. Seton Gordon, in his *Highways and Byways in the West Highlands* tells how:

> One of MacDougall's followers laid hands on the king and was killed for his rashness by a strong blow from the royal claymore, but with his dying grasp he tore off the king's cloak and with it the shoulder brooch.

> When Victoria sailed up Loch Tay (in 1842) the royal barge was steered by the chief of the MacDougalls, who wore the Brooch of Lorne in his plaid. The Queen so greatly admired the brooch that she asked MacDougall whether she might wear it during her historic row down the loch.

We can imagine the Queen's emotions as she savoured the romantic situation - the loch and the mountains almost unchanged since the days of Scotland's hero-king; the journey by boat, not so very different from the galleys the West Highland chiefs commanded; and gallant Captain MacDougall proudly wearing the very same brooch that had held together the cloak of the desperate hero. (1)

Victoria's escapades with Albert and based on Balmoral were innocent and great fun. She pottered about visiting old ladies and dispensing new petticoats. After the death of John Brown Senior, his widow moved down to Crathie, where the Queen regularly called on her for tea and to discuss how well the offspring were doing.

There were ascents of the big hills of the Eastern Grampians - Lochnagar, Morven, Ben Macdhui and so on. And there were their Great Expeditions of several days, usually incognito, with the additional excitement of not being spotted as who they were. And John Brown might be 'bashful' (drunk) in the evening and therefore unable to carry out his duties. Some of these days on the hills were very long, 35, 40, even 60 miles. Victoria and Albert had ponies for, perhaps, half the distance, but John Brown and other ghillies were on foot all day!

The period of widowhood was black - in every sense. Victoria retired from most of her official duties. Gradually she began to realise that there was a world out there that could be experienced without endangering her memories of Albert and in 1868, months after the publication of *Leaves*, Queen Victoria rented a villa in Lucerne, using it as a base from which she visited the Rigi (three years before the mountain railway was opened), Pilatus and the Rhone glacier. The royal gipsy was back in business! Even at the blackest, she did not cease to frequent Balmoral and Deeside, and in 1884 appeared *More Leaves from the Journal of A Life in the Highlands*, covering:

> The expeditions made by the Queen in her widowhood from 1862 to 1882, with the companionship of John Brown.

In her Preface to *More Leaves* Victoria wrote:

> ...to show how her sad and suffering heart was soothed and cheered by the excursions and incidents it recounts, as well as by the simple mountaineers, from whom she learnt many a lesson of resignation and faith, in the pure air and quiet of the beautiful Highlands.

It was in 1882 that Victoria's love affair with the Côte d'Azur began, when she spent the months of March and April at the Chalet des Rosiers, an Alpine-style concoction in Garavan, a luxury suburb in the last mile between Menton and the Italian frontier. She arrived by special train from London at a station built for the purpose, with a red carpet leading all the way to the villa and surrounded by cheering crowds. By Riviera standards the Chalet was fairly modest, being made of wood. An annexe had to be built and gas had to be installed for heating and cooking. Two neighbouring villas had to be taken over to accommodate Victoria's suite of forty. As usual, she was accompanied by family members, Leopold, the haemophiliac, who stayed at the neighbouring Hôtel Bellevue and was to return under his own steam, and Beatrice, her youngest daughter, who found it difficult to get away from her mother.

Menton is littered with plaques and street furniture, evidence of this and later visits by the Queen. There is a Hôtel Balmoral and a Residence of 'the Queen and Princes'. Victoria was always considerate of horses and in 1897 caused to be erected a *Fontaine de la Frontière,* an elaborate horse-trough for the poor, tired horses entering France, no doubt badly treated by their Italian masters. (PLATE 8A) A grandiose marble fountain near the old town, and bearing the royal coat of arms, complete with the supporters - the lion and the unicorn - records that it came from 'Her Britannic Majesty Victoria and in recollection of her stay at Mentone'.

Cannes was another wintering place where she kept up the Swiss atmosphere by staying at the Villa Edelweiss. In 1891 she spent the season at the Grand Hôtel de Grasse, but Grasse was too far from the sea and the surroundings were just a little too wild for the ageing Empress.

Eventually the Queen settled on Cimiez, on a hill above Nice, as her winter refuge for the 1890s. Cimiez today has an extravagant display of Belle Epoque villas, apartments and hotels. Victoria found winter at Cimiez like Balmoral in summer. Knowing her predilection, the Excelsior Hôtel Regina (PLATE 8B) was built and in her first year she took the 80 rooms for six weeks and 80,000 francs. The hotel had an internal telephone system - which Victoria refused to use - and a lift - which she used daily.

Her annual visit was organised like a military operation, beginning with the royal yacht *Victoria and Albert* taking the principals of the court to Cherbourg where the royal train began trundling across France at a gentle 50 kilometers per hour by day and forty by night, stopping for meals and between 8 and 9 am, when the Queen made her toilette. The gentle Sisi could be caustic on occasion, as when she said:

> One has been told that the Queen of England has rented the whole hotel, plus two villas, and has turned up with seventy people, some of them Hindoos... What joy to travel like a circus!

Pretty cool of Sisi, who was followed by a procession of underlings, horses, large dogs and her gymnastic apparatus.

The 'Hindoos', of course, were headed up by the Munshi, Abdul Karim, who, from 1887, had become the most important man in Victoria's life (John Brown having succumbed to erysipelas and whisky in 1883). Karim came from Agra and was first noted, when a 24-year old clerk, as one of two Indian waiters at the Queen's Golden Jubilee. 'Munshi' means teacher and in 1888 Karim was appointed 'Munshi and Indian Clerk to the Queen Empress at a salary of £12 per month'. As well as introducing curry to the Imperial menu he made himself indispensable to Victoria. With him she even spent a night at Glassalt Shiel on Loch Muick (still beloved by our present Royal family), as she had done with John Brown, but which she had not visited since his death.

It was quite symbolic how, in her early days Albert had learned Gaelic and her right-hand man had been a simple Highlander who spoke a variant of the language of the court. But as Empress she now had an exotic and suave Indian whose first language was Hindustani and who even had his mistress learning it. Like Brown, the Munshi was hated, and for the same reasons. He was low-born but acted as gatekeeper to the Imperial presence and was on a level of intimacy no courtier could attain. In addition, he was black and, very definitely, from a very foreign culture.

Victoria's days on the Riviera were not so very different from those of Franz-Josef, with the crucial difference that he was a despot trying desperately to hold together a ramshackle empire single-handedly, while she was the constitutional monarch of a country which would keep on going whether or not she interfered.

After a substantial breakfast - Victoria liked her food - the Queen dealt with the overnight dispatches and wrote letters of advice to her children and their children and all the other relatives scattered over the palaces of Europe. The afternoon was a time for visiting and being visited.

One of the ways by which Victoria earned the loyalty of her people was by noticing them and rewarding them. When on holiday in Cimiez, her generosity was observed and described. In the afternoons she would go out driving in the surrounding countryside in her donkey carriage, distributing sweets to the village children. Having taken out several trunks of 'trifles' - watches, chains, tiepins, rings, notecases, inkstands, photographs and the like - her hotel was like a souvenir shop. Throughout her stay she would give these tokens away. Commissioner Xavier Paoli, in charge of security on the Riviera, said:

From the prefect's wife to the lowest gendarme everyone received his little token and - marvellously - there was never a mistake nor a double issue in these gifts. The Queen remembered perfectly what she had handed out the previous year and maintained her 'gift book' with as much orderliness as the shopkeeper keeps his cash book.

As a great giver of presents and tokens she was not carelessly generous. Clearly she thought of people as individuals and tried to treat them accordingly. In systematically recording the details of each gift and its recipient she was not being the miserly housewife; she was making sure that her task of recognising those who had helped was fairly done. There was calculation in the process of dispensing rewards, but the impulse behind it was generous.

Erected in 1912 at the foot of the Excelsior Hôtel Regina garden. (PLATE 8C) Queen Victoria's statue is unusual in two respects. The inscription lists her full titles, including *Impératrice des Indes*, while the group portrays Victoria with motherly humanity. Instead of the usual embodiment of stiff authority, she is portrayed as gently receiving floral tributes from little local girls who swarm over her.

Believing that fiction may be a more powerful learning tool than history I used George MacDonald Fraser's Flashman to sum up his interpretation of the Empress Sisi. Victoria was an inveterate traveller, on business and for relaxation. But she was essentially a domestic being, her travel was safe and unexciting. Flashman has the words to describe her. In a tight hole he mentally reviews the women he has known. 'You never know what to expect on encountering royalty' is followed by a descriptive list, concluding: 'and tramping along looking like an out-of-work charwoman (our own gracious monarch).'

End Notes

1 The Brooch of Lorne has had a long and chequered history, having been taken in 1647, in the Civil War. It then passed through several hands until it was returned to the MacDougalls in 1824. It has remained at Dunollie Castle, the family home, till the present day.
David Caldwell, curator of the Scottish medieval collections at the National Museums of Scotland, has said:

It is a very important piece of west Highland art, but it dates from the mid 15th century, so cannot be Bruce's. Maybe the original brooch fell to pieces and this one was substituted for it.'

Epilogue

ON AUGUST 15 1947 the Union Jack came down in the new state of India. Jawaharlal Nehru became Prime Minister and Lord Louis Mountbatten, first Earl Mountbatten of Burma, ceased to be Viceroy but stayed on as Governor General. The previous day the new, independent state of Pakistan had been formed. So, after 71 years, the last of the great European empires had faded away and the letters IND. IMP. disappeared from our coins.

The King-Emperor George VI was a direct descendant of Queen Victoria, through Edward VII. Mountbatten was directly descended also, through Alice, Victoria's second daughter, and was thus related to the King (and to our present Queen). He was also Prince Philip's uncle. Like quite a number of those mentioned in this narrative, Mountbatten was murdered. In his case it was not by hate-crazed Indian fanatics, but (in 1979) by the post-Imperial brave boys at Mullaghmore, County Sligo in the Republic of Ireland. Poor Sisi had been a second choice for her killer, but Mountbatten was clearly a prime target for his killers!

A blimp was a balloon used for military purposes in the First World War. It had no rigid skeleton, was difficult to control and easily destroyed. David Low, cartoonist for the *Evening Standard*, created in 1936 Colonel Blimp, the embodiment of everything reactionary in the British ruling class. The collapse of the British Empire could be likened to the collapse of a punctured balloon. At the time of Victoria's death the world map was a patchwork with many patches, various in size, in red. Many patches were colonies and protectorates. Others, like Australia, were associations of colonies which moved towards independence from the mother country, although they maintained a loose political relationship - the Commonwealth - with the British crown and shared, in many cases, aspects of a common heritage.

Early in 1947 the Indian sub-continent was made up of the Empire of India and the Crown Colony of Ceylon. After many vicissitudes and much bloodshed there are now four independent states in the same area – India, Pakistan, Bangla Desh and Sri Lanka.

The demise of the other empires touched on here was more rapid and dramatic. Two years after Franz Josef's death his fragile empire was split up. Parts were hived off to the victors of World War I and new states were set up The old empire had been a hotch-potch of nationalities and so were the new states of Czechoslovakia and Yugoslavia - although they contrived to hang together for most of the twentieth century, before splitting again along ethnic lines.

The German empire collapsed in 1918. Alsace and Lorraine were handed back to France. The overseas possessions were shared out among the victors and a punitive peace created the ideal conditions for the rise of Hitler who saw himself as creating another German empire. His dream collapsed in flames and Germany was dismembered for another fifty years.

The Ottoman Empire, still with a toehold in Europe, was allied with Austria and Germany in World War I, was comprehensively defeated and, like them, was split up after the war. The presence of oil and aggressive governments has ensured that the Middle East is seldom off the front page.

Napoleon III was an empire-builder whose Second Empire saw the beginning of a great French colonial drive in Africa. His Imperial rule ended at Sedan, Alsace and Lorraine were ceded to the new German empire but, rather like our own empire, France, her overseas departments and her colonies and protectorates hung together until the great upsurge of nationalistic fervour after the Second World War. Again, however, there are still close bonds between the francophone countries.

Serious enough for the participants, in historical perspective Maximilian's Mexican Empire was a bit of a joke. No-one could say that Mexico's political history has been untroubled, with dictators, corruption and an overbearing northern neighbour. But they have not seen the need to import European aristocrats to solve their problems.

The Russian armies were unable to hold out to November 1918. The country collapsed in spectacular fashion and with it the rulers - to be replaced by a tyranny better organised than anything the Tsars had presided over. In the nineteenth century the Tsars had built up an empire in Central Asia. At the end of the twentieth century the component parts of the USSR re-asserted themselves, so that the massive monolith of the Soviet Union was split, in 1991, into fifteen independent sovereign states.

In this meltdown of empires, this Twilight of the Gods, where were the Gypsy Empresses? Did they see the end coming? Or did they just muddle along, doing what empresses had done since the beginning of time? If they ran away, what were they running from? Above all, was there a Big Idea to which they, more or less conformed?

This seems unlikely, as there seems to have been a degree of diversity of behaviour, albeit within fairly narrow limits. The lives of Franz Josef, his brother Maximilian and Napoleon III were closely entwined with each other as were, in consequence, the lives of their wives. All, on assuming power, made extravagant promises before God, in august company and in great cathedrals, that they would lead virtuous lives, protect the weak and rule wisely. In varying degrees each of them failed to honour their solemn promises.

Sisi's reaction was to run away for the best part of two years and for the rest of her life make occasional attempts to behave like an empress before retreating to her fantasy world of poetry and the sea. By the standards of the time she must be regarded as a failure. Although she had four children, only one was male and he was a poor specimen who could not face the reality of life.

Poor Carlota was none too stable before she was married. She had no children and suffered the humiliation of having a husband who clearly preferred to take his pleasures elsewhere. Her loyalty was strained to the limit by the crazy Mexican venture. The death of her husband at the hands of understandably enraged Mexican patriots and the indifference of those she thought ought to be sympathetic finished her off and she, too, ended her life in solitude.

Eugénie was quite different. The man she married was already a notorious philanderer and she could have had no illusions about him. She was also mature for a bride at that time. In what we might think of as the French style she took a great interest in politics and, as her husband's health deteriorated, got involved in government. Yet Eugénie must also be considered as a failure, since she had only the one son and he turned out to be an unpleasant young man who died as a result of his own stupidity.

In this study it must be quite clear that the empresses have not been treated equally. In terms of words each of Sisi and Carlota have been given more than the total for the three German empresses. It is easy to see why. Augusta was 61 when she became Empress, a role she occupied for sixteen years. The Empress Frederick ("Vicky') had a mere 99 days in which to make a mark. Wilhelm II's Augusta was unexciting, the embodiment of *Kinder, Küche und Kirche*. Yet there is a case for considering her to have been the ideal empress. She came from a modestly blue-blooded background. She was not cursed by high intelligence, nor did she trouble too much about the latest fashions. Simple she may have been but she was astute enough to capture the prize and produce a string of sons in quick succession without appearing to feel jealous about her husband's sexual freedom. Like the Ugly Duckling which became a swan she had fallen into wealth and position. Yet, when it all collapsed she stayed by her wastrel husband's side and went into exile with him, bitter though the experience was.

The Russian tsars had a romantic predilection for young blondes from other countries. With the passage of time their fancies turned elsewhere, and the question would come up - 'What is to be done?' Then we have the unedifying spectacle of the tsar twisting and turning at the prospect of a morganatic marriage. This despot, who could and did sign a decree sending a million men to their deaths, could not overrule a reactionary church and sycophantic advisers to produce a rational decision. The Russian Revolution had many causes, but a significant one was the great gulf between the goings-on of the Imperial family and the lot of ordinary Russians.

All these Emperors were totalitarian rulers in the sense that they might have advisers and even elected consultative bodies, but the final decision was in one man's hands only. With Victoria things were different. Her kingdom was a constitutional monarchy with the rules laid down in the late 17th century and continually being refined. Just before she took up her orb and sceptre the Great Reform Act of 1832 began a long revolution which widened the franchise to successive layers in the class structure - and to women. Gladstone and Disraeli travelled to Balmoral to discuss matters with the Queen and to be sure of her support - but the policies and decisions were theirs and not necessarily hers. In this year of Queen Elizabeth's Diamond Jubilee we are very conscious of the power and majesty of the state and its close connection with the church - and presumably, God. But we know that the real power lies with the cheering crowd outside the cathedral and with the grey men in suits inside they elected.

Perhaps this is the Big Idea we were looking for. Autocratic rule, the rule of the strong man, the man on the horse, may well have been appropriate when nations were being built and empires were being patched together from disparate societies, but it clearly failed as societies became more complex and, especially, as wars became just too big for any one person, however well supported, to handle.

In Britain, Victoria demonstrated that the monarch could have all the traits that contributed to nation-building. She was descended from an established line of kings and queens. She was crowned with elaborate ceremonial, anointed by the heads of the church and publicly acclaimed by her subjects. In England she was the head of the church. In her domestic life she was a model for her subjects, with a loving husband, earnest and intellectual, and a brood of children. She may not have herself been a reformer, but she associated herself with social progress and at the personal level had the common touch.

She could be all this without being involved in the sordid and disturbing details of government - wars, taxation, public health provision, legislation and the rest. As a matter of courtesy she would be consulted by her ministers - and as she aged her experience would be worth listening to - but they were the elected officers with the responsibilities and the power, who could be thrown out bloodlessly if they failed.

It is a strange and untidy thing, this constitutional monarchy, but if we look around it seems to have worked. All these great European empires have crumbled away, the British Empire as such has broken up, but over a century after Victoria's death we have a Queen celebrating a Diamond Jubilee, as popular and respected as ever her great great grandmother was. The Commonwealth still means something. Even the citizens of foreign republics find in her something to be admired.

Bibliography

Ina Caro, *Paris to the Past: Traveling through French History by Train* (WW Norton & Company, Inc., New York, 2011)

Christopher Clark, *Iron Kingdom: The Rise and Downfall of Prussia, 1600-1947* (Allen Lane, London, 2006)

Rosemary and Donald Crawford, *Michael and Natasha: The Life and Love of the Last Tsar of Russia* (Weidenfeld and Nicolson, London, 1997)

Andrew L Drummond and James Bulloch, *The Church in Victorian Scotland, 1843-1874* (Saint Andrew Press, Edinburgh, 1975)

Anne Edwards, *The Grimaldis of Monaco* (Harper Collins, London, 1992)

Carolly Erickson, *Alexandra, the last Tsarina* (Constable, London, 2001)

Byron Farwell, *The Great Boer War* (Wordsworth Editions, Ware, Herts, 1999)

Edgar Feuchtwanger, *Imperial Germany:1850-1918* (Routledge, London, 2001)

George MacDonald Fraser, *Flashman and the Tiger* (HarperCollins, London, 1999)

Martine Gasquet, *Les Femmes a la Belle Epoque sur la Côte d'Azur* (Gilletta, Nice, 2005)

Didier Gayraud, *Belles Demeures en Riviera, 1835-1930* (Gilletta, Nice, 2005)

Joan Haslip, *The Lonely Empress: Elizabeth of Austria* (Phoenix Press, London, 1965)

James Pope Hennessy, *Robert Louis Stevenson* (Jonathan Cape, London, 1974)

Bibliography

Alistair Horne, *Seven Ages of Paris* (Macmillan, London, 2002)

John House, *Impressionists by the Sea* (Royal Academy of Arts, London, 2007)

H Montgomery Hyde, *Mexican Empire* (Macmillan, London, 1946)

Robert Kanigel, *High Season in Nice* (Little, Brown, London, 2002)

Greg King, *The Last Empress* (Carol Publishing Group, New York, 1994)

John van der Kiste, *Dearest Vicky, Darling Fritz* (Sutton Publishing, Stroud, 2001)

Martin Kitchen, *A History of Modern Germany: 1800-2000* (Blackwell Publishing, Oxford, 2006

Ian Knight, *'A Minor Episode of the Campaign'* (in The Journal of The Anglo Zulu War Historical Society, Sixth Edition, December 1999)

Dr Enrique Lardé, *The Crown Prince Rudolf: his Mysterious Life after Mayerling* (Dorrance Publishing Co Inc, Pittsburgh, 1994)

James F McMillan, *Napoleon III* (Longman, Harlow, 1991)

Giles MacDonogh, *The Last Kaiser: William the Impetuous* (Weidenfeld and Nicolson, London, 2000)

Robert K Massie, *Nicholas and Alexandra* (Victor Gollancz, London, 1968)

Robert K Massie, *The Romanovs: The Final Chapter* (Jonathan Cape, London, 1995)

Andrei Maylunas and Sergei Mironenko, *A Lifelong Passion: Nicholas and Alexandra, Their Own Story* (Weidenfeld & Nicolson, London, 1996)

Michelin, *Guide de Tourisme - Vosges, Lorraine, Alsace* (Pneu Michelin, Paris, 1990)

Raoul Mille, *Ma Riviera - chroniques* (Gilletta, Nice, 2005)

The Gypsy Empresses

Edvard Radzinsky, *The Last Tsar:The Life and Death of Nicholas II* (Hodder and Stoughton, London, 1992)

Joanna Richardson, *Victoria and Albert* (Dent, London, 1977)

Jim Ring, *Riviera:The Rise and Rise of the Côte d'Azur* (John Murray, London, 2004)

Joseph Roth, *The Radetzky March* (2002 translation, Granta Books, London, 2002)

Desmond Seward, *Eugénie: The Empress and her Empire* (Sutton Publishing, Stroud, 2004)

Andrew Sinclair, *The Other Victoria* (Weidenfeld and Nicolson, London, 1981)

Ray Soweto, *The New Dawn: The Revelation of the 21st Century* (New Dawn Publishing, Knaresborough, 2008)

Hugues de la Touche, *Impératrices sur la Riviera: Naissance d'un art de vivre* (Thalia Edition, Paris, 2008)

GM Trevelyan, *History of England* (Longmans, Green, London, 1926)

Queen Victoria (ed. Arthur Helps), *Leaves from the Journal of Our Life in the Highlands* (The Folio Society, London, 1973)

CV Wedgwood, *The Thirty Years War* (Penguin Books, Harmondsworth, 1957)

Frances Welch, *The Russian Court at Sea* (Short Books, London, 2011)

Walter's Wiggles
The Random Thoughts of a Random Traveller
Walter Stephen
ISBN 1-906817-68-5   UK price £12.99

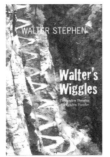

Spurred on by *Fernweh* – a longing for faraway places - Walter Stephen shares thoughts sparked off by destinations which have intrigued and attracted him. Using these places as inspiration for musings on subjects such as history, culture and science, Walter builds up a unique picture of the world that you won't find in any guide book.

But are these ramblings really as random as they seem? Soon his personal reasons for choosing each location become clear, with an awareness of the duality of man's relationship with the world coming into view. Facing his own mortality, Walter contemplates both the powerful beauty of the world and man's capacity for destruction in a book that is poignant, entertaining, informative and thought-provoking.

And just what are Walter's Wiggles? A unique escarpment path leading to Angels Landing in Zion National Park, Utah; one of the many fascinating places on Walter's travels, and part of a journey that is not as random as it at first seems.

Available directly from the author at the special price of £10 (p&p included).

Cheques should be made payable to:
Walter M Stephen
Hills of Home
82 Pentland Terrace
EDINBURGH
EH10 6HF

The Evolution of Evolution
Darwin, Enlightenment and Scotland
Walter Stephen
ISBN 978 1906817 23 7   UK price £12.99

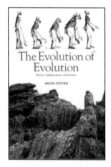

What led Darwin to form his theory of evolution? To what extent did the Enlightenment influence Darwin's work? How did Scots help Darwin to publish the most successful and controversial book of his time?

In 1825 Darwin began to study medicine at Edinburgh University, the seat of the Enlightenment. The Enlightenment had created a thirst for science. In his two years at Edinburgh, Darwin became involved with the people and ideas that were to shape the world's understanding of the natural sciences, including his concept of evolution and natural selection – and whose influence he was to acknowledge with ill grace.

The Evolution of Evolution *is a well researched and thoughtfully written book that recognises the importance of Scotland in the formation of evolutionary thinking and the role of Scots in both mentoring and influencing Charles Darwin throughout his life.*

(SCOTTISH REVIEW OF BOOKS)

Available directly from the author at the special price of £10 (p&p included).

Cheques should be made payable to:
Walter M Stephen
Hills of Home
82 Pentland Terrace
EDINBURGH
EH10 6HF

Walter Stephen is a former Chairman of the **Sir Patrick Geddes Memorial Trust** and is presently its Publications Convener. The following Trust publications are available directly from him at discounted prices.

Think Global, Act Local
Edited by Walter Stephen
ISBN 978 1842820 79 7   UK price £12.99

Town planning. Interest-led, open-minded education. Preservation of worthwhile buildings. Community gardens. All central to our society   but   first visualised by Sir Patrick Geddes. Seven major essays ranging from Edinburgh to India via Montpellier revealing Geddes as gardener, biologist, conservationist, social evolutionist, peace warrior and town planner.

One might get the impression that Professor Geddes is a vigorous institution, rather than a man.

A Vigorous Institution
Edited by Walter Stephen
ISBN 678 1905222 88 9   UK price £12.99

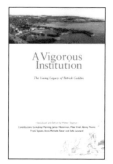

Twelve expert essays emphasising the living legacy of the work of Patrick Geddes in Britain, France, Catalonia, Italy and over 50 cities in India. How influential were his childhood and home experiences? How could an internationalist be so steeped in Scottishness? How much of an anarchist was he?

Each of the above is available directly from the author at the special price of £10 (p&p included).

Cheques should be made payable to:
Walter M Stephen,
Hills of Home
82 Pentland Terrace
EDINBURGH
EH10 6HF

All profits from these publications will go to the Sir Patrick Geddes Memorial Trust.

Where was Patrick Geddes born?
The Last Word?
Walter Stephen
ISBN 978-0-9555190-2-4   UK price £5.00

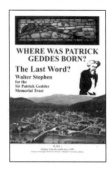

In a Da Vinci Code style of narrative, Walter Stephen describes the search for the Patrick Geddes birthhouse, (unknown until 2007). He brings forward hitherto unknown youthful influences on the great man and observes the special relationship between Deeside and the Royal family.

Exploration
Get to know your own Place and Work and Folk
Edited by Kenneth Mac Lean and Walter Stephen
ISBN 978-0-9555190-0-0   UK price £4.00

Replica of a regional survey manual of 1939, produced by the Leplay Society (founded by Geddes), edited by Mabel Barker (his goddaughter) and incorporating Geddes's interpretation of Leplay's famous triad of 'Place, Work, Folk'. Thoughtful background introduction.

Each of the above is available directly from the author at the special prices of £4(Where?) and £3(Exploration) (p&p included).

Cheques should be made payable to:
Walter M Stephen
Hills of Home
82 Pentland Terrace
EDINBURGH
EH10 6HF

All profits from these publications will go to the Sir Patrick Geddes Memorial Trust.